Crucified Love

Littleness, Spousal Love, and *Fiat* as the Instruments Jesus used in Enduring the Cross and the Means of a Soul Uniting with Him in Crucified Love

Dr. Mary Elizabeth Kloska, Th.D.

En Route Books and Media, LLC
St. Louis, MO

En Route Books and Media, LLC
5705 Rhodes Avenue
St. Louis, MO 63109

Contact us at **contact@enroutebooksandmedia.com**

Cover Credit: Mary Kloska
Copyright 2024 Mary Kloska

ISBN-13: 979-8-88870-263-5 and 979-8-88870-262-8
Library of Congress Control Number: 2024949306

All rights reserved. No part of this book may be reproduced, stored in a retrieval system, or transmitted in any form, or by any means, electronic, mechanical, photocopying, or otherwise, without the prior written permission of the author.

Acknowledgments

I would like to thank my old friend Dr. Ronda Chervin for generously and eagerly agreeing to be my director in this doctoral work and for her kind, faithful concern that this thesis met the highest grammatical standards.

I would like to thank Professor Anthony Lilles for not only reading this work to approve its theology, but for his very helpful insights, guidance and encouragement in making this thesis as strong and solid as possible. He went above and beyond the work of a reader taking over the role of director to help me develop my thought in full.

I would like to thank Laura Yanikoski for her many hours of counsel and help on arranging the references according to updated Chicago Manual Style requirements.

I would like to thank Dr. Cynthia Toolin-Wilson and Dr. David Clayton for accepting me into the Pontifex doctoral program and for all that Cynthia has done to walk me through the unfamiliar paths of doctoral academics.

I must thank Dr. Sebastian Mahfood, who originally suggested that I work towards my doctorate, for both his wisdom and humor throughout the process.

And, of course, I must also thank my parents who have greatly supported and encouraged me every step of the way.

Above all else, I am eternally grateful to sweet Jesus and his Mother for not only calling me to live such a beautiful spirituality of littleness, spousal love and the Cross, but also in sharing the wisdom of the Holy Spirit with me so that I have come to understand the theological implications of this vocation. Literally every insight and word written here is grace.

Table of Contents

Preface vii

Introduction 1

Chapter 1 What is Crucified Love? 7

Chapter 2 How Did Jesus Live His Interior Passion? In *Fiat* through Littleness and Love. 15
    Part 1: *Fiat* in Littleness (The Kenosis of Christ) 16
        Fiat and Kenosis 35
    Part 2: *Fiat* and Spousal Trinitarian Love 39

Chapter 3 Christ as the New Adam and Redeemer— Jesus as Priest, Altar, and Victim 59

Chapter 4 How Did Our Lady Live the Cross With Jesus? In *Fiat* Through Littleness and Love. 93
    Part 1: Our Lady's *Fiat* and Littleness—Innocence, Purity, Humility, Kenosis, Trust, Surrender, and Obedience 100
    Part 2: Our Lady's *Fiat* and Spousal Love 111
        Spousal Love With the Holy Spirit 112
        "Wife"—New Eve 117

Chapter 5 The Sorrowful Heart of Mary's *Fiat*— Our Lady as the New Eve, Helpmate of Jesus, the Eternal High Priest, Co-Redemptrix, and Mediatrix 131

Part 1: Our Lady as New Eve, Helpmate, Co-Redemptrix and Mediatrix 131
    Our Lady as Helpmate 138
    Co-Redemptrix 145
Part 2: Mary as Altar, Priest and Victim with Christ 169
    Mary as the Altar of Sacrifice 172
    Mary as Priest 174
    Mary's Offering of Christ, the Victim 178
    Mary as Victim—Mary Offers Herself 184
    The Joint Offering of Jesus and Mary 188
    Mary as Mediatrix 191

Chapter 6 How Does the Church Live the Cross with Jesus? In *Fiat* through Littleness and Love. 201

Chapter 7 The Saints Call to Littleness in the Church 211

Chapter 8 The Church and Each Soul Within Her as the "Bride, the Wife of the Lamb" 229

Chapter 9 The Saints Experience Nuptial Union with Christ on the Cross— Crucified Love is Marital Love 241

Chapter 10 The Saints' Call to the Cross and Co-redeeming Love— Priests, Altars and Victims with Christ 309
The Saints' Vocation to a Complete Fiat to God's Will as Jesus and Mary Lived 323

Conclusion 325

Works cited 331
    Primary sources 331
    Secondary sources 342

Works consulted 347
    Primary sources 347
    Secondary sources 348

Preface

In this work I will look at the concept of the crucified love of Christ—His immaculate, powerful, selfless love that was rejected, denied, abandoned, ignored, mocked and hated by the world, and yet a love that was never tainted in the smallest way by the evil response of others around Him. I will focus on the aspects of His humble littleness and spousal, trinitarian love, which held Him fast to the gift of Himself on the Cross in *fiat* to the Father's will. I will show how it is Christ's redemptive work in the Passion that makes Him the new Adam, lived out in the roles of Priest, Altar and Victim.

After laying the ground-work of crucified love as lived by Christ Himself, I will then lead the reader to see how Our Lady lived the Cross with Jesus, both through Her littleness and Her love which were the impetus behind Her *fiat* to the Father's will. I will show how Our Lady lived spousal love with the Father, the Son and with the Holy Spirit—and in particular how Her love union with Jesus on the Cross made her the 'woman/wife', the 'new Eve' of creation. I will explain Her role as the Helpmate of Christ and how through union with Him She lived as Co-redemptrix and Mediatrix of all grace. I will show Her congruity with Christ's role as Altar, Priest and Victim and how She is held up by the Church as a model for all Christians desiring to imitate Jesus and thus become saints.

Lastly, I will show how specific souls in the Church are called to imitate Our Lady in uniting with Jesus on the Cross through littleness and spousal love. I will particularly emphasize the need of each soul in the Church to surrender in *fiat* to the Father to His particular call to them—something that will only be realized as they imitate Jesus and Mary's littleness and spousal (crucified) love. It is through this that all members of the Church are called to be saints who live out the role of co-redeemers with Jesus and Mary, offering their hearts and lives as priests, altars and victims in union with them. This will be the source of their *fiats* to the Father's will as well. I will very specifically illustrate this through examples of many different saints and mystics, showing the pattern of God's fingerprints upon each of their lives through littleness, spousal love and the Cross regardless of their gender, age, culture and personal vocation. I will particularly use examples from the lives of the saints who experienced a mystical marriage with Christ, as well as a manifestation of the love of His Cross that imprints itself upon each soul He encounters. I draw heavily from the writings of the Carmelites, as well as those saints who visibly manifested the Passion of Christ through the stigmata, illness and martyrdom. I emphasize how it is not cruel punishment that they are enduring from God on the behalf of others, but instead a beautiful union of graced love that they share with Him through the experience of the Cross.

Throughout the entirety of this work, I will clearly argue that it is love that demanded the Cross from Christ and love that held Him steadfast upon it. It is the immaculate love of His Mother that united Her with Him in the work of the Cross and it is love that draws the saints to imitate Her in also being consumed by crucified love. Although I draw from the mystical writing and experiences of the saints who shared these graces with Christ, I also try to ground my arguments in the solid, objective theology of St. Thomas Aquinas, the

Church Fathers, saints and Popes who eloquently explained the science of love and the Cross.

Often in the Church there is the problem of Christians misunderstanding the suffering love of Christ. They do not see it as something that stems primarily from His great humility and pure love, nor do they see how deeply each and every soul is called to follow Our Lady's perfect imitation of Him in joining with His redemption on the Cross. Through analyzing these aspects of Christ's crucified love, one comes to see the majestic goal every soul on earth is called to seek—union with the crucified Jesus—and how accessible and gentle it is to follow Him by accepting the truth of one's own weak littleness put at the service of heroic love. My hope is that this work will not only show how Jesus suffered so perfectly and how His Mother united with Him in full, but also inspire many others to join them along with the saints in crucified love—a love so strong that it is willing to suffer—as true sons and daughters of God.

Throughout my entire life the Lord has called me to join Him in a deep union with His Heart's deepest love—being crucified love. He has taught me that it is not in being strong or powerful that I am able to unite with Him in such radical love, but rather by lowering myself and embracing littleness and the path of authentic humility that He is able to lift me close to His Heart on the Cross. While suffering may seem difficult for many in the world today to endure, Christ shows us on the Cross that it is actually easy if embraced by love. He says in Matthew 11:30 that His *'yoke is easy'* and His *'burden is light.'* This is because of love.

After spending years serving the persecuted Church in Eastern Siberia, I saw how the evil of Communism took God and love out of suffering—and suffering without Jesus is hell. Communists stole Christ from the Cross and laid the Russian people upon it 'without Him' in a way. I realized quickly as a missionary that only the presence of Jesus Christ and His love with the Russian people would be able to transform and uphold them in their suffering. Jesus' love changed the Cross from a place of hell to a place of union, hope and peace.

In today's world godlessness has spread much further than just the borders of communist Russia—it has taken over almost all countries on earth. The solution to an earthly hell that threatens humanity is a return to the Cross of Jesus Christ. Jesus crucified teaches humanity the upmost humility and most powerful love that comes with a Heart surrendering in full in *fiat* to the Father. Littleness, divine love and the Cross are not only the means by which Jesus redeemed the world, but are also the tools that Our Lady and all souls who follow Her example as a perfect disciple of Christ must use in order to be transformed and united with Him.

Our Lady is presented as central to the work of this thesis because as Christ proposes a way of littleness, spousal love and the Cross to humanity, Hers alone is the perfect response to Him of total conformity and surrender. In this She is clearly our Mother, modeling and teaching us through Her example how we are to answer Christ's call. She shows us that it is possible for a human to reach such heights of perfect love united one with Jesus. She not only teaches us this through Her life, but also wins grace for us through

Her '*fiat*' so that we can climb the same ladder of littleness, pure love and holiness through a crucified path with Her.

Jesus and Mary's examples of littleness, divine love and the Cross are extremely important in our modern times. The present world is inundated by examples of grandiose ambition, the growth of the human ego seeking at all cost to be the smartest, wealthiest, most powerful, popular, or important person. Even in the Church we see ugly competition and the evil effects of pride distort the beauty of God's call to individual souls. Littleness is the opposite goal of almost every person. Heroic, authentic, selfless love is rarely encountered in the world. And suffering—the Cross—is seen as something needing to be avoided at all costs. Yet, Christ came to preach to us a way of littleness, radical love and an embracing of the suffering of the Cross as the very means necessary for us to reach heaven. This perspective, which is so often overlooked and forgotten, is central to understanding the mysteries of the Catholic faith, as well as for individual souls to grow in holiness.

Humans need concrete illustrations in order to understand abstract ideas. This is where the importance of the example of the saints enters this work. By presenting concrete people who encountered Jesus' call to littleness, spousal love and the Cross in so many different ways, the reader can begin to understand how these virtues can take root in their own lives.

Introduction

At that time Jesus said, "I praise you, Father, Lord of heaven and earth, because you have hidden these things from the wise and learned, and revealed them to little children." (Mt 11:25)[1]

Christ, though he was in the form of God, did not count equality with God a thing to be grasped, but emptied himself, by taking the form of a servant, being born in the likeness of men. (Phil 2:6–11)

Son though he was, he learned obedience from what he suffered. (Heb 5:8)

Jesus Christ was in the beginning as *"the Word, and the Word was with God, and the Word was God. He was in the beginning with God. All things came to be through him, and without him nothing came to be"* (Jn 1:1–3). And yet, *"The Word became flesh and made his dwelling among us, and we saw his glory, the glory as of the Father's only Son, full of grace and truth"* (Jn 1:14).

---

[1] Scripture texts in this work are taken from the New American Bible, revised edition © 2010, 1991, 1986, 1970 Confraternity of Christian Doctrine, Washington, D.C. and are used by permission of the copyright owner. All Rights Reserved. No part of the New American Bible may be reproduced in any form without permission in writing from the copyright owner.

Jesus, as the Second Person of the Trinity, humbled Himself taking the form of man—placing His power at the service and in obedience to His Father as the ultimate act of charity. Jesus taught, *"Unless you turn and become like a child, you will not enter the kingdom of heaven. Whoever humbles himself like this child is the greatest in the kingdom of heaven"* (Mt 18:3–4). He Himself came to earth as a poor baby, born in the poverty of a stable. And by lowering Himself in a divine act of humility, His union with the Father was perfected by the fire of the Holy Spirit—the presence of love Himself as the Third Person of the Trinity that came forth from the union He shared as the beloved with the Father. Jesus' littleness placed at the service of love allowed the Father to uphold Him in power and majesty keeping Him steadfast to His Father's will of humanity's redemption even unto and through the Cross. Christ placed Himself below the Father—allowing the Father to pour forth His eternal love upon Him—thus glorifying Him through His obedience and suffering on the Cross. In scripture, we see this in Jesus' filial words spoken to His Father:

> *And now, Father, glorify me in your own presence with the glory that I had with you before the world existed.* (Jn 17:5)

> *Father, if you are willing, remove this cup from me. Nevertheless, not my will, but yours, be done.* (Lk 22:42)

> *And Jesus said, "Father, forgive them, for they know not what they do."* (Lk 23:34)

Introduction

Father, into Your hands I commend my spirit. (Lk 23:46)

In John 10:30, Jesus boldly claims *"The Father and I are one,"* thus proclaiming that the love of the Holy Spirit unites Them as one even as He lowers Himself in obedience to fulfill the Father's will. St. Augustine taught that Christ is the Beloved, the Father is the Lover, and the Holy Spirit is the eternal fruit of that love. We read in Question 37 of the *Summa theologica* that St. Thomas Aquinas and Gregory the Great claimed that "the Holy Spirit Himself is Love." Aquinas further explains, like Augustine, that *"there is expressed in the Holy Ghost, as love, the relation of the Father to the Son, and conversely, as that of the lover to the beloved."*[2] It is the littleness of Christ combined with the spousal love He shares with the Father that holds Him steadfast on the Cross.

Our Lady was immaculately conceived—yet in Her perfection, She also humbled Herself before the Lord. Her utter emptiness of self, allowed Her to be "full of grace" when the angel came to Her and asked Her to be the Mother of Jesus. She, like Christ, folded the greatness of Her favor before God beneath the wings of perfect obedience surrendering to His will in giving Her *fiat* to His request. The fire of the Holy Spirit's love united Our Lady so closely with the Heart of Her Son that She was at once His Mother and yet also His Spouse, His Bride, His Wife—the new Eve who would give birth to the new

---

[2] Thomas Aquinas, *Summa theologica*, trans. Fathers of the English Dominican Province (New York: Benziger Brothers, 1911-1925), I-II, q. 37, a. 1, https://www.newadvent.org/summa/.

Adam in the world. The humility and love that consumed Her at the moment of the Incarnation inflamed Her as one with Jesus and carried Her courageously and faithfully to endure His Passion and Death with Him. Her soul was pierced by the sword of His crucified love. In Her weakness as creature, She was carried through the suffering of His death to a resurrected life with Him.

Our Lady is an example for all of the Church—and for 2000 years, we have seen countless saints imitate Her perfect imitation of Jesus leading to Her perfect union with Him. This was not accomplished through saints achieving greatness, but rather recognizing their littleness and dependence on Christ and allowing the fire of the Holy Spirit's love to make them one with Him. It was Jesus' littleness and spousal love that held Him one with the Father through the Cross in *fiat*. Our Lady, the Church and each soul that is part of Her is called to be the "Little Wife Crucified of Christ."

For the purpose of this work, in using the word 'little' I am meaning humble, childlike, small, meek, dependent, weak, innocent, surrendered, docile, trusting and obedient. 'Little' does not mean imperfect, because Jesus embraced the littleness of humanity while still being perfect and He calls all souls to *'be perfect, just as your heavenly Father is perfect.'* (Mt 5:48) In fact, in Matthew 18:3 He holds up a child as the perfect example and ideal as one worthy to enter the kingdom of heaven. For the purpose of this work, the word 'wife' is being used as the woman created as both a gift and complimentary helpmate to her husband, who uses her freewill to subordinately participate in his work of obedience to God. This is something that an earthly wife models so that every soul in the Church can relate to

Christ as their Husband, as Israel related in such a way to God. In calling Our Lady and the Church the 'Little Wife Crucified' of Christ, I mean to say that both (Our Lady and the Church) are created to be humble, childlike, pure, dependent and docilely obedient in their role as servant and beloved Helpmate to Christ the eternal Bridegroom, who was faithful to the Father unto and through the Cross. By being so profoundly united to Jesus as His 'Little Wife', Our Lady and the Church will innately join Him in living out His Passion and Death.

Jesus insists that in order to follow after Him on the way of the Cross one must live *fiat* through embracing littleness and fiery spousal love. It was Our Lady's littleness and spousal love that held Her one with Jesus and the Father through the Cross in *fiat*. And all souls in the Church are called to imitate this path of littleness and spousal love to make them one with Jesus and the Father through the Cross in *fiat*.

Chapter 1

What is Crucified Love?

Love saved the world. In the beginning, humanity was created in love, by love, for love, and to love. This was the purpose, means and end of man's existence. Man was created to participate in divine love with God through obedience to his will. Obedience was the lifeline that kept God's Heart and man's heart united perfectly. When man committed sin and disobeyed God, his participation in God's life of love was broken. In sin, man used his own freewill to choose to shut his heart off from God's free gift. Sin is the rejection of the love of the Father. In man's closing his heart from grace through sin, evil began to tempt man away from all that God created good and, in this, suffering, division and death entered the world. When sin entered the world, a rift was made not only between man and God and between man and woman, but also within man himself. The original order of love established by God in creation was thrown into disarray. In order for this tear to be healed, Christ had to come to earth to mend humanity's relationship with the Father through obedience (an acceptance of love) and to pay back the divine debt owed to Him in justice. Jesus had to live out in His flesh that original purpose of man. He had to allow Himself to be created in love, by love, for love and to love and to fight with His will against the weakness of disobedience, choosing instead to surrender in *fiat* to His Father's will and love. It was in obeying the Father even on and through the Cross that Christ glorified Him.

Jesus had to come to earth as the Son of God to make visible the love that the Father was offering humanity anew, regardless of the cost of such a heavenly gift being offered to (and potentially rejected by) a fallen world. The effects of sin caused suffering and cruelty in a world that had been created perfect, and the price Jesus paid to heal the wound of sin and to restore man to his purpose, means and end of love was to embrace the suffering caused by man's disobedience and to love in and through the Cross—even unto death. The love of God as revealed in Jesus Christ was meant to be received by a grateful humanity and returned to Him in praise and adoration. Instead, humanity rejected, ignored, mocked and crucified the love of God given to Him in Christ. Yet instead of this destroying Jesus' love, it perfected it. And Christ took the blood that He shed as a consequence of others' sin and offered it back to His enemies as a bath which would purify, heal, enlighten and strengthen those seeking to return to the Father's embrace. In this way, we can see how the divine response of God to the hostility of man's sin was to take the consequences of that sin (suffering and death) upon Himself and offer the remedy of salvation.

Every Christian path follows after the bloody footprints of Christ down Calvary. The triumph of crucified love in the Resurrection is the greatest mystery of faith. And yet, it is not easy to follow Christ in suffering. One must use the 'tools' He used of littleness, humility, pure love and surrendered *fiat* to do so. And so, at the beginning of this thesis, we must first come to understand what is crucified love before we analyze how Jesus, His Mother and the saints used it as an instrument to carry souls to heaven.

Chapter 1: What is Crucified Love?

The crucified love of Christ is His total gift of Himself to us in the Incarnation and on the Cross, rejected by men through sin and yet completed in perfect love, accepted by Our Lady in full and offered to sinners until the end of time. The divine love of Christ is shown on Calvary by His trifold act as Priest, Altar, and Victim. This divine love is not limited by man's rejection through sin, but rather is perfected in selfless self-abnegation in obedience to the Father and as an act of worship to glorify Him. Through surrendering in a kenotic *fiat* by embracing littleness before the Father and in responding in total love with the Holy Spirit to the Father's gift, Christ was able to consummate His gift of self to both the Father and humanity on the Cross.

St. Francis of Assisi was known to often cry out, *"Love is not loved!"* in lament over the countless souls who remained indifferent to Jesus' gift of Himself on the Cross. This is the essence of the crucified love that Christ lived in His Passion. Jesus—the Second Person of the Holy Trinity—offered Himself in full to the Father on the Cross to save all men and women from hell. And yet, as He was presented in the Temple as an infant, Simeon prophesized, *"Behold, this child is destined for the fall and rise of many in Israel, and to be a sign that will be contradicted"* (Lk 2:34). Although He came to offer the merciful love of God to humanity, His gift of self was rejected, abandoned, betrayed, mocked, calumniated, belittled, and even killed. *"He was in the world, and the world came to be through him, but the world did not know him. He came to what was his own, but his own people did not accept him"* (Jn 1:10–11).

In this way, His perfect divine and human love for mankind was crucified.

And yet, Jesus' suffering was even deeper than all of this. Because He took the just punishments of man's sin upon Himself, His love of the Father also felt to be crucified. Jesus—the Light of the world—was left in darkness. He Who came to give us faith and hope was tempted with doubt and despair. This can be heard as He cried on the Cross, *"My God, My God, why have you abandoned me?"* (Mt 27:46). The experience of the rejection of His Father's love that Jesus took upon Himself on account of man's sin that He was redeeming did not taint nor lessen the perfect love and trust that Christ had towards the Father. His experience of filial love being crucified only showed the great magnitude, strength, and purity of His love all the more. In fact, regardless of His experience of crucified love, Jesus depended all the more on His Father and the Holy Spirit to uphold Him on the Cross—through embracing fully through kenosis a littleness before them and allowing the trinitarian love that they shared to mysteriously uphold Him.

All throughout His life, Christ spoke of being sent to earth in order to fulfill His Father's will. Jesus—as the Word of God incarnate—perfectly fulfilled the words spoken by His Father in Isaiah, *"So shall my word be that goes forth from my mouth; It shall not return to me empty, but shall do what pleases me, achieving the end for which I sent it"* (Is 55:11). He often repeated this Himself—twice clearly repeating Himself in Chapter 5 and then Chapter 6 of the Gospel of St. John: *"I cannot do anything on my own; I judge as I hear, and my judgment is just, because I do not seek my own will but the will of the one who sent me"* (Jn 5:30) and *"I came down from heaven not to do my own will but the will of the one who sent me"* (Jn 6:38). In the Gospel of Matthew, we read how He prayed in the Our Father, *"Thy will be done on earth as in heaven"* (Mt 6:10).

The will of the Father for humanity was that they lived in a continual love relationship with Him —both while on earth and then eternally in heaven. Once man destroyed this will of God by refusing to live in His love (something that included obedience to His commands), God's will became that man would be restored to right relationship with Him through His Son becoming their Savior. In John 6:40 Jesus clearly states, *"For this is the will of my Father, that everyone who sees the Son and believes in him may have eternal life, and I shall raise him [on] the last day."* Christ came to earth full of both an eternal love of the Father and for humanity and reconciled them together by fulfilling the Father's will, suffering the consequences of sin (being suffering and death) although He never committed sin and thus offering the merit of such selfless love back to humanity so that they could 'merit' heaven with Christ's Own merit. Jesus 'purchased' man from the consequences of His sin through His Own blood. Christ offered humanity His Own Sonship with the Father.

And Christ did not only seek the will of His Father when it was pleasant or easy to serve Him. Instead, Jesus strengthened His commitment to total surrender to His Father's will as He saw His Passion and death drawing near. In John 12, we read Him say, *"I am troubled now. Yet what should I say? 'Father, save me from this hour'? But it was for this purpose that I came to this hour. Father, glorify your name."* Then a voice came from heaven, *"I have glorified it and will glorify it again"* (Jn 12:27–28). As He prayed in the Garden of Gethsemane suffering already from mankind's sin and the closeness of His death, He said to His apostles, *"My soul is sorrowful even to death. Remain here and keep watch with me."* He advanced a little and fell prostrate in prayer, saying, *"My Father, if it is possible, let this cup pass from me; yet, not as I will, but as you will"* (Mt 26:38–39). And once the soldiers drew near and Peter tried to defend Him, He ratified His commitment to the Father's will that was to allow His own death in order to redeem the world. He said, *"Do you think that I cannot call upon my Father and he will not provide me at this moment with more than twelve legions of angels? But then how would the scriptures be fulfilled which say that it must come to pass in this way?"* (Mt 26:53–54). On the Cross Jesus suffered the seeming abandonment of His Father crying out, *"'Eli, Eli, lema sabachthani?'* which means, *"My God, my God, why have you forsaken me?"'* (Mt 27:45–46). Yet these were not simply arbitrary words expressing Jesus' feeling in that moment, instead they were a prayer of Psalm 22 which leads the soul praying it from the feeling of abandonment to a cry of hope and trust in God's great plan and provision even in the midst of feeling forsaken. This Psalm leads to the proclamation in verse 25, that the Lord *"...did not turn away from me, but heard me when I cried out."* And verse 32 refers to the deliverance brought to Christ by the Father. Even in the midst of feeling abandoned on the Cross, Jesus actively exercised faith and trust in His Father entrusting His spirit to Him when He died: *"Jesus cried out in a loud voice, 'Father, into your hands I commend my spirit'; and when he had said this, he breathed his last"* (Lk 23:46).

Chapter 1: What is Crucified Love?

In all of these examples, we see how Jesus—although one with His Father as the Second Person of the Trinity—lowered Himself through humility and laid His will at the service of His Father's will and plan for mankind. In this kenosis, we see the greatness and glory of Christ's divinity shine forth. St. Paul speaks of this in the great hymn of Philippians:

> *Have among yourselves the same attitude that is also*
> *yours in Christ Jesus,*
> *Who, though he was in the form of God,*
> *did not regard equality with God something to be grasped.*
> *Rather, he emptied himself,*
> *taking the form of a slave,*
> *coming in human likeness;*
> *and found human in appearance,*
> *he humbled himself,*
> *becoming obedient to death, even death on a cross.*
> *Because of this, God greatly exalted him*
> *and bestowed on him the name*
> *that is above every name,*
> *that at the name of Jesus*
> *every knee should bend,*
> *of those in heaven and on earth and under the earth,*
> *and every tongue confess that*
> *Jesus Christ is Lord,*
> *to the glory of God the Father.* (Phil 2:5–11)

St. Paul in Phil 2:7 states that Christ 'emptied Himself' or 'made Himself nothing'. The Greek word used in this original text is kenosis. Several Doctors of the Church draw from this notion of Jesus' kenosis the perfect blueprint of God's intention for humanity. Man was created to pour himself out in love before God and, in this, to fulfill the Father's will. Jesus models this to a fallen humanity. It was Christ's kenosis—His self-emptying—that was the springboard to His total fiat to His Father's will in all things, even unto His ultimate Passion and Death. In this next chapter we will explore how Jesus' kenosis leading through the Cross to the fulfillment of His Father's will is connected to the notions of 'littleness and love'.

Chapter 2

How Did Jesus Live His Interior Passion?
In *Fiat* through Littleness and Love.

Another way to speak of the 'littleness' of Christ is to speak of His kenosis. Jesus Christ—being both God and man—humbled Himself before the heavenly Father in an act of humility that made Him 'little'. He emptied His own will, beauty and love in order to receive His Father's will, beauty and love and to allow His Father to be glorified through Him. In this first section explaining the 'littleness' of Christ, I will use St. Cyril to emphasize the dual nature of Jesus Who fully suffered as Man while still being God. I will then use St. Thomas Aquinas' explanation of kenosis to show how Jesus emptied Himself (while still remaining God) in order to suffer with and for humanity. Next, I will use Pope St. John Paul II's explanation of their teachings to further clarify how Christ's kenosis (littleness) was used to conquer through the Cross. After explaining this act of Christ making Himself 'little' before the Father, I will explain how this kenosis was a tool that helped Him to surrender to the Father's will in a perfect *fiat*. I will then show how Jesus' kenosis was a manifestation of His love shared both with the Father and humanity. It was this love that helped Him in His work of redemption. In this second section I draw from St. Thomas Aquinas' teaching on the mutual indwelling of love, as well as from Pope St. John Paul II's *Theology of the Body*, Pope Benedict, St. Augustine and St. Francis de Sales' writings on the power of Christ's love as revealed in His Passion.

Part 1: *Fiat* in Littleness (The Kenosis of Christ)

In understanding the kenosis of Christ, one must first grasp the fullness of Jesus' divinity—something that was not lessened in any degree by the Incarnation. The *Catechism of the Catholic Church* (CCC) explains:

> After the Council of Chalcedon, some made of Christ's human nature a kind of personal subject. Against them, the fifth ecumenical council, at Constantinople in 553, confessed that "there is but one hypostasis [or person], which is our Lord Jesus Christ, one of the Trinity." Thus, everything in Christ's human nature is to be attributed to his divine person as its proper subject, not only his miracles but also his sufferings and even his death: "He who was crucified in the flesh, our Lord Jesus Christ, is true God, Lord of glory, and one of the Holy Trinity."[3]

Both St. Thomas Aquinas as well as St. Cyril of Alexandria explained that the fullness of Christ's divinity was in no means lessened by the Incarnation, rather Jesus took upon His divinity something new—that being a fallen human nature. This humble action of Christ—often referred to as His "self-emptying"—does not mean that He emptied His divine nature to take upon Himself human

---

[3] *Catechism of the Catholic Church*, 2nd ed. (Vatican City: Vatican Press, 1997), § 468.

nature as a replacement. Rather Christ's action is referred to as His *kenosis*, a Greek noun derived from the verb "to empty oneself" as we read in Philippians 2:7. Fr. Richard Conlin, a Canadian priest explained,

> Kenosis is the way of divine love: the Father gives away His Word to create the world and the Word empties Himself to bring the world back to the Father. In the paradox of divine love, Christ's hidden work in the world is revealed as the most powerful way to achieve the ultimate purpose of all creation: that God "who is the creator of all things may at last become 'all in all,' thus simultaneously assuring His own glory and our beatitude" (CCC 294).[4]

And so, in Jesus Christ's kenosis in the Incarnation He takes upon His divine nature the creaturely mode of existence. God is not abandoning His divine nature to replace it with humanity, rather God is freely choosing to live as a human being with all conditions of being finite, material, and mortal. St. Cyril explains, *"He made our poverty his own and we see in Christ the strange and rare paradox of Lordship in servant's form and divine glory in human abasement."*[5]

---

[4] Richard Conlin, "The Paradox of Divine Love: A Treatise on the Kenosis of Christ and Creation," The Prodigal Catholic Blog, November 16, 2016, https://prodigalcatholic.com/2016/11/16/the-paradox-of-divine-love-a-treatise-on-the-kenosis-of-christ-and-creation/.

[5] Cyril of Alexandria, *On the Unity of Christ* (New York: St. Vladimir's Seminary Press, 2015), 101.

Pope Benedict XVI in his book, *Behold The Pierced One*, beautifully explores the Incarnation of Christ as the Word that took on Flesh thus making the invisible, visible and the untouchable, touchable. He explains the Incarnation as something that in some ways has been developing over time in biblical history. He writes:

> In the Incarnation of the Logos we have the fulfillment of something that has been underway ever since the very beginning in biblical history. It is as if the Word has continually been drawing flesh toward itself, making it its *own* flesh, the sphere of its own self. On the one hand the Incarnation can only take place because the flesh has always been the Spirit's outward expression and hence a possible dwelling for the Word; on the other hand it is only the Son's Incarnation that imparts to man and the visible world their ultimate and innermost meaning.[6]

Pope Benedict XVI sees the ultimate expression of the Incarnation in God taking on flesh because of His transcending love for mankind, and this flesh being put at the service of Christ's Passion, Death and Resurrection. This becomes visible in the mystery of His Sacred Heart and the wounds of Christ still present in the Resurrection, which He allows the disciples to physically touch in order to ignite their faith. He continues:

---

[6] Pope Benedict XVI, *Behold The Pierced One* (San Francisco: Ignatius Press, 1984), 52.

Chapter 2: How Did Jesus Live His Interior Passion?

The Incarnation, certainly, does not exist for its own sake; of its very nature it is ordered to transcendence and hence to the dynamism of the Easter mystery. Its whole basis is the fact that, in His paradoxical love, God transcends Himself and enters the realm of flesh, the realm of the passion of the human being. Conversely, however, this self-transcendence on the part of God only serves to bring to light that inner transcendence of the entire creation which the Creator Himself has appointed: body is the self-transcending movement toward spirit, and, through the spirit, to God. Beholding the invisible in the visible is an Easter phenomenon. . . . Doubting Thomas, who needs to be able to see and touch before he can believe, puts his hand into the Lord's opened side; in touching, he recognizes what is beyond touch and yet actually does touch it; he beholds the invisible and yet really sees it: "My Lord and My God" (John 20:28).[7]

In quoting Bonaventure, Pope Benedict says, *"The wound of the body also reveals the spiritual wound. . . . Let us look through the visible wound to the invisible wound of love!"*[8] Pope Benedict XVI sees the wounds of the Incarnate Lord as the connection between man and the infinite. He says:

---

[7] Pope Benedict XVI, *Behold The Pierced One*, 53.

[8] Pope Benedict XVI, *Behold The Pierced One*, 53.

> But we can discern...the connection of body and spirit, of Logos, Spirit and body, making the incarnate Logos into a "ladder" which we can climb as we behold, touch and experience. All of us are Thomas, unbelieving; but, like him, all of us can touch the exposed Heart of Jesus and thus touch and behold the Logos himself. So, with our hands and eyes fixed upon this Heart, we can attain to the confession of faith: "My Lord and my God!"[9]

It is here in the incarnate Heart wound of the incarnate Christ where 'heart speaks to Heart', or rather, the human heart encounters and speaks to the very Heart of God.

This notion of Christ's incarnation put at the service of the easter mystery is something we can clearly see in Hebrews 4:14–16, where St. Paul sets the example of Christ's poverty taking on human nature as a source of comfort and strength for all people struggling in the spiritual life. He writes:

> Since then, we have a great high priest who has passed through the heavens, Jesus, the Son of God, let us hold fast our confession. For we have not a high priest who is unable to sympathize with our weaknesses, but one who in every respect has been tempted as we are, yet without sinning. Let us then with confidence draw near to the throne of grace, that

---

[9] Pope Benedict XVI, *Behold The Pierced One*, 54.

we may receive mercy and find grace to help in time of need. (Heb 4:14–16)

In 428, Nestorius, a new Bishop of Constantinople, argued that the divine nature of Christ could not be born, suffer, hunger or die—and therefore, he claimed that Our Lady was the Mother of Jesus the Man, but not the Mother of God. St. Cyril of Alexandria confronted this heresy boldly and his teaching led to the Nestorian controversy being condemned by the Council of Ephesus in 431 where Christ's hypostatic union was upheld and Our Lady was proclaimed the "Mother of God". St. Cyril refused to divorce the two natures of Christ and claimed that what God cannot experience in His eternal life, He certainly can experience through His hypostatic union in the Incarnation of Jesus Christ. St. Cyril taught: *"He suffers in his own flesh, and not in the nature of the Godhead."*[10] He further explains:

> Christ was hungry, and tired from the journey. He slept, climbed in a boat, was struck by the servants' blows, was scourged by Pilate, and was spat on by the soldiers. They pierced His side with a spear, and offered him vinegar mixed with gall. He also tasted death, suffered on the cross, and suffered the other insults of the Jews. They would say that all these things are applicable to the man, even though they may be "referred" to the person of the true Son. We believe, however, in one God the Father almighty, maker of all things

---

[10] Cyril, *Unity of Christ*, 130.

visible and invisible, and also in one Lord Jesus Christ, His Son. And we refuse to separate off the man Emmanuel as distinct from the Word, for we know that the Word became man like us, and so we say that the selfsame was truly God from God, while humanly he was man from a woman, just as we are. We maintain that because of the intimacy he had with His own flesh, he even suffered its infirmities; he retained the impassibility of His own nature, in so far as he was not only man but the selfsame was also God by nature.[11]

This idea of the theandric activity of Christ, Who performed all of His works fully as both God and man, was also taken up by St. Maximus the Confessor. He explained that this is why Jesus was able to unite all that was created back with His Creator. He said:

"God became man" in order to save lost man, and . . . united through Himself the natural fissures running through the general nature of the universe . . . to fulfill the great purpose of God the Father, recapitulating all things, both in heaven and on earth, in Himself, in whom they also had been created."[12]

---

[11] Cyril, *Scholia on the Incarnation* 35, in John Anthony McGuckin, *Saint Cyril of Alexandria and the Christological Controversy* (New York: St. Vladimir's Seminary Press, 2010), 332–33.

[12] Maximus the Confessor, "Ambigua 41," *On Difficulties in the Church Fathers*, vol. 2 (Cambridge, MA: Harvard University Press, 2014), 111,

St. Cyril further explained this hypostatic nature of Christ as both God and Man Who came to earth to restore all of fallen creation to the Father in his treatise, *Unity of Christ*:

> And indeed, the Only Begotten Word, even though he was God and born from God by nature, the "radiance of the glory, and the exact image of the being" of the one who begot him (Heb 1:3), he it was who became man. He did not change himself into flesh; he did not endure any mixture of blending, or anything else of this kind. But he submitted himself to being emptied and "for the sake of the honor that was set before him he counted the shame as nothing" (Heb 12:2) and did not disdain the poverty of human nature. As God he wished to make that flesh which was held in the grip of sin and death evidently superior to sin and death. He made it His very own, and not soulless as some have said, but rather animated with a rational soul, and thus he restored flesh to what it was in the beginning.[13]

In this we see that Christ's hypostatic union was not disrupted by His experience of suffering, rather it was closely related to His living out of littleness and love. It was precisely Jesus' divine humility put at the service of His human will that allowed Him to consciously choose to

---

https://churchlifejournal.nd.edu/articles/st-maximus-confessors-summation-of-early-partistic-thought/.

[13] Cyril, *Unity of Christ*, 54–55.

empty Himself in full, thus satisfying the Father for the debt of man's sin. Christ chose littleness through His kenosis.

In St. Thomas Aquinas' *Commentary on St. Paul's Letter to the Philippians,* he diligently expounds on the concept of Jesus embracing a littleness before God the Father in His kenosis. It is most clearly seen in his explanation of Philippians 2:6–9.

In his commentary, St. Thomas Aquinas draws forth the notion that Christ in all His majesty humbled Himself before the Father and therefore allowed Himself to be exalted—first, on the Cross, and then through the Resurrection in all glory. St. Thomas first points out Jesus Christ's majesty so that the depth of His self-emptying humility can be understood. He claims that the majesty of Christ's divinity is not replaced by a humble humanity—rather it remains in its fullness (*"though in the form of God,"* Phil 2:6) and Jesus instead humbles Himself by taking on something His divinity lacked, being a fallen human nature. He explains:

> He mentions Christ's majesty first, in order that His humility might be more easily recommended. In regard to His majesty he proposes two things, namely, the truth of His divine nature, and His equality. He says, therefore: *who,* namely, Christ, *though he was in the form of God.* For it is through its form that a thing is said to be in a specific or generic nature; hence the form is called the nature of a thing. Consequently, to be in the form of God is to be in the nature of God. By this is understood that He is true God: ["That we may be in His true Son, Jesus Christ" (1 Jn 5:20)]. However, it should not be

supposed that the form of God is one thing and God himself another, because in simple and immaterial things, and especially in God, the form is the same as that whose form it is.[14]

St. Thomas goes on to distinguish the important difference between Jesus being "in the form of God" rather than "in the nature of God":

> But why does he say, *in the form,* rather than "in the nature"? Because this belongs to the proper names of the Son in three ways: for He is called the Son, the Word and the Image. Now the Son is the one begotten, and the end of begetting is the form. Therefore, to show the perfect Son of God he says, *in the form,* as though having the form of the Father perfectly. Similarly, a word is not perfect unless it leads to a knowledge of a thing's nature; and so the Word of God is said to be in the form of God, because He has the entire nature of the Father. Finally, an image is not perfect, unless it has the form of that of which it is the image: "He reflects the glory of God and bears the very stamp of His nature" (Heb 1:3).[15]

---

[14] Thomas Aquinas, *Commentary to St. Paul's Letter to the Philippians* 2.2, trans. F. R. Larcher (Albany: Magi Books, 1969). Html-formatted by Joseph Kenny, https://isidore.co/aquinas/english/SSPhilippians.htm#22.

[15] Aquinas, 2.2.

And then Aquinas explains that Christ had the form of God perfectly precisely because of His humility—His self-emptying that led to a state of "littleness" in the Incarnation. The Word of God "*did not deem equality with God, something to be grasped.*" And St. Thomas was not referring to the humanity of Christ grasping at becoming a God—of course, Christ's perfect humanity would not dare to equate itself with God. It was rather that in His divinity that in essence was equal to the divinity of the Father that He lowered in humility both in the Incarnation and then in His Passion. The divine humility of Christ is shown in the human virtue of littleness. Jesus does not grasp at greatness itself, but rather shows great humility by willingly taking the powerless form of a slave. By Christ taking His power and using it to empty Himself as a slave, He gives birth to a new kind of littleness in which the Father is glorified. Christ's self-emptying in this way makes up for the disobedience of man and creates a path of divine humility for humanity to follow in His footsteps. Because Jesus shows His divine humility in a human self-emptying act which includes suffering man's consequence of sin, He atones for man's sin and heals the wound that humanity's grasping at divinity caused in the universe. When humanity seeks after and imitates Christ's littleness in faith, man enters into and participates in Jesus' atonement for sin. St. Thomas Aquinas explains:

> But does He have it perfectly? Yes, because He *did not count equality with God a thing to be grasped.* This can be taken two ways: in one way, of His humanity. But this is not the way Paul understood it, because it would be heretical; for it would

be a grasping [robbery] if it referred to His humanity. Therefore, it must be explained in another way, namely, of His divinity, according to which equality with God is said of Christ. It is contrary to reason to say otherwise: because the nature of God cannot be received in matter; but the fact that someone existing in a certain nature participates in that nature to a greater or lesser degree is due to the matter; which is not the case here. Therefore, we must say that He *did not count equality with God a thing to be grasped,* because He is in the form of God and knows His own nature well. And because He knows this, it is stated in John (5:18): "He called God His Father, making himself equal with God." But this is not a grasping, as it was when the devil and man wished to be equal to him: "I will make myself like the Most High" (Is 14:14); "You will be like God" (Gen 3:5), for which Christ came to make satisfaction: "What I did not steal must I now restore?" (Ps 69:4). Then when he says, *but emptied himself,* he commends Christ's humility: first, as to the mystery of the Incarnation; secondly, as to the mystery of the passion (Phil 2:8). In regard to the first: first, he mentions His humility; secondly, its manner and form (Phil 2:7).[16]

After establishing the great majesty of Jesus Christ, St. Thomas is able to show the depths of humility Jesus embodied through *"emptying himself, taking the form of a slave."* Aquinas clearly distinguishes

---

[16] Aquinas, 2.2.

between Christ not emptying out His divinity, but rather assuming a humanity He did not have upon Him—this humanity being corporal and capable of suffering. In this we clearly see how it was precisely this "littleness" of humanity embraced by the majesty of God in the Incarnation is what allowed Him to accomplish His work as Redeemer. This work of Redemption included the capability of taking human flesh and subjecting it perfectly to the will of the Father through the purification of divine love through enduring a suffering that could not diminish it. Rather, Christ's suffering and death elevated His love as the God-Man to an immaculate perfection. St. Thomas explains:

> He says, therefore, He *emptied himself*. But since He was filled with the divinity, did He empty Himself of that? No, because He remained what He was; and what He was not, He assumed. But this must be understood in regard to the assumption of what He had not, and not according to the assumption of what He had. For just as He descended from heaven, not that He ceased to exist in heaven, but because He began to exist in a new way on earth, so He also emptied Himself, not by putting off His divine nature, but by assuming a human nature.
>
> How beautiful to say that He *emptied himself*, for the empty is opposed to the full! For the divine nature is sufficiently full, because every perfection of goodness is there. But human nature and the soul are not full, but capable of fullness, because it was made as a slate not written upon.

Therefore, human nature is empty. Hence he says, He *emptied himself,* because He assumed a human nature.[17]

St. Thomas emphasizes the important fact that Jesus Christ did not take humanity on His divine nature as an accident—but rather in substance. By reiterating the hypostatic union of Jesus' two natures as God and man, Aquinas highlights that kenosis of Christ that led to salvation of humanity. It was in acting little before God (though He was in the form of God) that Jesus' greatness shown most perfectly. And in this He not only repaired the sin of man grasping at divinity through the disobedience of sin, but also laid forth a path that humanity could follow to participate in this gift of atonement with Him.

Finally, St. Thomas proves that it was the littleness of Christ put at the service of the Father's will in sublime obedience that allowed Him to endure His Passion and Death and then be glorified in the Resurrection. Jesus did not do this solely to shine holiness exteriorly upon fallen, sinful humanity (as bright light surrounding something decayed can cover it up by blinding the viewer from seeing it), rather He took humanity that was decaying and ill from sin upon Himself in both matter and form and transformed it, renewed it, healed it through His wounds offered to the Father in reparation for sin. His perfect obedience perfected the disobedience of man. And Christ did this in such a way that all men are capable and called to not only

---

[17] Aquinas, 2.2.

gaze upon this mystery, but instead partake in it by following His example of humility, obedience and heroic love. Aquinas concludes:

> Then when he says, He *humbled himself,* he commends Christ's humility as indicated in His passion: first, he shows Christ's humility; secondly, its manner (Phil 2:8). Therefore He was man, but very great, because the same one is God and man; yet He *humbled himself:* "The greater you are, the more you must humble yourself" (Sir 3:18); "Learn from me, for I am gentle and lowly in heart" (Mt 11:29).
>
> The manner and the sign of His humility is obedience, whereas it is characteristic of the proud to follow their own will, for a proud person seeks greatness. But it pertains to a great thing that it not be ruled by something else, but that it rule other things; therefore, obedience is contrary to pride. Hence, in order to show the greatness of Christ's humility and passion, he says that He *became obedient;* because if He had not suffered out of obedience, His passion would not be so commendable, for obedience gives merit to our sufferings. But how was He made obedient? Not by His divine will, because it is a rule; but by His human will, which is ruled in all things according to the Father's will: "Nevertheless, not as I will but as thou wilt" (Mt 26:39). And it is fitting that He bring obedience into His passion, because the first sin was accomplished by disobedience: "For as by one man's disobedience many were made sinners, so by one man's obedience many will be made righteous" (Rom. 5:19); ["The obedient

man shall speak of victory" (Prv 21:28)]. That this obedience is great and commendable is evident from the fact that obedience is great when it follows the will of another against one's own. Now the movement of the human will tends toward two things, namely, to life and to honor. But Christ did not refuse death: "Christ also died for sins once for all, the righteous for the unrighteous" (1 Pt 3:18). Furthermore, He did not flee ignominy; hence he says, *even death on a cross,* which is the most shameful: "Let us condemn him to a shameful death" (Wis 2:20). Thus, He neither refused death nor an ignominious form of death.[18]

The purpose of the majestic Word of God embodying the little weakness of humanity was to lift up humanity to the divine life that was lost through sin. As St. Athanasius famously stated, *"The Son of God became man so that we might become God."* God did not simply remain in heaven shouting words of instruction at humanity, leaving them broken and lost in their disobedience. Rather the Father chose to send His Word incarnate to take upon Himself the flesh, the struggle, the suffering, and death of humanity. He sent His Son to lead by example, to aid His people by coming to "dwell among them" (Jn 1:14) and by writing the will of God upon humanity and creation through His Own sweat, blood, and life. Only in this way could humanity be renewed.

---

[18] Aquinas, 2.2.

Pope St. John Paul II sheds a new light on St. Thomas' explanation of Christ's descending kenosis and ascending glorification. Drawing from St. Thomas Aquinas (who was formed in the school of St. Ambrose) and the teachings of St. John of the Cross, he explained this beautifully in his commentary on Philippians 2:6–10. He wrote:

> The Canticle unfolds in a double vertical trajectory: a first movement is one of descent followed by ascension. Indeed, on one hand, there is the humiliating descent of the Son of God when, in the Incarnation, he becomes man out of love for humankind. He plummets into the kenosis, the "emptying" of His divine glory, pushed to the point of death on the cross, the punishment of slaves who were least among men, thus making him a true brother of suffering humanity, sinful and rejected.
>
> On the other hand, there is the triumphant ascension which takes place on Easter Day, when the Father reinstates Christ in the divine splendor and he is celebrated as Lord by the entire cosmos and by all men and women now redeemed. We are placed before a magnificent re-reading of Christ's mystery, primarily the Paschal one. St. Paul, along with proclaiming the Resurrection (cf. 1 Cor 15:3–5), defines Christ's Paschal mystery as the "exaltation," "raising up," "glorification."
>
> Therefore, from the bright horizon of divine transcendence, the Son of God crossed the infinite distance between

Chapter 2: How Did Jesus Live His Interior Passion?

Creator and creature. He did not grasp on, as if to a prey, to His "equality with God," which was due to him by nature and not from usurpation. He did not want to claim jealously this prerogative as a treasure, nor use it for His own interests. Rather, Christ "emptied," "humbled" Himself and appeared poor, weak, destined for the shameful death of crucifixion; it is precisely from this extreme humiliation that the great movement of ascension takes off, described in the second part of the Pauline hymn (cf. Phil 2, 9–11).

God now "exalts" His Son… Christ appears in glory … He still bears the signs of the Passion, of His true humanity, but now reveals the splendor of divinity. Near to us in suffering and death, Christ now draws us to Himself in glory, blessing us and letting us share in His eternity.[19]

As if these texts from St. Cyril, St. Thomas Aquinas and Pope St. John Paul II were not enough to explain the notion of Christ's littleness (understood as His kenosis) as being the powerful means—along with love itself—of carrying Him through His Passion and Death, we finally look to a commentary on this idea laid forth by St. Ambrose (as presented by Pope St. John Paul II):

Let us conclude our reflection on the Pauline hymn with the words of St. Ambrose, who often uses the image of Christ

---

[19] John Paul II, General Audience, November 19, 2003, § 1–3, https://www.vatican.va/content/john-paul-ii/en/audiences/2003/documents/hf_jp-ii_aud_20031119.html.

who "emptied himself," humiliating himself and, as it were, annihilating himself (*exinanivit semetipsum*) in the Incarnation and His oblation on the Cross...The Bishop of Milan says: "Christ, hung on the tree of the Cross . . . was pierced by the lance, whereby blood and water flowed out, sweeter than any ointment, from the victim acceptable to God, spreading throughout the world the perfume of sanctification.... Thus, Jesus, pierced, spread the perfume of the forgiveness of sins and of redemption. Indeed, in becoming man from the Word which he was, he was very limited and became poor, though he was rich, so as to make us rich through His poverty (cf. 2 Cor 8: 9). He was powerful, yet he showed himself as deprived, so much so that Herod scorned and derided him; he could have shaken the earth, yet he remained attached to that tree; he closed the heavens in a grip of darkness, setting the world on the Cross, but he had been put on the Cross; he bowed His head, yet the Word sprung forth; he was annihilated, nevertheless he filled everything. God descended, man ascended; the Word became flesh so that flesh could revindicate for itself the throne of the Word at God's right hand; he was completely wounded, and yet from him the ointment flowed. He seemed unknown, yet God recognized him."[20]

---

[20] John Paul II, § 4, citing Ambrose, *Explanatio super Psalmos CXVIII* 3.8, *Saemo* IX (Milan-Rome: Biblioteca Ambrosiana, 1987), 131, 133.

In these words of St. Ambrose, we vividly see how Christ chose to annihilate Himself. Jesus used His majesty to empty Himself, to choose poverty and littleness and to literally pour out His life for the sake of man's salvation. As Jesus' Heart was pierced open by a lance after His death and blood and water flowed forth upon the earth, the Father raised Him up in glory in order to lift humanity back into right relationship with Himself.

It is clear through the reflections of these great saints of the Church that it was precisely the kenosis of Jesus Christ—the Second Person of the Trinity made incarnate in the womb of our Mother Mary—His embracing of "littleness" despite the great majesty of His nature—that enabled Him to fully embrace the Cross and bring salvation to humanity. And in this self-abnegation, God the Father raised Him up glorifying Him as King of kings and Lord of lords forever.

Fiat and Kenosis

It is important to note that it was not Christ's littleness itself that won eternal life for humanity. It was His littleness put at the service of God the Father's will. *"He who was God did not deem equality with God something to be grasped"* (Phil 2:6). We touched upon the notion of Christ's emptying Himself out before the Father and taking His Father's will upon Himself—accomplishing it in perfect obedience—as the instrument used to complete the act of redemption. Now we will more specifically look at how Christ conformed His will to the

Father. All throughout Scripture we hear Jesus exercising His will to conform it to His Father's will:

For I have come down from heaven, not to do my own will but the will of him who sent me. (Jn 6:38)

I can do nothing on my own. As I hear, I judge, and my judgment is just, because I seek not my own will but the will of him who sent me. (Jn 5:30)

So Jesus said to them, "Truly, truly, I say to you, the Son can do nothing of His own accord, but only what he sees the Father doing. For whatever the Father does, that the Son does likewise." (Jn 5:19)

Jesus said to them, "My food is to do the will of him who sent Me, and to finish His work." (Jn 4:34)

But I do as the Father has commanded me, so that the world may know that I love the Father. Rise, let us go from here. (Jn 14:31)

And going a little farther he fell on His face and prayed, saying, "My Father, if it be possible, let this cup pass from me; nevertheless, not as I will, but as you will." (Mt 26:39)

And he said, "Abba, Father, all things are possible for you. Remove this cup from me. Yet not what I will, but what you will." (Mk 14:36)

Father, if you are willing, remove this cup from me. Nevertheless, not my will, but yours, be done. (Lk 22:42)

It was through His trustful *fiat* surrender to the Father—even when the Father's will contradicted His Own human nature and preferences—that He completed His work as Priest, Altar, and Victim on Calvary. It was Jesus' obedience and faithfulness to His Father's divine plan of salvation for humanity that held Him strong in the face of weakness, suffering and a dreadful fear that overtook His sensibilities. *"In the days when he was in the flesh, he offered prayers and supplications with loud cries and tears to the one who was able to save him from death—and he was heard because of His reverence. Son though he was, he learned obedience from what he suffered; and when he was made perfect, he became the source of eternal salvation for all who obey him"* (Heb 5:7–9).

The conformity of Christ's will to that of His heavenly Father was an act of adoration and worship—He glorified His Father by accomplishing His will while on earth. When we worship God—we acknowledge His supreme worth. When we adore God—we lower ourselves before Him and beg or beseech from Him in prayer. Christ in His very *action* of kenosis in the Incarnation and on the Cross glorified the Father by magnifying His worth by enduring the greatest sacrifice in order to accomplish the Father's will (which was the redemption of His creation from sin). Christ's embracing of littleness through the humility and obedience of *fiat* and death on the Cross "begged" from the Father (Jesus "asked" through His body's, mind's, Heart's, soul's, and emotion's action of conformity to the Father's will in life and in death) salvation for all. In this way, Jesus' perpetual *fiat* on earth both in His words and in His actions as the Word was a prayer of perfect adoration and worship.

St. Therese of Lisieux said, *"For me, prayer is a surge of the heart; it is a simple look turned toward heaven, it is a cry of recognition and of love, embracing both trial and joy."*[21] Jesus' Sacred Heart was always afire with consuming divine love surging towards His Father in heaven in a *fiat*—"let it be done." His eyes were always on heaven. *"Jesus **raised His eyes to heaven** and said, 'Father, the hour has come. Give glory to your son, so that your son may glorify you'"* (Jn 17:1, emphasis mine). *"And taking the five loaves and the two fish, **He looked up to heaven** and said a blessing over them"* (Lk 9:16, emphasis mine). *"So they took away the stone. And **Jesus raised His eyes** and said, 'Father, I thank you for hearing me'"* (Jn 11:41, emphasis mine). His very being magnified the glory of the Father simply through His constant indwelling love that He shared with Him. Hebrews 1:3 says that Christ's very identity was so intertwined both as God and Man with the Father that He was *"the refulgence of His glory, the very imprint of His being, and who sustains all things by His mighty word."* And so in this way, Jesus' very breath, heartbeat, every movement,

---

[21] Thérèse of Lisieux, *The Story of a Soul*, C 25r, in *Catechism*, § 2558.

word and even aspiration of the Heart was a prayer and fire of loving praise of God the most high.

Christ's littleness—Christ's kenosis—was not passive. It was the active lowering of Himself before God the Father. It was the action of consciously taking the corporealness of humanity on Himself and choosing to forget Himself to bask in the will and the glory of the Father. In this He leaves humanity a clear example to follow. And in this we see a glimpse of the radiance of spousal trinitarian love.

Part 2: *Fiat* and Spousal Trinitarian Love

Not only was it Jesus' kenosis in the Incarnation and on the Cross that allowed Him to complete the work of redemption, but it was also His action of taking His will—surrendering it to the Father in *fiat*—and then allowing the Father to set His will and Heart on fire with divine love. Love, I would argue, fired Jesus one with the Father through a union of wills and fired Him one with humanity by emptying Himself out on the Cross for their salvation. St. Augustine explained in His work *On the Trinity* that God the Father is the Lover, God the Son is the Beloved and God the Holy Spirit is the Love between them personified. In Question 37 of the *Summa theologica* St. Thomas Aquinas quotes St. Gregory the Great as saying *"The Holy Spirit himself is Love."* In this analogy, we see why human spousal love is a reflection of the perfection of trinitarian love—where the Father and the Son infinitely love each other so fully that the third Person of the Holy Spirit is eternally begotten of that love. And it is this Third Person of the Trinity Who cements the Father and the Son together truly as one. St. Thomas Aquinas in Question 28 of the *Summa theologica* explains that one effect of love is mutual indwelling.

> It is written (1 Jn 4:16): "He that abideth in charity abideth in God, and God in him." Now charity is the love of God. Therefore, for the same reason, every love makes the beloved to be in the lover, and vice versa.
>
> I answer that, this effect of mutual indwelling may be understood as referring both to the apprehensive and to the appetitive power. Because, as to the apprehensive power, the beloved is said to be in the lover, inasmuch as the beloved abides in the apprehension of the lover, according to Philippians 1:7, "For that I have you in my heart": while the lover is said to be in the beloved, according to apprehension, inasmuch as the lover is not satisfied with a superficial apprehension of the beloved, but strives to gain an intimate knowledge of everything pertaining to the beloved, so as to penetrate into his very soul. Thus it is written concerning the Holy Ghost, who is God's Love, that He "searcheth all things, yea the deep things of God" (1 Cor 2:10).
>
> As the appetitive power, the object loved is said to be in the lover, inasmuch as it is in his affections, by a kind of complacency: causing him either to take pleasure in it, or in its good, when present; or, in the absence of the object loved, by his longing, to tend towards it with the love of concupiscence, or towards the good that he wills to the beloved, with

the love of friendship: not indeed from any extrinsic cause (as when we desire one thing on account of another, or wish good to another on account of something else), but because the complacency in the beloved is rooted in the lover's heart. For this reason, we speak of love as being "intimate"; and "of the bowels of charity." On the other hand, the lover is in the beloved, by the love of concupiscence and by the love of friendship, but not in the same way. For the love of concupiscence is not satisfied with any external or superficial possession or enjoyment of the beloved; but seeks to possess the beloved perfectly, by penetrating into his heart, as it were. Whereas, in the love of friendship, the lover is in the beloved, inasmuch as he reckons what is good or evil to his friend, as being so to himself; and his friend's will as his own, so that it seems as though he felt the good or suffered the evil in the person of his friend. Hence it is proper to friends "to desire the same things, and to grieve and rejoice at the same," as the Philosopher says (*Ethic.* ix, 3 and *Rhet.* ii, 4). Consequently, in so far as he reckons what affects his friend as affecting himself, the lover seems to be in the beloved, as though he were become one with him: but in so far as, on the other hand, he wills and acts for his friend's sake as for his own sake, looking on his friend as identified with himself, thus the beloved is in the lover.

In yet a third way, mutual indwelling in the love of friendship can be understood in regard to reciprocal love: inasmuch as friends return love for love, and both desire and do good things for one another.[22]

St. Thomas continues, explaining that *"The beloved is contained in the lover, by being impressed on his heart and thus becoming the object of his complacency. On the other hand, the lover is contained in the beloved, inasmuch as the lover penetrates, so to speak, into the beloved."* He speaks of the movement of love penetrating into the beloved and causing a kind of mutual indwelling.[23]

As one reflects on this explanation of the nature of love not only to bind two people together exteriorly, but also to cause a mutual indwelling where two people live with one heart, it is obvious that God Who is the perfection of Person would live this absolutely within Himself—causing the love that is shared between the Father and Son to not only manifest as the Third Person of the Trinity (the Holy Spirit), but to cause these three persons in one God to share an indwelling (through love) more profound than any human mind can fathom. If this trinitarian love of God is powerful enough to cause a divine mutual indwelling, then it must be not only the effect that comes from the incarnate Christ's adherence to the Father's will, but also the strength and impetus that holds Jesus fast and faithful to His identity of Redeemer in and through the Cross.

All throughout Scripture Jesus speaks about the unitive force of His love for the Father, a love so powerful and full that it could be

---

[22] Aquinas, q. 28, a. 2.

[23] Aquinas, q. 28, a. 2.

said that His love with the Father—their loves—are one. Jesus speaks so often in the Gospels about how the Father and He are one. The cause of this unity—a unity of nature, of will, and of heart so to say—is love. Over and over, Christ reflects on this indwelling love that He shares with the Father. We read:

*I do not ask for these only, but also for those who will believe in me through their word, that they may all be one, **just as you, Father, are in me, and I in you**, that they also may be in us, so that the world may believe that you have sent me. The glory that you have given me I have given to them, that they may be one even as we are one, I in them and you in me, that they may become perfectly one, so that the world may know that you sent me and loved them even as you loved me.* (Jn 17:20–23, emphasis mine)

"The Father and I are one." (Jn 10:30, emphasis mine)

In the beginning was the Word,
and the Word was with God,
and the Word was God.
He was in the beginning with God.
All things came to be through him,
and without him nothing came to be. (Jn 1:1–3)

"*What came to be through him was life,*
And this life was the light of the human race;

the light shines in the darkness,
and the darkness has not overcome it. (Jn 1:4–5)

The Father is the mouth—the fountainhead of all being and grace; the Son is the Word and the Spirit is the Breath of God within Him. The Father is the lamp—Christ is the light—the Holy Spirit is the bright warmth, the illumination. The Father is the fountain, Christ is the water, the Holy Spirit is the refreshment. The Father is the author, Christ is the life and the Holy Spirit is the sustainer. And it is the unity of their one love that inspired, led and fulfilled everything that Jesus Christ did on earth.

Not only was it Jesus Christ's love shared with His Father that upheld Him through His Passion and Death, it was also His spousal love for humanity. St. John of Avila wrote, *"If that love of Christ's soul toward God carried such tremendous force (because the gunpowder of grace that was driving it was infinite), and after having gone directly to wound the heart of the Father, it rebounds from there to the love of men, then with how much force and joy will it not turn upon them in order to love them and renew them?"*[24] And, *"You wished to go to the nuptial bed of the cross. . . . It does not seem, Lord, as if you are going to the cross, but to a wedding feast."*[25] Jesus Christ clearly taught that He did not come to earth simply to illumine humanity with the love He shared with the Father, but to also draw humanity into it,

---

[24] John of Avila, *On the Love of God; On the Priesthood*, ed. Idefonso Fernandez Figares (New York: IVE Press, 2012), 24.

[25] John of Avila, 28.

Chapter 2: How Did Jesus Live His Interior Passion?

allowing all people who cooperate with grace to partake in this love. In fact, He insists that if one wants to follow Him, to become and live as a child of God, to reach heaven—then He absolutely must enter in and be transformed by the love He shares with His Father and to *"remain in that love,"* even unto and through the Cross. He is very clear on this:

> *I am the true vine, and my Father is the vinedresser. Every branch in me that does not bear fruit he takes away, and every branch that does bear fruit he prunes, that it may bear more fruit. Already you are clean because of the word that I have spoken to you.* **Abide in me, and I in you. As the branch cannot bear fruit by itself, unless it abides in the vine, neither can you, unless you abide in me. I am the vine; you are the branches. Whoever abides in me and I in him, he it is that bears much fruit, for apart from me you can do nothing.** (Jn 15:1–18, 40, emphasis mine)

> *But when the Helper comes, whom I will send to you from the Father, the Spirit of truth, who proceeds from the Father, he will bear witness about me.* (Jn 15:26)

> *Jesus answered him, "If anyone loves me, he will keep my word, and my Father will love him, and* **we will come to him and make our home with him.**" (Jn 14:23, emphasis mine)

Whoever has my commandments and keeps them, he it is who loves me. And he who loves me will be loved by my Father, and I will love him and manifest myself to him. (Jn 14:21)

In order to draw man into this wellspring of divine love, God manifests Himself to His people as a Husband—culminating with His complete revelation of self through the Bridegroom Jesus Christ. Pope St. John Paul II speaks extensively about this in the audiences collected under the title A *Theology of the Body*. Beginning with his General Audience of September 15, 1982, the Holy Father expounds on this great love of God for His people, as well as specifically comparing Christ's bridal love for the Church as the example par excellence that all married couples should follow. He writes:

> . . . The love of Yahweh for the Chosen People can and must be compared to the love that unites bride and bridegroom, the love that should unite spouses. It would be good to quote many passages from Isaiah, Hosea, and Ezekiel. . . .[26]

To illustrate this tradition, we will limit ourselves for the moment to quoting a text from Isaiah. The prophet says:

Do not fear, for you will no longer blush;

---

[26] John Paul II, General Audience, September 15, 1982, § 94.7, in *Man and Woman He Created Them: A Theology of the Body*, trans. Michael Waldstein (Boston: Pauline Books and Media, 2006), 494.

Chapter 2: How Did Jesus Live His Interior Passion?

Do not be ashamed, for you will no longer be dishonored;
For you will forget the shame of your youth,
And the dishonor of your widowhood you will remember no more.
For your Creator is your husband,
Lord of hosts is his name;
The Holy One of Israel is your Redeemer,
The God of the whole earth his is called.
For like a wife forsaken and grieved in spirit the Lord has called you.
Is the wife of one's youth cast off, says your God?
For a brief moment I abandoned you,
But with immense love I will take you again. . . .
My steadfast affection shall not depart from you,
And my covenant of peace shall not waver,
Says the Lord, who has compassion on you. (Is 54:4–10)

. . . The love of God-Yahweh for Israel, the Chosen People, is expressed as the love of a human bridegroom for the woman chosen to be His wife through the conjugal covenant. . . .

Thus, in this text, God Himself in all His majesty as Creator and Lord of creation is explicitly called "husband" of the chosen people. This "husband" speaks about His great "affection," which will not "depart" from Israel, His wife, but will constitute a stable foundation of the "covenant of peace" with Him. . . . The "Lord of hosts" calls Himself not only "Creator" but also "Redeemer."[27]

In this, we see that God is not only the spring of all life, but also the preserver, the purifier, the savior of all life. He creates life like a Father and recreates life as the Son, the Bridegroom. Pope St. John Paul II explains:

> The first dimension of love and election, as a mystery hidden from ages in God, is a fatherly dimension and not a "conjugal" one. According to Ephesians, the first characteristic mark of that mystery remains connected with the very fatherhood of God, which is particularly brought out by the prophets (see Hos 11:1–4; Is 63:8–9; 64:7; Mal 1:6). The analogy of spousal love and of marriage appears only when the "Creator" and the "Holy one of Israel" manifests himself as "Redeemer." Isaiah says: "For your Creator is your husband, the Lord of hosts is His name; the Holy One of Israel is your Redeemer." (Is 54:5)
>
> Already in this text one can in some sense see the parallelism between "husband" and "Redeemer."
>
> . . . St. Paul, writing the letter to the People of God of the New Covenant and in particular to the Church of Ephesus, no longer repeats, "Your Creator is your husband," but shows how the "Redeemer" who is the firstborn Son and from ages

---

[27] John Paul II, General Audience, September 22, 1982, § 95.1–4, in *Theology of the Body*, 495–97.

Chapter 2: How Did Jesus Live His Interior Passion?

the beloved of the Father' reveals at the same time that His saving love, which consists in His gift of self for the Church, is a spousal love by which he marries the Church and makes her His own Body.[28]

This is clearly spoken by St. Paul in Ephesians 5:21–33:

> *For the husband is head of his wife just as Christ is head of the church, he himself the savior of the body. As the church is subordinate to Christ, so wives should be subordinate to their husbands in everything.*
>
> *Husbands, love your wives, even as Christ loved the church and handed himself over for her to sanctify her, cleansing her by the bath of water with the word, that he might present to himself the church in splendor, without spot or wrinkle or any such thing, that she might be holy and without blemish…*
>
> *This is a great mystery, but I speak in reference to Christ and the church.*

Here we not only see God referring to His people as His spouse or bride, but also as His wife. This is important as we later go on to show how Christ the new Adam redeems not only Our Lady as the 'woman/wife,' the new Eve, but also all of Her children who make up the Church.

---

[28] John Paul II, § 95:5–7, in *Theology of the Body*, 497–99.

Just as Jesus Christ lived kenosis (self-emptying) before the Father in the Incarnation and in His adherence to the Father's will, we also see in Ephesians how Christ lived a kenosis (self-emptying) before humanity. Here St. Paul expounds on how Christ "*handed himself over for her to sanctify her, cleansing her by the bath of water with the word.*" On the Cross, Jesus Christ poured out not only His blood, His tears, His strength, His worldly success, His power and His glory, but also all of His life and love in order to wash the Church from sin purifying her to the point of being totally translucent—brilliantly spotless and without blemish. St. Paul says that Christ—the Word of God incarnate—washes humanity with "the word," meaning that He washes His people with the Decalogue, the Old Testament prophesies, the canticles of the Psalms, His Own teaching and preaching. And yet, the gift of Christ the Husband goes even deeper—being the Word of God made flesh—He washes the Church and all souls brought to her fonts of baptism with His very self. He shares His very flesh and blood, soul and divinity with each member of His body through the Sacraments and by taking our sufferings, sin, and shame upon Himself on the Cross. Through His Passion and Death, through His wounds and tears, Jesus pours Himself out as a Bridegroom rushing forth with anticipatory love to possess His bride through a one-flesh union. A sermon popularly attributed to St. Augustine explains:

> Like a Bridegroom Christ went forth from his nuptial chamber. . . . He came even to the marriage-bed of the cross, and there, ascending it, he consummated a marriage. And when

he sensed the creature sighing in her breath, he surrendered himself to torment for his bride in a communication of love.[29]

In love on the Cross Jesus embraced fallen humanity as a beloved wife. He was willing to actively forget Himself in order to save her. He was willing to empty Himself out completely as a bridegroom hands himself over to his bride in full. In this way, His love of humanity drove Him to be bound on the Cross and His love held Him faithful even unto His Own Death.

Pope Benedict XVI similarly considers Christ's Passion and Death in terms of God's marital love for His people. He explains that through Christ's taking upon Himself the suffering of humanity, God and man become one. He speaks of this mystery in His book, *Jesus of Nazareth*:

> Jesus identifies Himself here as the "Bridegroom" of God's promised marriage with His people and, by doing so, He mysteriously places His own existence, Himself, within the mystery of God. In Him, in an unexpected way, God and man become one, become a "marriage," though this marriage—as Jesus subsequently points out—passes through the cross.[30]

---

[29] Augustine, "Homily on the Nativity of the Lord," *Sermo Suppositus* 120:8, Migne PL 39:1986, English translation from Brant Pietre, *Jesus the Bridegroom*, (New York: Image, 2014), 93.

[30] Benedict XVI, *Jesus of Nazareth—Holy Week: From the Entrance into Jerusalem to the Resurrection* (San Francisco: Ignatius Press, 2011), 1:252.

Each soul is united with Jesus as we are washed in the waters of Baptism, as He speaks the words of absolution over us in the Sacrament of Reconciliation—the words He spoke bloodied and battered on Calvary—*"Father, forgive them, for they know not what they do."* And each soul's one-flesh union with Christ is consummated in the Eucharistic sacrifice of Calvary—as we receive and are nourished by His body and blood in the Eucharist and allow this sacrament to transform us to be not only living tabernacles of His presence, but "little Christs" to all we meet. St. Paul in his letter to the Ephesians directs Christians to live in the love of Christ (a mutual indwelling proper to love itself as previously explained by St. Thomas Aquinas) and to imitate that love of His, which caused Him to hand Himself over to be crushed as seed is to make oil so as to be a sacrificial fragrant aroma before God: *"and live in love, as Christ loved us and handed himself over for us as a sacrificial offering to God for a fragrant aroma"* (Eph 5:2). Christ becomes "little" on the Cross (and in the Eucharist) to conquer human hearts—to come to possess them whole.

In his *Theology of the Body*, Pope St. John Paul II explains:

> On the basis of Christ's spousal love for the Church, the sacrament of redemption—fruit of Christ's redeeming love—becomes a permanent dimension of the life of the Church herself, a fundamental and life-giving dimension. It is the *"mysterium magnum"* of Christ and the Church, the eternal mystery realized by Christ, who "gave himself for her" (Eph 5:25),

uniting with her with an indissoluble love, just as spouses, husband and wife, unite in marriage.[31]

In this we see how Christ becomes 'little' and empties Himself out before the Father so that the Father's powerful love can rush through Him in full to touch, fill and transform humanity, who is like His Own bride. The union Christ consummates with humanity on the Cross happens as He takes His bride's punishment, wounds and weakness upon Himself and offers her in return His Own filial relationship with the Father. This union of Christ and His wife (the Church) is life-giving. It offers humanity eternal life that will never end.

In this way, Jesus Christ through littleness before the Father and before man—as well as consumed by love for the Father and for man—is bound fully to the Cross offering the Passion for the salvation of humanity. Christ does the will of the Father because He loves Him. And He loves humanity enough to die for its redemption both with a love that is the Father's (indwelling in love with the Father, Jesus loves humanity with the Father's very love which has become His Own), as well as with His Own love as the God-Man. And as Christ empties Himself for us and into us on Calvary (and through the Sacraments), He recreates us so that His love becomes our love and changes us into authentic children of God who are also capable of a reciprocal total self-emptying before God in response to His gift.

---

[31] John Paul II, General Audience, October 13, 1982, § 98.4, in *Theology of the Body*, 509.

Human souls find their new identity in Him. St. Frances de Sales in his *Treatise on the Love of God* beautifully explains:

> Divine love makes its abode in the most high and sublime region of the soul, where it offers sacrifice and holocausts to the divinity as Abraham did, and as our Savior sacrificed himself upon the top of Calvary, to the end that from so exalted a place it may be heard and obeyed by its people, that is, by all the faculties and affections of the soul. These he governs with an incomparable sweetness, for love has no convicts nor slaves, but brings all things under its obedience with a force so delightful, that as nothing is so strong as love nothing also is so sweet as its strength.... God having created man to His image and likeness, wills that as in himself so in man all things should be ordered by love and for love.[32]

This beautiful reflection by St. Frances de Sales can first be applied to the Man Christ Himself. The divine love of His Father made its abode in His soul where He offered sacrifices and holocausts surrendering to His Father's will in all things even unto death on a Cross. All men created in the image and likeness of Christ are called to imitate His example of self-emptying that leads eventually to the perfection of love. Humanity is drawn into this love of Jesus by Christ's offering of Himself both on their behalf to the Father as well

---

[32] Francis de Sales, *Treatise on the Love of God,* trans. Henry Benedict Mackey (Radford, VA: Wilder Publications, 2011), 52.

as to each individual soul. As each human heart receives this self-emptying gift of Jesus, it is inspired to make a return of his love back to the Father.

In St. Francis de Sales' reflection on the Song of Songs, he further expounds how this spousal love of a soul—wooed by Christ the Bridegroom—is enflamed by an overpowering desire for union with Him—even in His littleness and in His Cross. He writes of the bridal soul speaking:

> To be united heart to Heart, spirit to Spirit, to my God, my spouse, my life! When will the hour come in which I shall pour my soul into His Heart, and he will pour His heart into my soul, and thus happily united we shall live inseparable?![33]

This union of love will be consummated precisely on the Cross, where Christ pours Himself out for the Church and She responds with a gift of Herself in return. St. Frances de Sales later on writes that Mount Calvary is the *Academy of Love*. We see there the depth of Jesus' self-annihilation undergone for the sake of love alone, as well as how His love enflames the heart of His beloved to love with the same fire of love in return. He writes:

> Mount Calvary is the mount of lovers. All love that takes not its beginning from Our Savior's Passion is frivolous and dangerous. Unhappy is death without the love of the Savior,

---

[33] Francis de Sales, 58.

unhappy is love without the death of the Savior! Love and death are so mingled in the Passion of Our Savior that we cannot have the one in our heart without the other. Upon Calvary one cannot have life without love, nor love without the death of Our Redeemer. But, except there, all is either eternal death or eternal love: and all Christian wisdom consists in choosing rightly. . . . During this mortal life we must choose eternal love or eternal death, there is no middle choice.

O eternal love, my soul desires and makes choice of thee eternally! Ah! Come, Holy Spirit and inflame our hearts with thy love! To love or to die! To die and to love! To die to all other love in order to live to Jesus' love, that we may not die eternally, but that, living in thy eternal love, O Savior of our souls we may eternally sing: Vive Jesus! I love Jesus. Live Jesus whom I love! I love Jesus, who lives and reigns forever and ever. Amen.[34]

The entire purpose of Christ's self-gift of love is to draw His beloved into that love. This union of love inspires a soul to love as Christ does, disregarding suffering and claiming the marks of His Cross as most precious jewels. St. Ambrose explains, *"The soul that is espoused to Jesus Christ, and is voluntarily joined with Him on the*

---

[34] Francis de Sales, 425–26.

bed of the cross, considers nothing to be more glorious than wearing on his person the insignias and livery of the Crucified One."[35]

As we have seen in this chapter, Jesus Christ's littleness and spousal love are the greatest tools that enabled Him to live *fiat* to the Father's will in full on the Cross. He offers these tools to His beloved Bride and Wife, the Church, through His kenosis on Calvary so that each individual soul may be transformed by them and come to imitate them. It is Jesus' self-emptying love in His redemptive work of the Passion that makes Him the new Adam and He lives this out specifically in the roles of Priest, Altar and Victim. I will address how this is done in the following chapter.

---

[35] John of Avila, *On the Love of God*, 30.

Chapter 3

Christ as the New Adam and Redeemer— Jesus as Priest, Altar, and Victim

Through a total self-emptying in littleness and consummation by the fires of divine love, the Lord Jesus endured His Passion and Death on Calvary to restore humanity to the Father. In this paramount work of salvation, He fulfilled His mission as the new Adam, the Redeemer, the Priest, the Altar, and the Victim. These five titles of Jesus Christ are deeply intertwined and this connection is what we will unfold in this present chapter.

As we have established, Jesus Christ is the Bridegroom of the Church—laying down His life for the people of God for their salvation. His love for His people is inseparable from His sacrifice, which was a priestly work. Jesus came to earth with one purpose—to obey His Father's will which desired the redemption of His people. In Hebrews 3:1-2, we read that Jesus is *"the high priest of our confession, who was faithful to the one who appointed him."* This faithfulness Jesus would accomplish with the price of His Own blood. And this faithfulness that Jesus lived as the Son of the eternal Father restored all of humanity to a right relationship with Him. In this, Christ was the new Adam, the first-born of all creation.

In an ancient homily, St. John Chrysostom beautifully explains Jesus Christ as the new Adam and shows how He repaired all of the wounds given to humanity by the sinful fall of the first Adam:

You have observed His outstanding triumph, the splendid achievement of the cross. Now let me tell you something even more remarkable, the manner in which He gained His victory, and you will marvel all the more! Christ conquered the devil using the same means and the same weapons that the devil used to win. Let me tell you how this occurred.

The symbols of our fall were a virgin, a tree and death. The virgin was Eve (for she had not yet known man); then there was the tree; and death was Adam's penalty. And again, these three tokens of our destruction, the virgin, the tree and death, became the tokens of our victory. Instead of Eve there was Mary; instead of the tree of knowledge of good and evil, the wood of the cross; instead of Adam's death, the death of Christ.

Do you see then that the devil was defeated by the very means he used to conquer? By a tree the devil laid Adam low, and by a tree Christ defeated him. The first tree sent men to the world below, but the second called back those who had already gone down. The first tree buried man, already naked and a captive; the second revealed the victor naked to all the world.

The first death condemned those who were born afterward, but the second death raised up even those who were born before. Who will speak of the powers of the Lord? Though dead we became immortal. Such is the achievement of the cross. Do you now understand the victory and the way it was won? Learn now how this victory was achieved

Chapter 3: Christ as the New Adam and Redeemer

without any labor or effort of our own. We bloodied no weapons, nor stood on the battle line, nor bore any wounds, nor saw any fighting, and yet we won the victory. It was the Lord's combat, but ours was the crown. And since it is our victory, let us be like soldiers and raise joyous voices in song in praise of our achievement. Praising the Lord let us say: "Death is swallowed up in victory. O death, where is your victory? O death, where is your sting?"

All this was the glorious result of the cross. The cross is our trophy raised against the demons, our sword against sin, and the sword Christ used to pierce the serpent. The cross is the Father's will, the glory of the Only-begotten, the joy of the Spirit, the pride of the angels, the guarantee of the Church, Paul's boast, the bulwark of the saints and the light of the entire world.[36]

In Genesis, we see how God created Adam, placed him in the Garden, created Eve and entrusted her to him and instructed them not to eat of the fruit of the tree of good and evil. In this divinely instituted arrangement, Eve should have been looking at Adam to protect, provide for and guide her, and Adam should have been looking at God. But instead, the serpent tempted Eve and, in that

---

[36] John Chrysostom, Homily *De coemeterio et de cruce*, in International Commission on English in the Liturgy, *The Liturgy of the Hours* (New York: Catholic Book Publishing Co., 1975), 4:1660.

moment, Eve was looking at her own desires in sin, and Adam was looking at her. The divine order was inverted.

Yet this sad story of how impurity entered the world does not end on a hopeless note. Jesus came as the new Adam—the sacrificial Adam—Who was to restore the original purity lost by Adam and Eve's sin as well as to restore humanity's right relationship with God through obedience. Jesus lived perfect purity, and He gifts that to humanity on the Cross. Where Adam allowed his wife Eve to tempt him to sin, Christ seeing that His "Wife" (humanity) had fallen in sin, stays to fight for Her salvation through the sacrifice of His Own life. All that was broken in man and woman's purity by original sin was healed by Jesus' Incarnation, and especially by His perfection of love shown by His total sacrifice on the Cross. For all of His life, Jesus lived the perfect relationship with the Father—the sort of relationship God intended for humankind from the beginning. Adam and Eve had grasped at the forbidden fruit in the garden of Eden. Jesus did not grasp anything, instead He docilly received all that the Father ordained for Him. *"Though he was in the form of God, did not regard equality with God something to be grasped. Rather, he emptied himself, taking the form of a slave, coming in human likeness; and found human in appearance, he humbled himself, becoming obedient to death, even death on a cross"* (Phil 2:6–8).

Adam and Eve disobeyed. Jesus obeyed unto DEATH! Adam and Eve ate the fruit of the forbidden tree and thus entered darkness and had to be thrown from the Garden. Jesus willingly entered the Garden to suffer and pray. He was invited back into that Garden to redeem the sin which had occurred there. And Jesus also in obedience had to eat the fruit of a tree—the horrific fruit of the Cross. This fruit was not pleasing to Jesus' eye or taste (as the "forbidden fruit' had been to Adam and Eve), for it was a symbol of everything which hurt His Father, whom He dearly loved. And yet in obedience, He had to "drink His cup." Jesus' love had to conquer all sin and death let into the world by Adam and Eve's sin. And in His surrender, in His *fiat*, in His trust in His Father for everything He needed (a trust that was not even broken by what seemed to be His Father's abandonment on the Cross), He made all things new. Where Eve said, "Take and eat" to her husband, giving sin to humanity, Jesus says "Take and eat" to humanity, offering His very body on the Cross and in the Eucharist as a remedy to that sin. In this, humanity was given the chance to become children of God. It is clear that Jesus' work as the Redeemer clearly identifies Him also as the new Adam Who offers eternal life.

It is written, "The first man, Adam, became a living being," the last Adam a life-giving spirit. But the spiritual was not first; rather the natural and then the spiritual. The first man was from the earth, earthly; the second man, from heaven. As was the earthly one, so also are the earthly, and as is the heavenly one, so also are the heavenly. Just as we have borne the image of the earthly one, we shall also bear the image of the heavenly one. (1 Cor 15:45–49)

A contemporary of St. John Chrysostom—the Doctor and Father of the Church, St. Augustine—further developed this idea of Jesus Christ, the new Adam. Augustine claims that Adam was not stuck between the two options of abandoning his wife in sin or joining her in her sin. There was a third option of *sacrifice*—Adam could fight to free his wife from the grasp of Satan by staying to sacrifice on her behalf. Adam did not do this in the garden of Eden, and thus he himself is guilty of committing sin right along with his wife. But Jesus Christ came to earth as the new Adam—and He *did* sacrifice Himself completely to rescue His wife, the Church, from eternal death and hell. Professor John Cavadini explains St. Augustine's interpretation as thus:

> That Adam had some alternative is clear from the contrasting story of the second Adam. Christ did not abandon us, and, though he joined us sinners, he did not enter into a fellowship of sin with us. He was prepared, in mercy, to sacrifice his own life for Eve, now in the person of the church, the new Eve (which presumably includes the old Eve). Adam had the chance, it would seem, to somehow "save" Eve by his own compassionate mercy, but he preferred to take advantage of Eve, committing himself to the complacent truncation of the imagination, the "myth" of the false alternatives. Part of his construction of these false alternatives is revealed in the story he tells God in order to explain what happened. As Augustine sees it, Adam blamed Eve, expecting that God would judge her and vindicate him. . . . This is a "false compassion" that displaces "the true compassion of self-sacrifice."
>
> Adam, in following Eve into sin enacts a simulacrum of mercy justified by a myth. Moreover, in ratifying and

consummating Eve's original sin, Adam transformed it into original sin in the strict Augustinian sense. Original sin is the son of Adam, namely the willing of and the creation of a fallen solidarity.[37]

This work of being the Savior of the world—the new Adam—was a priestly work. It was common for first-century Jewish bridegrooms to be dressed as a priest. As Dr. Brant Pitre explains in his book, *Jesus the Bridegroom*:

> [This] is true for the Bridegroom-Messiah. When the time comes for His wedding day on the cross, Jesus "decks himself as a priest" (1QIsaiah 61:10) in order to offer the nuptial sacrifice of His own flesh and blood, through which God will be united to His people in a new and everlasting covenant.[38]

A priest offers sacrifice to atone for sin—and Jesus Christ came to earth as the new Adam to offer the sacrifice of His Own body and blood to redeem humanity. Jesus did not come only as the Eternal High Priest of His people, but as a *compassionate, merciful* High Priest—One Who loved His people with a love greater than His love of His Own life. He loved humanity as a bridegroom loves his bride.

---

[37] John Cavadini, "Spousal Vision: A Study of Text and History in the Theology of Saint Augustine," *Augustinian Studies* 43, nos.1/2 (2012): 127-48, https://doi.org/10.5840/augstudies2013431/213.

[38] Brant Pitre, *Jesus the Bridegroom* (New York: Image, 2014), 109.

And yet, He was a priestly Bridegroom that would willingly take upon Himself the weakness and sin of His bride and offer the total sacrifice of Himself on the Altar of the Cross to save His beloved.

> *Therefore, since we have a great high priest who has passed through the heavens, Jesus, the Son of God, let us hold fast to our confession. For we do not have a high priest who is unable to sympathize with our weaknesses, but one who has similarly been tested in every way, yet without sin. So let us confidently approach the throne of grace to receive mercy and to find grace for timely help.* (Heb 4:14–16)

Jesus was the Priest-Shepherd, Who not only offered sacrifice on behalf of His people, but with great love *"freely laid down his own life"* (Jn 10:8) to protect them and provide for them as a bridegroom would do for his bride, or a father would do for his child. Jesus Christ's love on the Cross was intimate and personal for the souls He had come to save. In His work of Redeemer, we see aspects of Jesus' love that encompass both the sacrificial, spousal nature of a love willing to pour himself out completely in self gift to his beloved, as well as a fatherly love willing to sacrifice himself in order to protect and ensure the salvation of the one entrusted to his care.

St. Francis de Sales beautifully expresses the passionate love that Jesus Christ, the Eternal High Priest, had for the children of God. His mercy and compassion are evident here:

The high priest of the Law wore upon his back, and upon his bosom, the names of the children of Israel, that is, the precious stones upon which the names of the chiefs of Israel were engraved. Ah! Behold Jesus our chief bishop, and see how, from the instant of his conception, he bore us upon his shoulders, undertaking the charge of redeeming us by his death, even the death of the cross. . . . This soul of Our Savior knew us all by name and by surname; but above all in the day of his passion, when he offered his tears, his prayers, his blood and his life for all, he breathed in particular for thee these thoughts of love: Ah! My eternal Father, I take to myself and charge myself with all poor Theotimus's sins, to undergo torments and death that he may be freed from them, and that he may not perish but live. Let me die, so he may live; let me be crucified so he may be glorified. O sovereign love of the Heart of Jesus, what heart can ever bless thee as devotedly as it ought!

Thus, within his maternal breast the divine heart foresaw, disposed, merited and obtained all the benefits we have, not only in general for all, but also in particular for each one, and his breasts of sweetness provided for us the milk of his influences, his attractions, his inspirations and sweetnesses by which he draws, conducts and nourishes our hearts to eternal life. Benefits do not inflame us unless we behold the eternal will which destines them for us, and the Heart of Our Savior who has merited them for us by so many pains, especially in his death and passion.[39]

This new priestly Adam Who had come to save the world as both a kind Shepherd and King lived loving sacrifice in all that He did, said, and prayed. In every atom of His being, He fulfilled Romans 12:1 where St. Paul urges Christians to *"present your bodies as a living sacrifice, holy and pleasing to God; this is your spiritual worship."* In this way, He was the Priest making the sacrifice, the Victim being sacrificed and His very body was the Altar upon which this sacrifice was made. Hans Urs Von Balthasar explains:

> The image of a shepherd who demonstrates his authority as the "Chief Shepherd" (1 Pt 5:4) by dying for his sheep (and thus seemingly abandoning them) is every bit as paradoxical as the image in Hebrews of the high priest who appears—living—before God "with his own (outpoured) blood" (Heb 9:12). In essence it is the same image and the same paradox, in fact, since on both occasions the absolute authority derives precisely from the absolute commitment. For Jesus the "Good (that is, right) Shepherd" and simultaneously also the "great high priest" (Heb 4:14).[40]

---

[39] Francis de Sales, *Treatise on the Love of God*, 424–25.

[40] Hans Urs Von Balthasar, *Priestly Spirituality*, trans. Frank Davidson (San Francisco: Ignatius Press, 2013), 86.

To be a priest is to be anointed. And it is to be set aside—specially consecrated—to offer sacrifice. The very name Christ comes from the Greek word *christos*, which means "the anointed one." Jesus Christ was not only the Priest offering the sacrifice on Calvary, but He was simultaneously the Lamb of God—the sacrifice being offered. From the beginning of his ministry, St. John the Baptist proclaimed Christ's identity as the Lamb of God: *"Behold, the Lamb of God, who takes away the sin of the world!"* (Jn 1:29). The Israelites would have immediately understood this connection with the paschal lamb they offered each year at Passover, pouring his blood over their doorposts to save them from death. In this way, Jesus was also the Victim. St. John Chrysostom says that, *"when Mass is being celebrated, the sanctuary is filled with countless angels who adore the Divine Victim immolated on the altar."*[41] And the altar on which this sacrifice was offered was the Altar of His Heart, of His *fiat*. This has been clearly shown in the beautiful artwork depicting the Sacred Heart of Jesus aflame with a fire of love pouring forth blood. Jesus is the burning bush—always burning with a fire of love—and yet, never destroyed. *"For our God is a consuming fire"* (Heb 12:29).

St. Paul's letter to the Hebrews is rich with depictions of Christ, the new Eternal High Priest—describing Him as merciful and compassionate, faithful, eternal, holy, undefiled, and perfect. All of these

---

[41] John Chrysostom, *On the Priesthood*, trans. W. R. W. Stephens (Monee, IL: CreateSpace Independent Publishing Platform, 2014), 95.

characteristics were necessary for the new Adam to recreate fallen humanity through the sacrifice of His pouring out of His life on Golgotha. Jesus was a merciful and compassionate High Priest. The word compassion comes from the Latin word *compassio* meaning "to suffer with." Christ came to earth to suffer with humanity and thus raise them to the glory of children of God. He did not come to be feared as a severe judge, but rather to be loved and trusted as a gentle Savior. Isaiah writes:

> *Here is my servant whom I uphold,*
> *my chosen one with whom I am pleased,*
> *upon whom I have put my spirit;*
> *he shall bring forth justice to the nations,*
> *not crying out, not shouting,*
> *not making his voice heard in the street.*
> *a bruised reed he shall not break,*
> *and a smoldering wick he shall not quench,*
> *until he establishes justice on the earth;*
> *the coastlands will wait for his teaching.* (Is 42:1–4)

Here we read the prophetic description of the coming Messiah as One Who establishes justice and order in a gentle, meek and humble manner. Because He would 'not cry out' nor shout, not threaten nor place a burden too heavy upon His people which in turn might break their strength, He was not one to be feared. His yoke would truly be easy and His burden light. Christ would take upon His Own shoulders the brunt of the just punishment man deserved for His sin and through His Own expiation offer back to man the peace that comes with rightly ordered love.

The book of Hebrews provides another colorful description of Jesus as the Messiah, the Eternal High Priest—describing Him not as a far-off detached Savior bestowing salvation on humanity from afar, but rather drawing man to Himself as a wounded lamb gone astray that needs a strong, gentle shepherd to carry him home. The justice that Christ procures is not one that comes through angry vengeance inducing fear, but rather one that comes through sacrificial love provoking trust.

> *You have not approached that which could be touched and a blazing fire and gloomy darkness and storm and a trumpet blast and a voice speaking words such that those who heard begged that no message be further addressed to them. . . . No, you have approached Mount Zion and the city of the living God, the heavenly Jerusalem, and countless angels in festal gathering, and the assembly of the firstborn enrolled in heaven, and God the judge of all, and the spirits of the just made perfect, and Jesus, the mediator of a new covenant, and the sprinkled blood that speaks more eloquently than that of Abel.* (Heb 12:18–24)

Jesus was incarnate—sharing flesh and blood with His children so as to keep them very close to His Heart. He searches out lost, sinful man and *"carrying him upon his shoulders"* (Lk 15:5) He pleads with humanity, *"Come to me, all you who labor and are burdened, and*

I will give you rest. Take my yoke upon you and learn from me, for I am meek and humble of heart; and you will find rest for yourselves. For my yoke is easy, and my burden light" (Mt 11:29–30). Christ meekly, yet boldly, proclaimed, *"I came so that they might have life and have it more abundantly. I am the good shepherd. A good shepherd lays down his life for the sheep"* (Lk 10:10–11). This self-offering was not something Jesus simply allowed to happen to Himself (as a passive Victim), but instead something He consciously, actively offered as the Priest. *"This is why the Father loves me, because I lay down my life in order to take it up again. No one takes it from me, but I lay it down on my own. I have power to lay it down, and power to take it up again"* (Lk 10:17–18).

Jesus, as the new priestly Adam, takes the burden of sin upon His Own shoulders and pays the necessary price to ransom us from hell. He does this bodily, concretely, and thus He more intimately understands our sufferings, temptations, and struggles. He not only wants to help us with those, but to take them upon Himself.

> *For we do not have a high priest who is unable to sympathize with our weaknesses, but one who has similarly been tested in every way, yet without sin.* (Heb 4:14)

Jesus knows the struggles man has against the world, flesh and devil as man is tempted to sin while necessarily drawing from the strength of God to fight against such temptations. Christ's knowledge of suffering is not just intellectual knowledge, but something He has experienced Himself in the flesh. And through His

Own struggles and pain, Jesus has been able to make a way for man to follow His example of patience and holiness even in the midst of difficulty. It is Christ's incarnated experience of suffering and death in His Own flesh (which He did not deserve) that He expiated the sins of all of humanity and thus showed to them the way to follow His merciful footsteps in suffering well for the sake of His Father's justice:

> *Now since the children share in blood and flesh, he likewise shared in them, that through death he might destroy the one who has the power of death, that is, the devil, and free those who through fear of death had been subject to slavery all their life. Surely, he did not help angels but rather the descendants of Abraham; therefore, he had to become like his brothers in every way, that he might be a merciful and faithful high priest before God to expiate the sins of the people. Because he himself was tested through what he suffered, he is able to help those who are being tested.* (Heb 2:14–18)

As we meditate on the depths of Jesus' kenosis and His priestly, suffering, sacrificial love as a spousal Messiah, we see clearly how Christ is both compassionate and merciful. Humanity deserved hell because they broke their relationship with God through sin. Christ empties Himself taking upon Himself human nature with the consequences of sin although He Himself never disobeyed the Father. Jesus chooses to enter into hell to suffer the consequences of sin in His sinless being, thus expiating sin for the rest of humanity. His descent into hell is echoed in His words from the Cross, *"My God, My God, why have you abandoned me?"*. As He prays Psalm 22 it is clear that this Psalm is written prophetically about His death on the Cross. It speaks about His enemies surrounding Him, mockery ensnaring Him, feeling abandoned even by the Father and lost in darkness. And yet it then reaches to heaven with a hopeful hymn of praise, proclaiming His perfect faith in the conquering of death through His resurrection which will praise the Father Who delivers Him. In praying this Psalm, He declares that He will *"live for the Lord"* and offer praise to the Father Who delivers Him.

Romano Guardini in his book *The Lord* beautifully explains both the depths of Jesus' kenosis (emptying Himself in order to suffer) as well as the nobility of His love that remained faithful to His Father's will regardless of the cost. As we read the violence of suffering Christ endured juxtaposed with the gentleness of His response to all the Father permitted, we realize how it is precisely His humility (littleness) and love that upheld Him in completing the work of man's salvation. Guardini explains:

> The plunge from God towards the void which man in his revolt had begun (chute in which the creature can only despair or break) Christ undertook in love. Knowingly, voluntarily, he experienced it with all the sensitiveness of his divinely human heart. The greater the victim, the more terrible the blow that fells him. No one ever died as Jesus died, who was life itself. No one was ever punished for sin as he was, the Sinless One. No one ever experienced the plunge down the vacuum

of evil as did God's Son—even to the excruciating agony behind the words: "My God, my God, why hast though forsaken me?" (Mt 27:46). Jesus was really destroyed. Cut off in the flower of his age; his work stifled just when it should have taken root; his friends scattered, his honor broken. He no longer had anything, was anything: "a worm and not a man." In inconceivable pain "he descended into hell," realm in which evil reigns, and not only as the victorious breaker of its chains. This came later; first he had to touch the nadir of a personally experienced agony such as no man has ever dreamed. There the endlessly Beloved One of the eternal Father brushed the bottom of the pit. He penetrated to the absolute nothingness from which the "re-creation" of those already created (but falling from the source of true life toward that nothingness) was to emerge: the new heaven and new earth.

Christ on the cross! Inconceivable what he went through as he hung there. ... Everything, without reserve—body, heart and spirit given over to the illimitable flame of omnipresent agony, to the terrible judgment of assumed world-sin that none can alleviate and whose horror only death can end. Such the depths from which omnipotent love calls new creation into being.[42]

---

[42] Romano Guardini, *The Lord*, trans. Elinor Castendyk Briefs (Washington, DC: Regnery Publishing, Inc., 2013), 466–67.

In His descent into hell Christ offered atonement for sin. In what we read here from Guardini He proved His identity as the compassionate, Eternal High Priest. He also shows that He is faithful. He is faithful to the Father in doing His will and He is faithful to His sheep laying down His life for them.

Jesus is also described in Hebrews as the faithful High Priest. This is of great importance as we meditate on His identity as the new Adam. The first Adam was not faithful—he disobeyed; he fell in sin. The second Adam carried out His work with absolute fidelity. He was not remiss in any way in His sacerdotal duties. Hebrews 3:6 states that *"Christ was faithful as a son placed over his house."* It was Jesus' absolute humility and passionate love for His Father and His Father's will that carried Him through His work of High Priest par excellence—that of offering His Own body, blood, soul, and divinity as the paschal lamb. He was the Word of God that said, *"Behold, here I come, Lord, to do your will"* or *"I delight to do your will, my God; your law is in my inner being!"* (Ps 40:8–9). And as Christ delighted to do the will of the Father, the Father delighted in His Son's accomplishment of His will:

> *For just as from the heavens*
> *the rain and snow come down*
> *and do not return there*
> *till they have watered the earth,*
> *making it fertile and fruitful,*
> *giving seed to the one who sows*
> *and bread to the one who eats,*

> *so shall my word be*
> *that goes forth from my mouth;*
> *my word shall not return to me void,*
> *but shall do my will,*
> *achieving the end for which I sent it.* (Is 55:10–11)

In this passage of Isaiah, we see how Christ—the Word of God—came down from heaven only to do the will of the Father. The eternal Word of God became "little" as He was planted in the ground of humanity (Our Lady's womb) and watered humanity it by His blood, sweat, tears and *fiat* making it fertile again in the fruitfulness of fulfilling God's will. He primarily did this through sacrifice and in this His work was priestly. Christ was not only to offer arbitrary sacrifices, but rather the Own sacrifice of His corporal nature. He became the sacrifice. He became the Victim. Again, it is repeated in Hebrews 10:5–7:

> *For this reason, when he came into the world, he said:*
> *"Sacrifice and offering you did not desire,*
> *but a body you prepared for me;*
> *holocausts and sin offerings you took no delight in.*
> *Then I said, 'As is written of me in the scroll,*
> *Behold, I come to do your will, O God.'"*

Jesus freely embraced the Father's will, regardless of the difficulty or cost. He said, "'I am troubled now. Yet what should I say? 'Father, save me from this hour'? But it was for this purpose that I came to this hour. Father, glorify your name.' Then a voice came from heaven, 'I have glorified it and will glorify it again'" (Jn 12:27–28).

Jesus Christ is completely faithful in His work as Bridegroom, High Priest, and Messiah all of the way *to the end*. This is why His last words on the Cross were *"It is finished"* (Jn 19:30). In Latin He says, *"Consumatum Est,"* which literally means "It is consummated." Jesus Christ, the Bridegroom, has consummated His marriage to humanity completely through His work of redemption. Pope Benedict XVI writes in his work *Jesus of Nazareth*:

> In John's account, Jesus' last words are "It is finished!" (Jn 19:30). In the Greek text, this word (*tetelestai*) points back to the very beginning of the Passion narrative, to the episode of the washing of the feet, which the evangelist introduces by observing that Jesus loved His own "to the end (*telos*)" (13:1). This "end," this ne plus ultra of loving, is not attained in the moment of death. He has truly gone right to the end, to the very limit and even beyond that limit. He has accomplished the utter fullness of love—He has given himself.
>
> In our reflection on Jesus' prayer on the Mount of Olives in Chapter 6, we encountered a further meaning of this same word (*teleioum*) in connection with Hebrews 5:9: in the Torah it means consecration, bestowal of priestly dignity, in other words, total dedication to God. I think we may detect this same meaning here, on the basis of Jesus' high-priestly prayer. Jesus has accomplished the act of consecration—the priestly handing over of himself and the world to God—right

to the end (Jn 17:19). So in this final word, the great mystery of the cross shines forth. The new cosmic liturgy is accomplished. The cross of Jesus replaces all other acts of worship as the one true glorification of God, in which God glorifies himself through him in whom he grants us His love, thereby drawing us to himself.[43]

The Eternal High Priest offers the highest liturgy possible. To understand the role of Jesus as the Eternal High Priest, one first must understand the essence of liturgy. Liturgy itself was introduced by God Himself in the Old Testament. He instructed man on the proper way to adore and praise God, as well as how to offer atonement for their sin after the fall. In liturgy a communal people come together to give glory to God—worshiping His holiness and repairing the justice due to Him that is denied through sin. In liturgy a priest is set aside from the rest of the people and especially consecrated to God to offer this sacrifice for the people.

In the Old Testament, we see many examples of this. For example, we read in Genesis that after the flood Noah offered a sacrifice of praise and thanksgiving on behalf of his family and his offering was pleasing to God:

Then Noah built an altar to the LORD, and choosing from every clean animal and every clean bird, he offered burnt offerings on the altar. When the LORD smelled the sweet odor,

---

[43] Benedict XVI, *Jesus of Nazareth*, 1:223.

> *the LORD said to himself: Never again will I curse the ground because of human beings, since the desires of the human heart are evil from youth; nor will I ever again strike down every living being, as I have done.* (Gen 8: 20-21)

Later on, we see Moses instructed with the details of the Passover that was a deep prophetic foreshadowing of Christ's Own Passion and Death, as well as the setting up of the Levitical priesthood. In Job 1:5 we also read about Job offering sacrifices to atone for the sins of his children.

Sacrifice as a form of adoration rightly ordered the Israelites' hearts to their subservient place before God. It was also an action intended to atone for sin (although full atonement could only come through Jesus Christ Himself). And lastly, it drew the community together in remembrance of God's merciful presence among them. God encouraged His people to exercise their gift of memory, often exhorting them to build an altar of remembrance when His presence revealed itself in a place or to yearly keep particular days set aside and anointed for prayer in remembrance of what the Lord had done among them. These first liturgies were performed by a priest figure and included a victim offered to God on an altar. But, as we read in Hebrews, such sacrifices had to be offered over and over again on behalf of the people for they were imperfect and offered by imperfect people.

Jesus Christ came as the Eternal High Priest. He was set aside and consecrated by God to offer the one eternal sacrifice on behalf of man that would forever open the gates of heaven to him. Although

Chapter 3: Christ as the New Adam and Redeemer

Christ was the Eternal High Priest, He also was the immaculate Victim that was being offered and this eternal sacrifice was offered on the Altar of His body crucified. His Passion and Death was an act of worship and reparation. In the Holy Mass we are drawn back into this one eternal moment both in our memory, as well as mystically in a very real way. Because Jesus was human, He had the matter of His body to offer as a Victim. Because He was divine His sacrifice was eternal and, therefore, not only atoned for the sins of one man, but instead for all of humanity and it had cosmic consequences for all of creation.

In the Garden of Edan before the fall, Adam and Eve offered their sinless bodies and souls to God as a living sacrifice to glorify and worship Him. Later on, Adam and his sons offered sacrifice of their first fruits to adore the Father, as well as to repair for what they had denied God by their disobedience in sin. Christ, the new Adam, offered Himself as the first fruit of creation to both offer fitting praise to the Father (in worship), as well as to restore creation to Him. Whereas Old Testament sacrifice cries to the Father an apology for the sin of man, Jesus' sacrifice actually repairs the effects of that sin making 'all things new.' Priests in the Church today offer the sacrifice of the Mass *in persona Christi* as they enter into the Eternal Priesthood of Christ to offer the eternal sacrifice on the Cross made present in the Eucharist. In this eternal sacrifice creation is continually recreated in and through Jesus Christ.

As we read in the excerpt from Pope Benedict XVI above, Jesus the Eternal High Priest completed what the Old Testament sacrifices foreshadowed. He loved completely. He loved unto the end.

His gift on behalf of man was total. This is the sort of sacrifice offered by not only a Priest, but by a priestly Bridegroom. And the perfection of His sacrifice gave the greatest possible glory to God—a glory that was not only absolute, but also eternal.

Not only was Christ a faithful High Priest, but He was a "forever" High Priest. In the Old Testament, the high priests were taken from the line of Levi and generation after generation sons would replace their fathers—for their offering to God in reparation did not take away sin, but instead covered sin in a plea for God's mercy. Only Jesus Christ, Himself sinless and yet willing to offer Himself in atonement, could complete the single act of pure reparation needed to remove sin completely and restore humanity to the possibility of right relationship with God:

> *For Christ did not enter into a sanctuary made by hands, a copy of the true one, but heaven itself, that he might now appear before God on our behalf. Not that he might offer himself repeatedly, as the high priest enters each year into the sanctuary with blood that is not his own; if that were so, he would have had to suffer repeatedly from the foundation of the world. But now once for all he has appeared at the end of the ages to take away sin by his sacrifice. Just as it is appointed that human beings die once, and after this the judgment, so also Christ, offered once to take away the sins of many, will appear a second time, not to take away sin but to bring salvation to those who eagerly await him.* (Heb 9:24–28)

Chapter 3: Christ as the New Adam and Redeemer

Jesus alone—as the immaculate Victim and Eternal High Priest—could offer one sacrifice that was sufficient to atone for all of man's sin and was worthy enough to give the Father all of the glory He deserved. It is the blood of Christ that offers eternal praise. Yet Jesus goes beyond this necessary work of adoration and through His blood enters into fallen humanity to repair and recreate the places of man's wounds and weakness from sin into places where God's image can once again be reflected in perfection.

> *But when Christ came as high priest of the good things that have come to be, passing through the greater and more perfect tabernacle not made by hands, that is, not belonging to this creation, he entered once for all into the sanctuary, not with the blood of goats and calves but with his own blood, thus obtaining eternal redemption. For if the blood of goats and bulls and the sprinkling of a heifer's ashes can sanctify those who are defiled so that their flesh is cleansed, how much more will the blood of Christ, who through the eternal spirit offered himself unblemished to God, cleanse our consciences from dead works to worship the living God....* (Heb 9:11–14)

Jesus' very identity as the new Adam was priestly and He never dies—so His one perfect act of sacrifice on Calvary endures eternally. Hebrews 7:17 states, "*For it is testified: 'You are a priest forever according to the order of Melchizedek.'*" And "*because he remains forever, [he] has a priesthood that does not pass away. Therefore, he is always able to save those who approach God through him, since he lives forever to make intercession for them"* (Heb 7:24–25). This is humanity's eternal hope—that we have an Eternal Priest Who forever will be faithful in redeeming us. *"This we have as an anchor of the soul, sure and firm, which reaches into the interior behind the veil, where Jesus has entered on our behalf as forerunner, becoming high priest forever according to the order of Melchizedek"* (Heb 6:19–20). And, *"The main point of what has been said is this: we have such a high priest, who has taken his seat at the right hand of the throne of the Majesty in heaven, a minister of the sanctuary and of the true tabernacle that the Lord, not man, set up"* (Heb 8:1–2).

We also see in Hebrews how it was the "littleness" and humility of Christ—along with the fire of His indwelling love with the Father—that held Christ eternally faithful in His offering, His self-gift. Because of Jesus' complete kenosis, He was emptied of all worldliness. He was perfectly innocent and pure:

> *It was fitting that we should have such a high priest: holy, innocent, undefiled, separated from sinners, higher than the heavens. He has no need, as did the high priests, to offer sacrifice day after day, first for his own sins and then for those of the people; he did that once for all when he offered himself. For the law appoints men subject to weakness to be high priests, but the word of the oath, which was taken after the law, appoints a son, who has been made perfect forever.* (Heb 7:27–28)

His breath was the very breath of the Father. His being made translucent through the humble purity of His love enabled His sacrifice to be eternally perfect. He not only knew no sin, but temptation did not even leave a trace of evil in Him. He was like man *"in all ways, but without sin"* (Heb 4:15). He was separate from those priests before Him who had themselves committed transgressions and, therefore, needed first to purify themselves before they offered sacrifice to purify others. And since He never once disobeyed His Father through sin, He was worthy not only to be the Priest, but the unblemished offering (Victim) Himself. And His obedient acceptance of the Cross purified His love which radiates through all time and space—thus, leaving all the possibility of claiming the redemption He offers humanity and also the hope of following in His footsteps.

> *In the days when he was in the flesh, he offered prayers and supplications with loud cries and tears to the one who was able to save him from death, and he was heard because of his reverence. Son though he was, he learned obedience from what he suffered; and when he was made perfect, he became the source of eternal salvation for all who obey him, declared by God high priest according to the order of Melchizedek.* (Heb 5:7–10)

In all of this we see that Christ not only was the immaculate High Priest, but also the spotless Victim being offered. In the Old Testament God demanded a spotless lamb be offered on Passover and He promised that its blood poured over the doorpost would save the Israelites from the angel of death. In the same way, Christ was the spotless Lamb of God Whose blood was poured out on the wood of the

Cross, thus saving all of humanity from eternal death. In John 1:29 we hear St. John the Baptist proclaim, *"Behold the Lamb of God who takes away the sins of the world!"* And at every Mass the priest holds up the Eucharistic Heart of Christ and likewise says, *"Behold the Lamb of God!"* In essence he is saying, *"Behold the one who was sacrificed as a victim for the sins of the world."*

In the Last Supper, Christ the Eternal High Priest takes the bread and transforms it into Himself, offering it as a Victim of love both to the Father on behalf of humanity and to humanity as their own spiritual food. Jesus takes His Own Heart in His hands and breaks it in two and invites us to look upon His wounded love and to receive Him. Every sacrifice that Jesus offers is something He does because of His capacity to suffer in His human nature. It is His human mind, emotions, body and Heart that feels pain and through which He prays by offering a sacrifice of praise to the Father by doing His will. In this way Christ is not only the Priest offering an eternal sacrifice on our behalf, but He also is the Victim (sacrifice) Himself.

Jesus also is the Altar on which the sacrifice is offered. It is the corporealness of His body on the Cross that is the Altar on which the sacrifice is offered. Every pain, every drop of blood that Jesus shed was poured out upon the Altar of His body and Heart on the Cross. Like in 1 Kings 18:38 when the fire of God came down and consumed the altar and sacrifice of Elijah, so too the fire of God's love explodes from heaven upon the Altar of Christ's Heart on the Cross consuming it in full. Like the burning bush that was set on fire and yet not consumed, so the Heart of Jesus is the Altar upon which love burns incessantly and yet never annihilates Him. Every sacrifice offered is given on the Altar of His Heart burning with love. In all of this it is clear that Christ the new Adam is not only the Eternal Priest, but the sacrifice (Victim) and Altar as well.

St. Peter Chrysologus beautifully explains this three-fold identity of Christ as the Priest, Victim and Altar and takes it even further to apply it to each member of the Church who make up His body. Our Redeemer, Jesus Christ, in emptying Himself totally before the divine love of the Father by accomplishing His will, is the new Adam—Eternal High Priest—eternally perfected by His *fiat*. He invites the Christian to enter into Him in confidence and to follow His new and living way of love:

> *Therefore, brothers, since through the blood of Jesus we have confidence of entrance into the sanctuary by the new and living way he opened for us through the veil, that is, his flesh, and since we have "a great priest over the house of God," let us approach with a sincere heart and in absolute trust, with our hearts sprinkled clean from an evil conscience and our bodies washed in pure water. Let us hold unwaveringly to our confession that gives us hope, for he who made the promise is trustworthy.* (Heb 10:19–23)

In an ancient sermon, St. Peter Chrysologus exhorts all Christians to accept Jesus' gift as the Priest, Victim and Altar and to imitate Him in their own lives. He speaks of not only Christ's call to littleness, spousal love and the Cross, but shares how Jesus exhorts all Christians to follow Him on this way. He explains how all those who follow Him must empty themselves before the Father's will and take up their Cross. He speaks of the power of not only being a Priest Who offers the sacrifice of One's Own life, but also the love that pushes Him on to also be the very Victim and Altar of that sacrifice. His appeal to such limitless self-emptying sacrifice is an appeal of a lover encouraging His beloved. First, Christ quells the fear that rises in a man when he sees the price of sacrifice. He explains His Own suffering as something not to be feared or dreaded as evil powerlessness, but instead something He chose in love to bear out of love for those who He loved. After encouraging man to not fear such great love, He exhorts Him to trust in His love and to courageously follow His way of the Cross with His Own self-gift to the Father. We read:

> Listen to the Lord's appeal: In me, I want you to see your own body, your members, your heart, your bones, your blood. You may fear what is divine, but why not love what is human? You may run away from me as the Lord, but why not run to me as your father? Perhaps you are filled with shame for causing my bitter passion. Do not be afraid. This cross inflicts a mortal injury, not on me, but on death. These nails no longer pain me, but only deepen your love for me. I do not cry out because of these wounds, but through them I draw you into my heart. My body was stretched on the cross as a symbol, not of how much I suffered, but of my all-embracing love. I count it no less to shed my blood: it is the price I have paid for your ransom. Come, then, return to me and learn to know

me as your father, who repays good for evil, love for injury, and boundless charity for piercing wounds.[44]

After this He calls humanity to not only accept His suffering and death, but to courageously choose to embrace it themselves as a means of gaining heaven for Himself and those for whom He intercedes. He explains every Christian's role as priest, altar and victim as part of the body of Christ Who was the ultimate Priest, Altar and Victim. He explains this vocation to the Cross with such simplicity and love that those who hear Him cannot help but be inspired to follow Him on His Cross' way:

> Listen now to what the Apostle urges us to do. *I appeal to you*, he says, *to present your bodies as a living sacrifice.* By this exhortation of his, Paul has raised all men to priestly status.
>
> How marvelous is the priesthood of the Christian, for he is both the victim that is offered on his own behalf, and the priest who makes the offering. He does not need to go beyond himself to seek what he is to immolate to God: with himself and in himself he brings the sacrifice he is to offer God for himself. The victim remains and the priest remains, always one and the same. Immolated, the victim still lives: the priest who immolates cannot kill. Truly it is an amazing

---

[44] Peter Chrysologus (Sermo 108: PL 52, 499-500), in *The Liturgy of the Hours*, 2:770-772.

sacrifice in which a body is offered without being slain and blood is offered without being shed...

The Apostle says: *I appeal to you by the mercy of God to present your bodies as a living sacrifice.* Brethren, this sacrifice follows the pattern of Christ's sacrifice by which he gave his body as a living immolation for the life of the world. He really made his body a living sacrifice, because, though slain, he continues to live. In such a victim death receives its ransom, but the victim remains alive. Death itself suffers the punishment. This is why death for the martyrs is actually a birth, and their end a beginning. Their execution is the door to life, and those who were thought to have been blotted out from the earth shine brilliantly in heaven.

... Paul says: *I appeal to you by the mercy of God to present your bodies as a sacrifice, living and holy.* The prophet said the same thing: *Sacrifice and offering you did not desire, but you have prepared a body for me.* Each of us is called to be both a sacrifice to God and his priest... Let your heart be an altar. Then, with full confidence in God, present your body for sacrifice. God desires not death, but faith; God thirsts not for blood, but for self-surrender; God is appeased not by slaughter, but by the offering of your free will.[45]

---

[45] Peter Chrysologus (Sermo 108: PL 52, 499-500), in *The Liturgy of the Hours,* 2:770-772.

Jesus not only presents Himself in all majesty to humanity as the new Adam, Priest, Sacrifice and Altar, but also calls humanity to have confidence in Him—trusting Him to similarly purify us and transform our sinful nature into true children of God. In this we become part of His work as priests, victims and altars ourselves.

Our Lady is the one human who received Jesus' gift of Self most perfectly—thus we recognize Her as the new Eve with an Immaculate Heart. She is a mirror of His crucified love. As His Helpmate She perfectly partakes with Him in His work as Priest, Victim and Altar. Mary's work with Christ is subordinate and dependent upon Him as the Redeemer, and yet Her Self-offering to Him in His work is full. The next section will show how Our Lady perfectly participated with Christ in His work of redemption, imitating His littleness, spousal trinitarian love and *fiat* before the Father's will. And this will be followed by a chapter explaining how Her participation with Christ made Her the new Eve, His Helpmate, Co-redemptrix and Mediatrix of all graces to mankind.

Chapter 4

How Did Our Lady Live the Cross With Jesus? In *Fiat* Through Littleness and Love.

Simeon blessed them and said to Mary his mother, "Behold, this child is destined for the fall and rise of many in Israel, and to be a sign that will be contradicted (and you yourself a sword will pierce) so that the thoughts of many hearts may be revealed." (Lk 2:34–35)

Standing by the cross of Jesus were his mother and his mother's sister, Mary the wife of Clopas, and Mary of Magdala. When Jesus saw his mother and the disciple there whom he loved, he said to his mother, "Woman, behold, your son." Then he said to the disciple, "Behold, your mother." And from that hour the disciple took her into his home. (Jn 19:25–27)

Our Lady, who was born as the Immaculate Conception, was simultaneously destined to be the Queen Mother of Sorrows. From the first *fiat* She gave to God at the Annunciation, She simultaneously was consenting to and offering Her *fiat* on Calvary. The Child to be born of Mary was the Savior of the world and as His Mother She would partake in that act of redemption with Him. In fact, it was Her perfect reception of His gift of salvation that preserved Her from the stain of sin at Her own conception.

The first time that Our Lady offered Jesus to the Father in the Presentation in the Temple She was told of the mystery of suffering that lay before Her and Her Son. One day while standing at the foot of the Cross on Calvary She would make a second offering of Her Son to the Father—She would consent to Her own flesh and blood in Her Son suffering and dying to save humanity. In the Byzantine *Akathist to Our Lady of Sorrows—Softener of Evil Hearts* we pray:

Oikos XI

"O my Son and Pre-eternal God, Fashioner of all creation! O Lord, how canst Thou endure the suffering on the Cross?" the pure Virgin cried, saying: "By Thy awesome birth, O my Son, I have been exalted above all mothers, but woe is me! Now when I see Thee, my womb burns within me." But we shed tears remembering thee, and cry out to thee:

Rejoice, thou who didst see the voluntary passion of thy Son on the Cross!

Rejoice, thou who didst see thy beloved Son sore wounded!

Rejoice, ewe lamb, seeing thy Son as a lamb being led to slaughter!

Rejoice, thou who didst see the Deliverer of the wounds of soul and body covered with wounds!

Chapter 4: How Did Our Lady Live the Cross with Jesus?

Rejoice, thou who didst see thy Son rise from the dead!

Rejoice, much-sorrowing Mother of God, turn our sorrows into joy and soften the hearts of evil men![46]

In this prayer we read of the mystery of Our Lady in Her little, humble submission to the Father offering Her little, humble Son to Him on the Cross. It is evident that the Mother imitates Her Son in His kenotic love of the heavenly Father. And it is both Her humility and passionate love for Jesus that not only keeps Her faithfully close to Him in His suffering, but also completes that sacrifice with Him. The language of this Akathist beautifully intertwines images of Christ's littleness, love, suffering and *fiat*, but also uses the image of Our Lady as a mirror that reflects these things in Her own life. It begins to show us a glimpse of what we will reflect on in this chapter: that Jesus' wounds become also the wounds of His holy Mother's Heart.

The holy abbot St. Bernard exquisitely expounds on this vast mystery and beauty of Our Lady's mystical martyrdom with Christ. After being the "Fruit-Bearer" allowing the Word of God to take flesh within Her, She continued Her fecundity by giving birth to souls through a one-flesh love union anchored in *fiat* with Her Son on Calvary. He explains:

---

[46]"Akathist to the Mother of God—Softener of Evil Hearts," *Eirenikon: Towards Orthodox-Catholic Reconciliation* (blog), https://eirenikon.wordpress.com/akathist-to-the-mother-of-god-softener-of-evil-hearts/.

The martyrdom of the Virgin is set forth both in the prophecy of Simeon and in the actual story of our Lord's passion. The holy old man said of the infant Jesus: He has been established as a sign which will be contradicted. He went on to say to Mary: And your own heart will be pierced by a sword.

Truly, O blessed Mother, a sword has pierced your heart. For only by passing through your heart could the sword enter the flesh of your Son. Indeed, after your Jesus—who belongs to everyone, but is especially yours—gave up His life, the cruel spear, which was not withheld from His lifeless body, tore open His side. Clearly it did not touch His soul and could not harm Him, but it did pierce your heart. For surely His soul was no longer there, but yours could not be torn away. Thus, the violence of sorrow has cut through your heart, and we rightly call you more than martyr, since the effect of compassion in you has gone beyond the endurance of physical suffering.

Or were those words, "Woman, behold your Son," not more than a word to you, truly piercing your heart, cutting through to the division between soul and spirit? What an exchange! John is given to you in place of Jesus, the servant in place of the Lord, the disciple in place of the master; the son of Zebedee replaces the Son of God, a mere man replaces God himself. How could these words not pierce your most loving heart, when the mere remembrance of them breaks ours, hearts of iron and stone though they are!

Do not be surprised, brothers, that **Mary is said to be a martyr in spirit**. Let him be surprised who does not remember the words of Paul, that one of the greatest crimes of the Gentiles was that they were without love. That was far from the heart of Mary; let it be far from her servants.

Perhaps someone will say: "Had she not known before that He would not die?" Undoubtedly. "Did she not expect him to rise again at once?" Surely. "And still she grieved over her crucified Son?" Intensely. **Who are you and what is the source of your wisdom that you are more surprised at the compassion of Mary than at the passion of Mary's Son? For if He could die in body, could she not die with him in spirit? He died in body through a love greater than anyone had known. She died in spirit through a love unlike any other since His.**[47]

Here St. Bernard lays forth the interior martyrdom of Our Lady. In the beginning of this thesis, we discussed Christ's littleness and passionate love that held Him faithful in *fiat* even unto His Passion and Death on the Cross—thus making Him not only the Redeemer, but also the new Adam, the eternal Bridegroom Priest, Victim and Altar. And so, through our reflection on Our Lady's relationship with Him, we will come to see how clearly She followed His footsteps in all of this. She allowed His redemption to take such deep root in Her Own Heart and soul that She, too, lived an extreme littleness, self-emptying, surrender and love before the Father. She, too, lived

---

[47] Bernard of Clairvaux, *Sermo in dom. infra oct. Assumptionis* 14-15, *The Liturgy of the Hours*, 4:1401–2, emphasis mine.

subordinately, yet also in union with Him, the role of Co-redemptrix, Mediatrix, new Eve and Bridal priest, victim and altar as His Helpmate and Mother. She was the servant of the crucified and yet also His Mother. And this two-fold role plunged Her into a mystical martyrdom with Him in all of the suffering He endured on earth.

Mary's destiny as the Mother of God was bound up with the destiny of the Son of God to such a degree that they could be said to have shared one Heart. Jesus told St. Bridget, *"Her heart was in My heart and that is why I can say that My Mother and I have saved mankind as with one heart: I by suffering in My heart and My flesh, and She by the sorrow of the heart and for love."*[48] It is through Her surrender to the Father and love union (through the Holy Spirit) with Christ that She became our Mother and intercessor in heaven. This is beautifully portrayed in this Byzantine prayer:

Troparion (Apolytikion) — Tone 5

Soften our evil hearts, O Theotokos, and repel the attacks of those who hate us, / and loosen all the rigidity of our soul. / For beholding your holy image, / we are filled with compunction by your compassion and loving kindness toward us, / and we kiss your wounds; / for we are terrified by the darts with which we wound you. / O Compassionate Mother, / do not let us perish because of our hardness of heart, / or our

---

[48] Paul Philippe, *The Blessed Virgin and the Priesthood*, trans. Dorothy Cole (Chicago: Henry Regnery Company, 1955), 61.

neighbor's hardness of heart, / for you are truly the Softener of Evil Hearts.[49]

This prayer reflects both the depths of Our Lady's suffering with Christ, as well as the power He fills Her with on account of Her gift to Him of such a complete self-oblation. Because His wounds become Her wounds, She is a powerful intercessor before God. Satan, who is the most prideful and selfish creature, cannot stand to remain close to such a humble, obedient, self-immolating creature. The love of Christ that comes to live in the Heart of Our Lady burns the evil one away. And each soul entrusted to Her motherly Heart prays that it also would burn our sin away, helping us reach the heights of virtue Christ calls us to embrace.

The Blessed Mother by means of littleness and spousal love surrendered in a total *fiat* to the Father with and for Jesus crucified. In this way, She fully participated in His Passion as is evident both through Her presence on Calvary and participation in the Eucharistic sacrifice that perpetuates Jesus' gift on the Cross. By fully receiving the gift of salvation into Her Heart, Our Lady joins Christ, the new Adam, not only as His Mother but also as His "Woman"—His "Wife"—the new Eve. In this way, She is Mediatrix, Co-redemptrix, and a Helpmate of Jesus, the Eternal High Priest. She, as the first and most perfect disciple, also lives in union with Him as an Altar, a Priest, and a Victim. Christ, the new Adam, and Our Lady, the new

---

[49] "Akathist to the Mother of God—Softener of Evil Hearts."

Eve, are united in the Incarnation, on the Cross, and in the Eucharist through their united flesh and *fiat*.

Part 1: Our Lady's *Fiat* and Littleness—Innocence, Purity, Humility, Kenosis, Trust, Surrender, and Obedience

Our Lady's littleness was ever present in Her soul from the first moments of Her conception and birth. St. Francis de Sales says about the Infant Mary, the Maria Bambina:

> Come close to Her cradle, think of the virtues of this holy infant. Question the angels, the cherubim and seraphim, ask them if they are equal in perfection to this little girl, and they will tell you that She infinitely surpasses them. See them surround Her cradle. Then as they regard Her a little more closely, ravished and beside themselves, they proceed in their admiration: Who is this that comes forth like the dawn, as beautiful as the moon, as resplendent as the sun, as awe-inspiring as bannered troops?[50]

---

[50] Francis de Sales, "Sermon on the Nativity of the Blessed Virgin Mary," September 10, 1620, in *The Sermons of Saint Francis de Sales on Our Lady* (Gastonia, NC: Tan Books, 1987) available at https://salesianliterature.wixsite.com/spirituality/copy-of-sermons-on-our-lady-7.

The Blessed Mother was immaculate in Her conception and remains radiantly translucent in holiness—in purity, humility, and love—in heaven. Since She was conceived without original sin and never committed the tiniest fault against the heavenly Father's perfect plan for Her creation, Our Lady remained in a state of holy childhood and littleness before the Trinity all of the days of Her life. This spiritual childhood kept Her innocent and humble Immaculate Heart continually open, docile, surrendered, obedient, and dependent on the Father in trust in every moment of Her existence. Her mystical life was hidden deep within Her soul and yet radiated its effects upon all of humanity and creation.

St. Louis de Montfort in *True Devotion to Mary* writes of this great virtue of littleness in Mary, particularly by reflecting on the aspect of Her great hiddenness. Our Lady remained little and hidden during Her lifetime so that Christ would be magnified more greatly within and around Her. Each soul that strives to imitate Jesus and Mary in the virtue of littleness would benefit greatly from particularly meditating on this aspect of hiddenness. Christ hid His divinity by taking on human nature. Mary hid the unmatchable supernatural gifts bestowed upon Her as the Mother of God. And all Christians are called to follow the same path of remaining content with being hidden, unknown and humble so that God can radiate profoundly to the world through them. St. Louis de Montfort writes:

> It was through the Blessed Virgin Mary that Jesus came into the world, and it is also through Her that He must reign in the world.

Because Mary remained hidden during Her life She is called by the Holy Ghost and the Church "Alma Mater," Mother hidden and unknown. So great was Her humility that She desired nothing more upon earth than to remain unknown to Herself and to others, and to be known only to God.

In answer to Her prayers to remain hidden, poor and lowly, God was pleased to conceal Her from nearly every other human creature in Her conception, Her birth, Her life, Her mysteries, Her resurrection and assumption. Her own parents did not really know Her and the angels would often ask one another, "Who can She possibly be?" for God had hidden Her from them, or if He did reveal anything to them, it was nothing compared with what He withheld.

God the Father willed that She should perform no miracle during Her life; at least no public one, although He had given Her the power to do so. God the Son willed that She should speak very little although He had imparted His wisdom to Her;

Even though Mary was His faithful spouse, God the Holy Ghost willed that His apostles and evangelists should say very little about Her and then only as much as was necessary to make Jesus known.

Mary is the supreme masterpiece of Almighty God and He has reserved the knowledge and possession of Her for himself. She is the glorious Mother of God the Son who chose to humble and conceal Her during Her lifetime in order to foster Her humility. He called Her "Woman" as if She were a stranger, although in His heart He esteemed and loved Her above all men and angels. Mary is the sealed fountain and the faithful spouse of the Holy Ghost where only He may enter. She is the sanctuary and resting place of the Blessed Trinity where God dwells in greater and more divine splendor than anywhere else in the universe, not excluding His dwelling above the cherubim and seraphim. No creature, however pure, may enter there without being specially privileged.[51]

Mary was so hidden that not only did She conceal the great graces of God bestowed upon Her from people who She encountered, but also, She in many ways remained hidden from Herself. Mary was the only creature who never looked at the graces God was giving Her. She never looked in a mirror at Herself. Everything in the Heart of Mary was for God. Her little heartbeat from the beginning of Her conception beat 'Father, Abba, Fiat, Magnificat' just as Her Son's Heart beat the same thing. Because Our Lady was immaculate and never sinned, nothing ever obstructed the fulfillment of Her living as the creature God intended Her to be. In other words, Mary truly lived the perfection of what God wanted for Her to be as 'Mary' every millisecond of Her life. This made Her grow exponentially in grace every moment of Her existence, and this growth of grace and love continues eternally in Her life in heaven. Because of

---

[51] Louis de Montfort, *True Devotion to Mary* (Coppell, TX: Christ the King Libraries, 2020), 5.

all of this, Mary was the most radiant catalyst for God's glory that any creature could be (besides Jesus Christ Himself). And yet, this brilliant light remained hidden under the obscurity of ordinary life as a Hebrew woman. Mary kept Her dazzling life with God within the confines of Her own hidden Heart. She emptied Herself before Him—both directly in prayer as well as His presence living in those She served in the world. Just as Christ, Who was in the form of God and yet did not grasp at equality with God, but rather emptied Himself and took the form of a slave, so, too, Our Lady full of grace did not grasp at that very grace bestowed upon Her, but rather emptied Herself and took the form of a slave. She said in Luke 1:38, *"Behold, I am the handmaid of the Lord. May it be done to me according to your word."* It is in the Annunciation that we see the depths of Mary's kenosis—Her choice for the little, humble way of Her Son. This was lived in a great hiddenness.

Our Lady existed for God, in order to proclaim and magnify His glory in all things. When She prayed the Magnificat at Her visitation to Elizabeth She exclaimed, *"My soul magnifies the Lord and my spirit exults in God my savior"* (Lk 1:46–47). She recognized that it was because He had *"looked upon his handmaid's lowliness"* (Lk 1:48) which She surrendered to Him that led to His *"lifting up the lowly"* (Lk 1:52). Cardinal Newman writes thus about Our Lady's humility and hiddenness in God, saying that it is *"Mary's prerogative to be the Morning Star, which heralds in the sun. She does not shine for Herself, or from Herself, but She is the reflection of Her and our*

Redeemer, and She glorifies Him. When She appears in the darkness, we know that He is close at hand."[52]

Our Lady's childlike Heart before the presence of the heavenly Father not only retained the perfection of purity and humility, but enabled Her to penetrate the very depths of divine knowledge and love because of Her translucent holiness. As She contemplated the mysteries of God *"pondering on them within her heart"* (Lk 2:19) She was transformed by them allowing the love of God (the Holy Spirit) to find His resting place within Her.

In this we see how Our Lady's humble 'littleness' is intertwined with Her immaculate love. Because Our Lady was so empty of Herself, the Holy Spirit was able to consume Her in full. Purity is the presence of God. Our Lady was empty of self and full of God, thus Her entire being radiated translucent purity and beauty. This was all used by Our Lady as an instrument to bestow merciful love on others. Our Lady was closer to God than any other human besides Jesus Christ Himself. Our Lady, in virtue of justice, did not need to put Herself on equal footing with sinful men, nor was She expected to lower Herself to the level of being their servant. Yet She lived more than anyone else the words of Christ in Matthew 20:28, *"I did not come to be served but to serve and to give my life as a ransom for many."*

St. Ildephonsus expounds on this three-fold mystery of Mary's purity, humility and mercy:

---

[52] John Henry Newman, *The Mystical Rose* (Strongsville, OH: Scepter Publishers, Inc. 1996), 130–31.

You are the rose of paradise, which is held lovingly in the hand of the King of heaven! For you are the perfect bloom of virginal beauty and the Queen of all virgins, the Empress of all holy maidens unmatched in radiance and peerless in immortal chastity.[53]

Similarly you, O mistress, are raised up most high of all, by virtue of your sanctity and singular purity. Your Immaculate Heart is raised up to the uppermost rank in the seraphic courts, closest to the inaccessible light of the unseen Father. With the gentle eyes of a dove you lovingly contemplate his luminous divinity. With the fearless and penetrating eyes of an eagle you boldly perceive the depths of his majesty. And your every action proceeds with the greatest sureness –with unfailing certainty and assurance, born of true piety.... **O Mary! For you are indeed the very perfection of sanctity, the complete plenitude of grace, and the luminous fire of God's ardent love.**[54]

"Most serene Queen and inviolate Mother of God–Virgin pure, holy and immaculate–we praise your purity, while we marvel at your humility. But even more lovingly –for it is ever sweeter and more needful to the sinner –we invoke your mercy and clemency. **Your perfume is the gift of the Holy**

---

[53] Ildephonsus of Toledo, *Crown of the Virgin: An Ancient Meditation on Mary's Beauty, Virtue, and Sanctity*, trans. Robert Nixon (Gastonia, NC: Tan Books, 2020), 65.

[54] Ildephonsus of Toledo, 74, 76, emphasis mine.

Spirit. This Spirit rests in you, illuminating you, and inflaming you with his love. Your Fruit is truly eternal –the fragrance of which fills the world, the taste of which delights the faithful heart, the splendor of which surpasses even the sun and its noontide magnificence![55]

It was Mary's purity and humility in "littleness" that informed and strengthened Her Heart in an absolute surrender of *fiat* to the Father's will. If Our Lady had not the perfection of humility and love as She had, She would never have been able to remain sinless. Humility and love were the footsteps Our Lady used to always conform Her will in *fiat* to the will of Her heavenly Father. St. Maximillian Kolbe explains Her purity, humility and *fiat*—and it is these tools that later Mary will use to unite with Jesus fully in His Passion.:

> The Immaculata is the work of God and like every other such work is without comparison and entirely dependent upon her Creator. She is simultaneously the most perfect and most holy work of God for, as St. Bonaventure maintains: God can create a greater and more perfect world, but He cannot exalt a creature to higher dignity than that to which He exalted Mary.
>
> The Immaculata is the final "line of demarcation" between God and creation. She is a faithful image of divine perfection and holiness.

---

[55] Ildephonsus of Toledo, 35, emphasis mine.

The Immaculata never had the slightest trace of sin or stain of fault in her. Her love was always of the fullest, without the smallest imperfection. She loved God with her whole being, and love united her from the first moment of her existence in so perfect a manner to God that the angel at the Annunciation could say: "Full of grace, the Lord is with thee." She is, therefore, created of God, belonging to God, a reflection of God, an image of God, a child of God and the most perfect of human beings.

She is an instrumentality of God who with total awareness freely permits herself to be led by God and, in agreement with His will she desires to do only that which He commands, and acts in keeping with that will as perfectly as possible, without the smallest withdrawal of her will from the will of God. In the perfect use of the power and privileges entrusted to her, she fulfills always and, in all things, only and exclusively the will of God. This she does in love of God and in the Holy Trinity. This love of God reaches such heights that it calls down the fruits of God's love.[56]

St. Edith Stein also saw the connection between Our Lady's littleness and spousal love as the tools She will use to *fiat* to the Cross. She speaks of Mary's spiritual childhood as the source of Her perfect

---

[56] Maximillian Kolbe, *The Will to Love—From the Writings of St. Maximilian Kolbe*, trans. Regis N. Barwig, ed. Charles Madden and Daniel Gallio (Libertyville, IL: Marytown Press, 1998), 35–36.

fiat that leads to motherhood—the Word taking flesh within Her. And it is this gift of the Incarnation that will be completed on Calvary. Professor Dianne Traflet, STD, explains:

> She could be fruitful because she was always empty of self. She could give her "yes" to motherhood because she first had given her "yes" to childhood, that is, her assent as handmaiden. Her ability to recognize herself as a handmaiden indicates her childlike humility and her mature readiness to become a mother. Her spiritual childhood necessarily preceded her motherhood. Edith explained that "motherhood was transfigured" when "God chose as the instrument for his incarnation a human mother."
>
> ... In that holy motherhood, Mary "watches over his childhood; near or far, indeed, wherever he wishes, she follows him on his way; she holds the crucified body in her arms; she carries out the will of the departed. But not as her action does she do all this: she is in this the handmaid of the Lord; she fulfills that to which God has called her. And this is why she does not consider the child as her own property: she has welcomed him from God's hands; she lays him back into God's hands by dedicating him in the Temple and by being with him at the crucifixion."[57]

---

[57] Dianne Marie Traflet, *St. Edith Stein: A Spiritual Portrait* (Boston: Pauline, 2008), 95, citing Edith Stein, "Ethos of Women's Professions" in

The "littleness" of Our Lady was the source of Her *fiat* that gave us our Redeemer. Just as Jesus Christ lived a great kenosis in His Incarnation and on the Cross, so too Our Lady lived Her own kenosis—completely emptying Herself before God in the Annunciation placing Her body, mind, emotions, Heart, soul, will, and future at the service of the Father's will, the Holy Spirit's love and the Son's life. Her humility, surrender and obedience to God allowed Her to become the Mother of the Redeemer, and, in union with Him, the Mother of the redeemed. It is also this kenosis of Our Lady that allowed Her to unite so deeply with Her Son on the Cross.

Our Lady did not think about Herself, Her wants, Her desires, Her "needs." No, instead like a child perfectly trusting Her heavenly Father, Our Lady emptied Herself into the hands of His loving providence. This allowed Him to fill Her with gifts beyond all human understanding: the gift of His Son taking flesh within Her and the gift of suffering with Him on earth to give birth to souls into eternity. Because Our Lady remained in this state of "littleness" all of the days of Her life, Christ held Her close to His Heart uniting with Her both in the pain of the Passion as well as in the joy of His Resurrection.

The Collected Works of Edith Stein, vol. 2, *Essays on Woman*, trans. Freda Mary Oben (Washington, D.C.: ICS Publications, 1987), 47.

Part 2: Our Lady's *Fiat* and Spousal Love

St. Alphonsus de Liguori, referring to a supposed sermon of Augustine, said that *"Mary was that only one who merited to be called the Mother and Spouse of God."*[58]

Our Lady's relationship with God is multifaceted. Where human relationships are finite, the divine grace and love in a soul's relationship with God elevates it to a level so profound that there is always an element of mystery in it. *"Our life is hidden in Christ in God"* (Col 3:3). God espoused the Israelite people to Himself saying, *"I will betroth you to me forever: I will betroth you to me with justice and with judgment, with loyalty and with compassion; I will betroth you to me with fidelity, and you shall know the LORD"* (Hos 2:21–22). And so being a Daughter of Israel, Our Lady took part in such a relationship with God. And yet, the Blessed Mother's individual role and commission by God to be preserved from original sin and to conceive and bear the Son of God to the world was unique and higher than how all other souls who came before and after Her were called.

In some ways, Mary merits the title "Spouse of the Eternal Father" simply because He asked Her to receive His Word into Her body and soul and to become the Mother of His Son. *"For your husband is your Maker; the LORD of hosts is his name, Your redeemer, the Holy One of Israel, called God of all the earth"* (Is 54:5). And yet, being

---

[58] Alphonsus de Liguori, trans. and ed. Eugene Grimm, *The Glories of Mary* (New York: Redemptorist, 1931), 304, citing Augustine, *Sermo Suppositus* 208a.11, Migne PL 39:2134.

a Daughter of the Father from the beginning of time, Our Lady lived a deep spiritual childhood with Him. A father begets life and it was the heavenly Father Who knit Mary together in Her mother Anna's womb. *"You formed my inmost being; you knit me in my mother's womb. I praise you, because I am wonderfully made; wonderful are your works! My very self you know. My bones are not hidden from you, when I was being made in secret, fashioned in the depths of the earth. Your eyes saw me unformed; in your book all are written down; my days were shaped, before one came to be"* (Ps 139:13–16).

Spousal Love With the Holy Spirit

While Our Lady primarily lived a relationship of spiritual childhood before God the Father, She lived as the holy Spouse of the Holy Spirit from the first moment of Her conception. This is why when the angel Gabriel was sent by God from heaven to Her in the Annunciation, he greeted Her calling Her "full of grace" (*"Hail, favored one! The Lord is with you."* Lk 1:28). And after greeting Her, the angel proposed to Our Lady an even deepening of the Holy Spirit's gift of Himself to Her:

> *The Holy Spirit will come upon you, and the power of the Most High will overshadow you. Therefore, the child to be born will be called holy, the Son of God.* (Lk 1:35)

Chapter 4: How Did Our Lady Live the Cross with Jesus?

And in the angel's annunciation of the Incarnation to St. Joseph, he clarified again that Our Lady was so deeply penetrated by the Holy Spirit that Jesus Christ was conceived within Her:

Joseph, son of David, do not be afraid to take Mary your wife into your home. For it is through the Holy Spirit that this child has been conceived in her. (Mt 1:20)

Just as an earthly husband is joined to his wife and a child takes flesh within her, no less was Our Lady joined to the Holy Spirit as Her Spouse so that the Son of God takes flesh within Her.

On May 2, 1990 at a General Audience, Pope St. John Paul II explained:

[Mary] is also the virgin-bride to whom it is granted conceiving and bearing forth the Son of God: the unique fruit of the nuptial love of God toward humanity, represented and summarized comprehensively as it were in Mary.

Descending upon Mary in the Annunciation, the Holy Spirit is the One who, in the Trinitarian relationship, expresses in His Person God's nuptial love, that love that is "eternal." In that moment the Holy Spirit is, in a unique way, the God-Spouse. In the mystery of the Incarnation the Holy Spirit effects the human conception of the Son of God while maintaining the divine transcendence. . . .

In this divine espousing of humanity, Mary responds to the announcement of the angel with the love of a bride, capable of responding and adapting perfectly to the divine election. As a result of all of this, from the time of St. Francis of Assisi, the Church calls the Virgin the "spouse of the Holy Spirit." Only this perfect nuptial love, profoundly rooted in the complete virginal self-giving to God, could enable Mary to become the "Mother of God" in a conscious and worthy way, in the mystery of the Incarnation.

In the Encyclical *Redemptoris Mater* I wrote: "The Holy Spirit had already come down upon her, and she became His faithful spouse at the Annunciation, welcoming the Word of the true God, offering "the full submission of intellect and will . . . and freely assenting to the truth revealed by him," indeed abandoning herself totally to God through "the obedience of faith," whereby she replied to the angel: "Behold, I am the handmaid of the Lord; let it be to me according to your word"" (26).

Mary, with this act and gesture, totally reverses the act of Eve, and becomes, in the spiritual history of humanity, the new Bride, the new Eve, Mother of all the living, as the Doctors and Fathers of the Church have stated frequently. She will be the type and model, in the New Covenant, of the nuptial union of the Holy Spirit with each of us and with all of the human community.[59]

---

[59] John Paul II, General Audience, May 2, 1990, English translation available at https://tobinstitute.org/the-holy-spirit-and-mary-model-of-the-nuptial-union-of-god-with-humanity/.

Chapter 4: How Did Our Lady Live the Cross with Jesus?

Here Pope St. John Paul II exquisitely explains the nuptial union of Our Lady with the Holy Spirit. And because of Her total response of self-abandonment and obedience to the Holy Spirit's divine nuptial invitation of love, She stands as an example for all souls in their relationship with God.

Adam and Eve were created by the Breath of God (which is the Holy Spirit) and were meant to be consumed by His presence all the days of their lives. In rejecting through disobedience and sin this gift of God's continual presence with them, they were separated from Him. In the Immaculate Conception Our Lady was created with the same overflowing presence of God within Her. Because She never sinned, there was never any absence of God within Her. And yet, the Holy Spirit Who created Her entered into a new relationship with Her at the Annunciation. God's presence ever flowing within Her was transformed from being that of the creator and sustainer of life, to a new dimension of nuptial spouse. Our Lady did not choose Her own creation, yet in the Annunciation She was given a choice to enter into a new relationship with God. She was always joined to Him and yet in Her *fiat* the Holy Spirit filled Her in a new marital way making the Word of God flesh within Her womb. Our Lady who had been created as the Daughter of the Most High was transformed into His Mother. She was proposed to by God because She already was His beloved immaculate Bride. She was able to respond in such freedom and fullness because of His presence welling up from within Her. And yet, at the moment of Her consent, She was joined to Him in a new marital way. At the moment of Her *'Fiat'*, Her marriage to God was consummated and His Word took flesh within Her. In this

She became the new Eve, the true 'Mother of all the living.' She was the perfection God intended for woman from the beginning.

St. Maximillian Kolbe also spoke of this mystery in his writings, most particularly how Our Lady as the Immaculate Conception was God's Spouse and masterpiece. He focuses on the identity of the Holy Spirit as Love. This ties in with what we already discussed in Pope St. John Paul II. It is the love of God in the Holy Spirit that created Mary, that sustained Mary, that proposed to Mary, that answered in Mary and that brought about the Incarnation in Mary. This same love would later uphold Mary in the interior martyrdom She would suffer as the Mother of the Redeemer and it is this love that would glorify Her eternally in heaven as our Queen. He writes:

> The Immaculata is in an ineffable manner united to the Holy Spirit as His Spouse, but in a manner incomparably more perfect than human words can express. . . . On what does this dwelling of the Holy Spirit in the Virgin Mary depend? He himself is love in her, the love of the Father and the Son, a love by which God truly does love himself, the love of the whole Blessed Trinity, a fruitful love, a conception. . . . The Holy Spirit lives in the Immaculata, in her soul, her being, and renders her fruitful from the very first moment of her existence and throughout her life and forever. This abeternal Immaculate Conception in the womb of her soul immediately initiates the divine life, her Immaculate Conception.[60]

---

[60] Maximillian Kolbe, *The Will to Love*, 37.

Chapter 4: How Did Our Lady Live the Cross with Jesus?

It is clear from St. Maximillian Kolbe that it is the Holy Spirit Who espouses Our Lady in Her conception, Who inspires Her *fiat* at the Annunciation, Who makes Her fruitful in the Incarnation and Who ultimately unites Her to Christ on the Cross—making them beat and bleed with one Heart as the new Adam gives birth to a redeemed humanity and the new Eve stands by faithful as His Helpmate and Compassioner. In this next section we will discuss Mary's role as the 'Woman-Wife' of God and the new Eve.

"Wife"—New Eve

Our Lady as the Spouse of the Holy Spirit gives birth to the Son of God. And yet, Mary also is considered both the Mother and the Wife of Christ—who with Him gives birth to a new humanity. The Blessed Mother as the new Eve participated with Jesus, the new Adam, in His act of redemption. It was Our Lady's intense love relationship with the Father (as His perfect little Daughter) as well as Her spousal relationship with both the Holy Spirit and Christ, that sealed Her union with the Heart of God and carried Her through the Passion and Death of Jesus.

In St. Thomas Aquinas' *Summa theologica,* the Angelic Doctor explains both the unitive quality and the mutual indwelling effect of love. He speaks of the compenetration of hearts that takes place between two people who share a deep love, and this is something experienced in a perfect degree by the Hearts of Jesus and Mary.

Dionysius said that *"every love is a 'unitive love'"* (*Div. Nom.* iv).[61] St. Thomas explains how *"the beloved is present within the lover"* who *"wills good to him, just as he wills good to himself"* to such a degree that the beloved is *"called a man's 'other self.'"* In this *"mutual indwelling . . . the beloved is said to be in the lover . . . while the lover is said to be in the beloved,"* where each one *"strives to gain an intimate knowledge of everything pertaining to the beloved, so as to penetrate into his very soul."* He describes this love as intimate as *"the bowels of charity,"* a love that *"is not satisfied with any external or superficial possession or enjoyment of the beloved; but seeks to possess the beloved perfectly, by penetrating into his heart, as it were."*[62] The unity and compenetration of hearts that exists between two souls who deeply love each other

> reckons what is good or evil to his friend, as being so to himself; and his friend's will as his own, so that it seems as though he felt the good or suffered the evil in the person of his friend. Hence it is proper to friends "to desire the same things, and to grieve and rejoice at the same," as the Philosopher says (*Ethic.* ix, 3 and *Rhet.* ii, 4). Consequently in so far as he reckons what affects his friend as affecting himself, the lover seems to be in the beloved, as though he were become one with him: but in so far as, on the other hand, he wills and acts for his friend's sake as for his own sake, looking on his

---

[61] Aquinas, *Summa theologica*, I-II, q. 28, a. 1.

[62] Aquinas, q. 28, a. 1.

friend as identified with himself, thus the beloved is in the lover."[63]

He concludes saying that the *"mutual indwelling in the love of friendship can be understood in regard to reciprocal love: inasmuch as friends return love for love, and both desire and do good things for one another."*[64]

We already referred to this explanation of love by St. Thomas Aquinas in the section where we discussed the unitive love within the Trinity. And yet, it is important to reference this love again here—as we apply the trinitarian love shared by the Father and the Son as an image of what Adam and Eve were called to share with God, and then through God with each other. In their failure to do this through sin (which caused a rift between both their hearts with God and each other), we find the ultimate example of human love reflecting this depths of Trinitarian love in the love shared between the Hearts of Jesus and Mary—the new Adam and the new Eve. What St. Thomas is describing about love in general is all the more true about the perfection of love found between the Heart of Our Lady and God—between the Heart of the Queen Mother and Her Son the King—between the Heart of the new Eve with Her Husband, the new Adam. St. Louis de Montfort in True Devotion to Mary says:

---

[63] Aquinas, q. 28, a. 1.
[64] Aquinas, q. 28, a. 2.

Lord, you are always with Mary and Mary is always with you. She can never be without you because then she would cease to be what she is. She is so completely transformed into you by grace that she no longer lives, she no longer exists, because you alone, dear Jesus, live and reign in her more perfectly than in all the angels and saints. ... So intimately is she united to you that it would be easier to separate light from the sun, and heat from the fire. I go further, it would even be easier to separate all the angels and saints from you than Mary; for she loves you ardently, and glorifies you more perfectly than all your other creatures put together.[65]

Pope Bl. Pius IX explained how this union of compenetrating love between the Hearts of Jesus and Mary was the means through which Mary helped Christ to crush the head of Satan and bring about the redemption of mankind:

> The Fathers and ecclesiastical writers, enlightened by instruction from on high, taught that . . . just as Christ, the Mediator between God and men, by taking our nature, cancelled the decree of condemnation against us, triumphantly nailing it to the Cross, so too the most holy Virgin, intimately and indissolubly united to Christ, became with Him the everlasting enemy of the venomous serpent, and thus shared with

---

[65] Louis de Montfort, *True Devotion to Mary*, 25.

her Son His victory over the serpent, crushing as she did the serpent's head with her virginal foot.[66]

Mary existed in the mind of God when He created Eve after Her image. Because Our Lady was sinless and completely obedient to God at all times, She is the prototype of the woman-wife that God intended to create in the world. It was because of Her Immaculate Conception and total surrender to God, trusting in complete obedience to all He asked of Her not only in Her *fiat* in the Annunciation but through the Cross and all the days of Her life, that She is "Woman" *par excellence*. The Blessed Mother's total obedience in *fiat* to God contrasted strongly the total disobedience of Eve. In this, Our Lady became the new Eve, who responded generously and docilly to the Father's will as the gift given to Christ — the new Adam — not only to be His Mother, but also to be His Helpmate. Because of Her Immaculate Heart, She fulfills exactly what the Father intended for woman to be. In this, Her identity not only reflects Genesis' account of the creation of man and woman, but also perfects it because She fulfills His commands to woman completely. In this She is taken to be the archetype of Scripture's many references to the perfect beauty of "the woman."

---

[66] Pius IX, Apostolic Constitution *Ineffabilis Deus*, December 8, 1854, in Gabriel M. Mesina, "Christ and Mary Revealed In Genesis 3:15," *Missio Immaculatae*, vol. 13, no. 3 (May/June 2017), https://missiomagazine.com/christ-mary-revealed-genesis-315/.

Although Our Lady was the Mother of Christ, She was also redeemed by Him. By receiving this redemption fully into Her soul — never blocking through sin any drop of His gift of grace — Mary was completely consumed by God and lived His possession of Her to the full. Our Lady as the immaculate prototype of the Church was the new Eve. As in Genesis, God created Eve from the side of Adam, the Blessed Mother was immaculately conceived through the grace that flowed from the "side of Christ" on the Cross. Washed in the blood of Christ from the first moment of Her conception, She was formed to be "His Woman," "His Wife," the "second half" of Him. Our Lady shared one flesh and blood and Heart and soul with Jesus —in the Incarnation, in the Eucharist, on the Cross. Looking upon Her immaculate perfection Christ could say, like Adam, *"This one, at last, is bone of my bones and flesh of my flesh; This one shall be called 'woman,' for out of man this one has been taken"* (Gen 2:23). Because of Our Lady's perfect union with God from the moment of Her creation She truly lived as His Wife, "clinging" to Him as spoken of in Genesis through Her *fiat*. And Mary did not cling to Christ simply for Herself. She clung to Christ in order to be a gift and Helpmate to Him. First, She was the gift of Woman to Him as His Mother. And later, She was the gift of Woman to Him as His Helpmate in redemption.

In the Incarnation, the Word became flesh within the womb of Mary. And on the Cross Jesus says, *"It is consummated,"* (Jn 19:30) where the flesh given to Him by Mary is united in a new and deeper way with Her (and the entire Church) through His suffering love. Pope St. John Paul II in his *Theology of the Body* explains that although God's love is a "fatherly love" in the beginning of creation, that love is transformed into a spousal love analogous to a "husband" when it is manifested in Jesus Christ as the Redeemer.[67] In a similar way, Our Lady's love for Jesus in the beginning was that of a Mother, but it is transformed into a spousal love analogous to a "Wife" when it is manifested in Her role as His Helpmate in redemption.

Adam and Eve's relationship in Genesis prophetically points to Jesus and Mary's relationship in the New Testament. In fact, Jesus in the Incarnation fulfills what it means to be a Man, Husband to humanity and Son of the Father better than Adam did in the beginning. The word husband comes from "husbandry" or "gardener." Adam was placed in the garden of Eden to care for creation, to cultivate life, and to protect and nurture divine life in the heart of his gift of a wife in Eve. The Word of God made flesh in Jesus Christ left His Father in heaven to come down to earth to cling to His Wife (humanity) manifested perfectly in the union He had with Mary in the Incarnation, on the Cross and in the Eucharist. He came to earth to care for creation in the most perfect way of redeeming its fallen state caused by Adam's sin. He came to protect, nurture and eventually save His Wife, the Church. And we see this done in a perfect way with Mary first in Her Immaculate Conception, and second because She freely and immaculately consented in Her will to cooperate with this gift of grace won for Her by Christ. She always said *fiat* to God. She always said *fiat* to Christ, the 'Gardener-Husband' and His work. As His 'Wife' Mary was a gift to Jesus as Eve was meant to be a gift to Adam, given to support Him in His work of redemption. She was His

---

[67] John Paul II, § 95.4, in *Theology of the Body*, 497.

Helpmate by willingly participating in His work of restoring creation by crucified love in the Incarnation and through the Cross.

As Jesus obeyed the Father in the work of redemption, so, too Our Lady as His Helpmate offered Her obedient *fiat* with and to Him. And this total reception of Christ's gift of salvation and Her return in the gift of Herself to Him, Mary is acting as His 'Woman-Wife' *par excellence*. Our Lady's maternal love is transformed into spousal love that makes Her a fruitful Wife in helping the children He entrusts to Her under the Cross. Through Mary's spousal love as a Helpmate to Christ, She freely participates in a subordinate way as His 'Woman-Wife' in His mission of restoring humanity to God. Her maternal love for Christ is transformed into a maternal love with Christ for Her spiritual children. In this, She is a model for all of the Church called into a similar union with Christ as our Savior.

The *Catechism* says that *"those who are united with Christ will form the community of the redeemed, the 'holy city' of God, 'the bride, the **wife of the Lamb**.'"*[68] In this way, all souls in the Church are called to imitate Our Lady. All are called to accept to be recreated through the blood coming from the side of Christ on the Cross and to allow Him to lay His life within them in order to possess them whole. This is the glorified state Our Lady lived all of the days of Her life. And this is how all souls are called to imitate Her example. In the creation story, it says that, *"The man and his wife were naked without shame"* (Gen 2:25). When the immaculate Christ is joined by His immaculate Mother at the foot of the Cross and united in one *fiat*, their purity

---

[68] *Catechism*, § 1045, emphasis mine.

of union has no trace of the shame of sin. All souls are called to courageously follow the example of Our Lady in this —allowing themselves to be stripped of pride, washed in Christ's blood and transformed into pure transparent vessels of His love as She was.

Our Lady is able to live this original vocation of Woman/Wife because Her Immaculate Conception preserved Her original innocence. This littleness before God to whom She always docilely surrendered in full allowed Him to fill Her with the completeness of His gifts of the Holy Spirit. He placed His Own courage and love within Her Heart which led Her to follow Jesus back into the darkened Garden of Gethsemane where He went to redeem sin through perfect obedience. Whereas Eve gave Adam the fruit in disobedience to God, Christ entered the Garden to feed the Church (including Our Lady) the fruit of obedience even unto death. He prayed, *"My Father, if it is possible, let this cup pass from me; yet, not as I will, but as you will"* (Mt 26:39). Instead of eating from a forbidden tree, Jesus was crucified on it. He—the Light of the World—was consumed with darkness to give humanity Light. And Our Lady followed Him into the darkness of Calvary in order to be His Helpmate by joining Her tears to His blood. Jesus' *"work and toil"* of *fiat* on the Cross (Gen 3:17) was united with Her painful *"labor"* with Him (Gen 6:16). His suffering of body was united with Her suffering of soul and in this She was "His Woman" (a Helpmate and Gift) *par excellence*. Mary perfectly reflected the obedience of Her Son and joined Her own *fiat* to His, thus magnifying the Lord.

When one looks at the Genesis account of God's creation of man and woman, one sees that in the beginning to be a "woman" simply meant to be a "wife."

> *The LORD God said: It is not good for the man to be alone. I will make a helper suited to him. . . . So the LORD God cast a deep sleep on the man, and while he was asleep, he took out one of his ribs and closed up its place with flesh. The LORD God then built the rib that he had taken from the man into a* **woman**. *When he brought her to the man, the man said: "This one, at last, is bone of my bones and flesh of my flesh; This one shall be called "***woman***," for out of man this one has been taken. That is why a man leaves his father and mother and clings to his* **wife**, *and the two of them become one body. The man and his* **wife** *were both naked, yet they felt no shame."* (Gen 2:18, 21–25, emphasis mine)

One can see that when God created "woman" it was precisely to be a "wife" to "her man." There is something written in the very heart and identity of woman that her nature is to be a gift and helpmate to God, to man and to humanity. When Eve disobeys God, the Holy Spirit immediately speaks to her of the "Woman" *par excellence* who would be born immaculately and who through flawlessly obeying God would crush the head of Satan. In Genesis 3:15, the Holy Spirit speaks of Our Lady, the immaculate new Eve, as the one who would eventually stomp on the head of the devil through giving birth to the Savior and participating in His work of redemption by always

Chapter 4: How Did Our Lady Live the Cross with Jesus?   127

obeying the Father with Him. We read of this in Genesis 3:15 where God says, *"I will put enmity between you and the **woman**, and between your offspring and hers; They will strike at your head, while you strike at their heel."*[69] And we read of this being accomplished in the book of Revelations where it is written about the glory of Mary as both the "Woman" and "Wife": *"A great sign appeared in the sky, a **woman** clothed with the sun, with the moon under her feet, and on her head a crown of twelve stars,"* (Rev 12:1, emphasis mine) and *"Behold the Bride, the **Wife** of the Lamb"* (Rev 21:9, emphasis mine).

The etymology of "wife" means "woman." In the original Greek, Hebrew and Latin texts of Scripture, the translation of the word for "woman" is synonymous with the word for "wife." In the very beginning when God created "woman," He was creating a "wife" who would complete man. This is evident in the Latin texts of Scripture where the same noun *uxor* (meaning "wife") is used in Genesis 2:23–24, Ephesians 5:25, 28, 31–32 (where it speaks of husbands and wives), and Revelation 21:9 and 19:7. When one looks at the Hebrew text, one can see that it is also the same word (*ashe*) that is used for both "woman" and "wife" in Genesis 2:22–25 and Genesis 3:15. A similar thing can be seen in the Greek wording of the New Testament. In Matthew 19:5, John 2:4, 19:26, Ephesians 5: 21–33, and Revelations 12:1, 21:9, 19:7, the Greek word *gune*—like the Hebrew, a word identical for "woman" and "wife"—is used.

To be a "woman" as the Father created her to be in the beginning is to be a "wife." Because of Eve's disobedience, she ripped her

---

[69] Emphasis mine.

identity in half disordering it. As a woman, she was not a gift or helpmate to man. Instead of drawing man into a deeper union with God through *fiat*, Eve separated him from God by tempting him (Adam) to sin. Eve fed her children disobedience by listening to Satan, eating the apple, and offering it to Adam. Our Lady, on the contrary, nursed Her offspring with perfect obedience and love by surrendering in *fiat* to all that the Father asked of Her every day of Her earthly life, but especially emphasized from the Annunciation to Calvary. In this, Our Lady fulfilled God's desire for what it means to be a "Woman-Wife" most perfectly.

Jesus Himself emphasizes His Mother's identity as the ideal "Woman-Wife" by the way He addresses Her in Scripture. In John 2:4 and 19:26, Christ Himself addresses His Mother as "Woman" (*gune*). This was in no way to degrade their relationship, but instead was to compliment Her using a word that reflected back to Genesis and what it meant to be a woman in the beginning. At the wedding at Cana Jesus said to His Mother, "**<u>Woman</u>**, *what is this between you and me?*" (Jn 2:4, emphasis mine) –in Greek, this sentence meaning the same thing as "**<u>Wife</u>**, *what is this between you and me?*" In this, Jesus was transforming, deepening and elevating their relationship from that of Mother and Son to that of the new Adam and His Helpmate the new Eve. Christ was calling His Mother by a name which originally meant that She was a Gift and Helpmate to "Her Man." Our Lady's work as Christ's Helpmate (His "Woman/Wife") begun in a visible way in Cana at the beginning of His public ministry, but it culminated on the Cross. It was on Calvary that Jesus once again called His Mother "Woman" (in Greek *gune*, the same word for

"Wife"). At that moment when the Sacred Heart of Jesus and the Immaculate Heart of Mary were consumed and united in one *fiat* to the sacrifice of Christ's life for the salvation of the world, their union bore fruit in the Church. This fruit was visible in Our Lady's new son, St. John. St. John was a symbol of all of the children who were born of the one united *fiat* of the new Adam and new Eve on Calvary.

It was precisely because Our Lady was a Helpmate to Christ by uniting Her sufferings to His that He was able to lay His life within Her in full. This is what makes Our Lady so powerful—it is in Her littleness, Her humble surrender, Her bold *fiat*. It is through Mary's pure Heart being completely conformed to Christ as "His Woman/Wife" that He is able to share His redemption with Her and defeat evil in the world through Her.

In the next chapter we will further explore this idea of Mary as the new Eve, the Helpmate of Jesus crucified and thus, a Co-redemptrix who assists Him in His mission and a Mediatrix of grace to all of the children of God.

Chapter 5

The Sorrowful Heart of Mary's *Fiat*— Our Lady as the New Eve, Helpmate of Jesus, the Eternal High Priest, Co-Redemptrix, and Mediatrix

Part 1: Our Lady as New Eve, Helpmate, Co-Redemptrix and Mediatrix

> Rejoice, through whom joy shall shine forth;
> Rejoice, through whom the curse shall vanish.
> Rejoice, fallen Adam's restoration;
> Rejoice, redemption of Eve's tears.[70]

Eve heard the word of the devil and took it to her heart and obeyed it—thus sin entered the world. Mary heard the Word of God and took this Word to Her Heart (into Her very womb!) and thus the redemption of mankind was incarnated on earth. It was Mary's *fiat* that undid the curse brought upon humanity by Eve.

---

[70] Romanos the Melodist, "Akathist Hymn to Theotokos," first statis, in *Akathist Hymn and Small Compline*, trans. N. Michael Vaporis (Brookline, MA: Holy Cross Orthodox Press, 2015), available at https://www.goarch.org/-/the-akathist-hymn-and-small-compline.

St. Justin Martyr wrote, "*Eve . . . conceiving the word from the serpent, brought forth disobedience and death. But Mary . . . when the angel announced to her that the Spirit of the Lord would come upon her . . . answered: Be it done to me according to your word.*"[71] Christ "*was made man of the Virgin, so that the disobedience brought on by the serpent might be cancelled out in the same manner in which it had begun.*"[72]

Words have power. God created the world with the Word. God said, *"Let there be light."* And there was light. St. John speaks of this at the beginning of his Gospel when he writes:

> *In the beginning was the Word,*
> *and the Word was with God,*
> *and the Word was God.*
> *He was in the beginning with God.*
> *All things came to be through him,*
> *and without him nothing came to be.*
> *What came to be through him was life,*
> *and this life was the light of the human race;*
> *the light shines in the darkness,*
> *and the darkness has not overcome it.* (John 1:1-5)

---

[71] Justin Martyr, *Dialogue with Trypho* 100, in William Most, *Mary In Our Life* (Garden City, NY: Image Books, 1963), 24.

[72] Justin Martyr, *Dialogue with Trypho* 100, in Most, 24.

Chapter 5: The Sorrowful Heart of Mary's *Fiat*

The purpose of God's word is to create life and to give light. Man's gift of speech was given to reflect this purpose of God's word. Words are like capsules that bring forth the spirit of a person present in their hearts. *"A good person out of the store of goodness in his heart produces good, but an evil person out of a store of evil produces evil; for from the fullness of the heart the mouth speaks."* (Lk 6:45) Words can carry life, light and love to people as God's Word did in the beginning. Or if people speak from a heart of sin, it can carry death.

Jesus' words always created Life and gave forth Light. When He met sick people, He would say 'Be healed' and they would be healed. To the dead He would say, 'Rise up' and they would rise up. To the raging storm He would say, 'Be still' and it would be still. To those in darkness He would say, 'See!' and they would see. His words brought into effect what they meant. They always came from His divine Heart of love, and so they gave forth not only Life, but also a brilliant heavenly teaching of Light. They bestowed upon those who listened to it a knowledge that they are loved as children of God.

When the word of God encounters a soul that has separated itself from Him in sin, it converts that soul. It purifies it. When words go forth from the mouth of a prophet to others who need to repent, those words burn like fire. But it is not a fire that comes to destroy. It is a fire that transforms the listener as fire refines gold. Jeremiah said about the word of God bubbling forth from within him, *"I say I will not mention him, I will no longer speak in his name. But then it is as if fire is burning in my heart, imprisoned in my bones; I grow weary holding back, I cannot!"* (Jer 20:9) The word of God always brings forth life, light and love because the word of God always brings with it the very presence of Himself.

When Adam was created in Genesis, the Lord instructed him to name all of the animals. In this work Adam was participating in the life of God, speaking life and truth to the world around him. When Eve was finally created and brought to him, he said, *"This one shall be called 'woman,' for out of man this one has been taken."* (Gen 2:23) In Genesis 3:20 we read that, *"The man gave his wife the name "Eve," because she was the mother of all the living."* Even after her fall in sin, Adam identified Eve's true purpose on earth had been to bring forth life in this world. Yet because of her disconnect with God from sin, she gave forth life that included the effects of sin, being suffering and death.

Our Lady created sinless and always keeping Her will subject to the will of God in *fiat* brought forth the true Word of God that would restore life, light and truth to humanity. Because of Her obedience, the Word became flesh under Our Lady's Heart and sprung forth from Her womb as a triumphant remedy to man's sin. The Word of God spoken by the Father to create the universe in the beginning now took flesh in Our Lady to recreate a fallen humanity. The Word of God within Her gave forth heavenly love, wisdom, light and power.

St. Irenaeus stated:

> Just as she [Eve] ... being disobedient, became a cause of death for herself and the whole human race: so Mary ... being obedient, became a cause of salvation for herself and the

whole human race. . . . For in no other way can that which is tied be untied unless the very windings of the knot are gone through in reverse: so that the first joints are loosed through the second, and the second in turn free the first. . . . Thus, then, the knot of the disobedience of Eve was untied through the obedience of Mary.[73]

Pope St. John Paul II developed this theme by reflecting on the teaching of St. Iranaeus in audiences dedicated to the role of Mary in salvation history. He not only juxtaposed Our Lady's obedience with Eve's disobedience, but also went the further step to say that it was Mary's obedience that actually contributed to the restoration of Eve:

St. Justin and St. Irenaeus speak of Mary as the new Eve who by her faith and obedience makes amends for the disbelief and disobedience of the first woman. According to the Bishop of Lyons, it was not enough for Adam to be redeemed in Christ, but "it was right and necessary that Eve be restored in Mary" (*Demonstratio apostolica*, 33).[74]

---

[73] Ireneus, *Against Heresies* 3.22.4, in Most, 25.

[74] John Paul II, General Audience, October 15, 1997, § 4, in Arthur Burton Calkins, "The Mystery of Mary Coredemptrix in the Papal Magisterium," *Mary Co-redemptrix: Doctrinal Issues Today*, ed. Mark Miravalle (Goleta, CA: Queenship Publishing, 2002), 61.

In a General Audience on October 25, 1995, Pope St. John Paul II described in depth how this understanding of Our Lady as the new Eve was referred to by the Fathers of the Church, but it was not systematically developed theologically until the 10th century.

> At the end of the second century, St. Irenaeus, a disciple of Polycarp, already pointed out Mary's contribution to the work of salvation. He understood the value of Mary's consent at the time of the Annunciation, recognizing in the Virgin of Nazareth's obedience to and faith in the angel's message the perfect antithesis of Eve's disobedience and disbelief, with a beneficial effect on humanity's destiny. In fact, just as Eve caused death, so Mary, with her "yes" became "a cause of salvation" for herself and for all mankind (cf. *Adv. Haer.*, III, 22, 4; SC 211, 441). But this affirmation was not developed in a consistent and systematic way by the other Fathers of the Church.
>
> Instead, this doctrine was systematically worked out for the first time at the end of the 10th century in the Life of Mary by a Byzantine monk, John the Geometer. Here Mary is united to Christ in the whole work of Redemption, sharing, according to God's plan, in the Cross and suffering for our

salvation. She remained united to the Son "in every deed, attitude and wish" (cf. *Life of Mary*, Bol. 196, f. 123 v.).[75]

Just as in the beginning Eve was created to be a helpmate to Adam, so too Our Lady, the new Eve, was given to be a Helpmate to Jesus Christ, the new Adam:

> The universal motherhood of Mary, the "Woman" of the wedding at Cana and of Calvary, recalls Eve, "mother of all living" (Gen 3:20). However, while the latter helped to bring sin into the world, the new Eve, Mary, cooperates in the saving event of Redemption. Thus, in the Blessed Virgin the figure of "woman" is rehabilitated and her motherhood takes up the task of spreading the new life in Christ among men.[76]

> Having created man "male and female" (cf. Gen 1:27), the Lord also wants to place the New Eve beside the New Adam in the Redemption. Our first parents had chosen the way of sin as a couple; a new pair, the Son of God with his Mother's cooperation, would re-establish the human race in its original dignity.[77]

---

[75] John Paul II, General Audience, October 25, 1995, § 2, in Mark Miravalle, *With Jesus: The story of Mary Co-Redemptrix* (Goleta: Queenship Publishing, 2003), 71.

[76] John Paul II, General Audience, April 23, 1997, § 3, in Calkins, "Mary Coredemptrix in the Papal Magisterium," 62.

[77] John Paul II, General Audience, April 9, 1997, § 3, in Calkins, 62.

This beautifully explains how Our Lady not only displayed the ultimate virtue whereas Eve exhibited vice, but takes it a step further to show how She participated in Christ's redemption of man. On July 23, 1997, Pope St. John Paul II said that, *"Christ is King not only because he is Son of God, but also because he is the Redeemer; Mary is Queen not only because she is Mother of God, but also because, associated as the new Eve with the new Adam, she cooperated in the work of the redemption of the human race."*[78]

But what exactly does it mean that Our Lady as the new Eve was the "Helpmate' of Christ in the work of His redemption?

Our Lady as Helpmate

Fr. Paul Phillippe, O.P., clearly explains the Blessed Mother's role in the priesthood of Jesus Christ by taking his reader back to St. Albert the Great's understanding of Our Lady as created by God to be a companion and co-adjutor of Christ crucified. In his book *The Blessed Virgin and the Priesthood,* he explains:

> St. Albert the Great says that the Blessed Virgin was not chosen by the Lord to be a minister, but to be a spouse and help, after the words of Genesis: "Let us make for him a helpmate like unto himself" (Gen 11:18). The Most Holy Virgin is not a Vicar, (that is to say an instrument), but a coadjutor and a **companion** participating in the reign as She participated in

---

[78] John Paul II, General Audience, July 23, 1997, § 2, in Calkins, 64.

the Passion. . . . The wounds that Christ received in His body, She felt in Her Heart.[79]

What then is the Role of Mary in the Passion? Nothing more than that of a help to Christ, "a help like unto himself" as St. Albert the Great says. For Mary is not formally a priest on Calvary, but only the associate of the Sovereign Priest. It is by Her union of charity with Christ that She collaborated in the Redemption, it is by Her Immaculate Heart that She is our Mother, as it is by His Sacred Heart that Jesus brought us into life.[80]

What we read here is an astounding insight into the unitive nature and power of love. St. Albert is claiming that because love united the Hearts of Jesus and Mary perfectly, the same love caused Our Lady to feel mystically in Her Heart the same wounds that Christ suffered in His body and soul. His suffering became Her suffering because of Her love. And although Christ alone redeemed man through the perfect offering of His suffering and death to the Father in expiation for sin, Our Lady collaborated with Him by offering to the Father along with Jesus Her own suffering that She endured on account of love of Her crucified Son. Hans Urs Von Balthasar also

---

[79] Paul Phillippe, *The Blessed Virgin and the Priesthood* (Chicago: Henry Regnery Company, 1955), 36, emphasis mine.

[80] Phillippe, 61.

explained this mystery beautifully in his book, *Priestly Spirituality*, saying:

> His is a sacrifice that in the burning fire of suffering consumes within itself the entire god-forsakenness of the sinner—and thus it is not only the cost physically but also the most spiritually agonizing sacrifice of all. What, then, is Mary's position now in relation to this divine and human sacrifice?... **She embraces it with him, since She does not revoke Her Yes (*fiat*) but remains faithful to it to the last. She lets it be done. She offers to the Father, as She always has done, this self-sacrificing, sacrificial Victim, but in such a way that this offering (oblatio) is for Her the most heartrending renunciation, only thereby making Her oblation truly into a sacrifice, the surrender of what is dearest of all. How much sooner would the Mother suffer in the place of Her Son all that he has to undergo! How terrible it is to have to assent to this sacrifice, which, from a worldly perspective, is the most meaningless and hopeless of all!** And when in Holy Mass, during the Canon, the Church again and again speaks of a sacrifice offered and recalls that it is not only the sacrifice of the Son that is commemorated but that the Church herself fully participates in the act of sacrifice, where else has She truly realized what this Her offering to the Father of the Son, costs Her except at that moment when, in Mary, She offered up Her Son to the Father? Sinners in the Church cannot in fact realize this; they must be glad, rather, that Christ offers himself for them. And the Church

does not exist except in real subjects. **Alone, this all-holy woman, and at most just a few others who have been purified to the point of purest love, can gauge what sword it is that pierces the heart of the Church when She for Her part sacrifices to the Father this self-sacrificing Lamb.**[81]

Here Van Balthasar explains this work of love that Our Lady completed with Christ perfectly because of Her Immaculate Conception, but that also all Christians who make up the body of Christ are called to offer with them as well. To the degree one is united with Christ in love is the degree they will participate with Him in His Passion and Death. Our Lady was consummately united with Jesus because of Her superb love union with Him. In this She not only loved as a Mother, but also fulfilled the role of the new Eve with Christ, the new Adam. By participating in Her Son's Passion both as His Mother as well as Helpmate, Our Lady simultaneously fulfilled the roles of a Mother offering Her Son, as well as the Woman/Wife helping Her eternal Husband give birth to all souls making Her the true *"Mother of all the Living."* (Gen 3:20). St. Edith Stein explains:

> Following Her Son to Golgotha and suffering with Him in His agonizing work of redemption, Mary was "the archetype of followers of the Cross for all time," who "stood by the side of the Redeemer." Mary's love for her Son never wavered. Even a pierced heart could not destroy her love; perhaps,

---

[81] Von Balthasar, *Priestly Spirituality*, 49, emphasis mine.

indeed, it intensified and expanded. Like Mary who battled against evil as "co-redeemer by the side of the Redeemer," all women are to be willing to join the fight for the kingdom.[82]

The new Eve stands beside the new Adam on the threshold between the Old and the New Covenants. God chose as the instrument for His Incarnation a human mother, and in her He presented the perfect image of a mother. From the time that she learns she is to bear a son she is completely at the service of this mission. He is given to her by God and in fidelity to God she must look after Him. Her existence until the hour of His birth is one of composed expectancy; then in a life fully surrendered to service, she takes careful note of all words and signs which anticipate something of His future course. With all reverence for the divinity hidden in Him, she still maintains authority over Him when He is a child; in true perseverance, she participates in His work until His death and beyond it. But before the annunciation of her election, this woman called to the most exalted maternity had not wanted marriage and motherhood for herself; and this was against every tradition of her people.[83]

---

[82] Traflet, *St. Edith Stein: A Spiritual Portrait*, 99.

[83] Stein, *Essays on Woman*, 2:189.

Chapter 5: The Sorrowful Heart of Mary's *Fiat*

St. Edith Stein continues Her powerful teaching of Mary, the Mother turned Co-redeeming Helpmate echoing the same sentiments of St. Albert the Great:

> And thereby, **as Co-redeemer by the side of the Redeemer.** . . . In Mary, we do not see the Lord (as we do in a priest), but we see her always by the Lord's side. Her service is rendered directly to Him: through the prayer of intercession, she intercedes with Him for humankind; she receives from His hands graces to be bestowed and does indeed transmit them. She does not represent the Lord but assists Him. Her position is thus analogous to that of Eve by the side of the first Adam. But Mary is beside Jesus not for His sake but for ours. She is the mother of the living not because all succeeding generations come from her but because her maternal love embraces the whole Mystical Body with Jesus Christ its head. In her virginity, she is the pure prototype of womanhood because she stands beside Him who is the prototype of all manhood and because she leads all humanity to Him. In this womanhood devoted to the service of love, is there really a divine image? Indeed, yes. A ministering love means assistance lent to all creatures in order to lead them toward perfection. But such love is properly the attribute of the Holy Spirit. Thus, we can see the prototype of all feminine being in the Spirit of God poured out over all creatures. It finds its most perfect

image in the purest Virgin who is the bride of God and mother of all mankind.[84]

Scattered throughout her writing, St. Edith Stein refers to Our Lady as the new Eve, Co-redeemer, and Helpmate of Jesus. In her work *The Science of the Cross*, she concludes what Dionysius claimed that, *"The divinest of all divine work is to co-operate with God in the salvation of souls."*[85] But She sees in Our Lady a cooperator who transcends all other people who devote their lives to working with Christ for the salvation of souls. The Blessed Mother helps Him beyond simply a human way, entering into a divine work that reaches a supernatural level beyond all others. She said, *"Mary leaves the natural order and is placed as Co-Redemptrix alongside the Redeemer."*[86] It is Our Lady's littleness (and kenotic self-emptying), Her Heart's consummation in divine love and Her perpetual *fiat* that allow Christ to hold Her perfectly one with Him on the Cross.

But how is this Lady, the Helpmate of Christ, our Co-redeeming Mother?

---

[84] Stein, 2:189, 191, emphasis mine.

[85] Edith Stein, *The Science of the Cross: A Study of St. John of the Cross*, eds. Lucy Gelber and Romaeus Leuven, trans. Hilda C. Graef (Washington, DC: Henry Regnery Co., 1960), 215.

[86] Stein, 215. See also M. F. Perella, "Edith Stein. Ebrea, carmelitana, martire," *Palestra del Clero* 78 (1999), 695.

Co-Redemptrix

> *He said in reply, "Have you not read that from the beginning the Creator 'made them male and female' and said, 'For this reason a man shall leave his father and mother and be joined to his wife, and the two shall become one flesh'? So they are no longer two, but one flesh. Therefore, what God has joined together, no human being must separate."* (Mt 19:4–6)

These were the words that Jesus spoke when questioned about the insolubility of marriage. And in His answer in general about the immorality of divorce, He referred back to the original plan of God for man and woman *"in the beginning."* Because Our Lady was immaculate, She actually fulfilled the original blueprint that the Father had for woman when He created Her. Archbishop Fulton Sheen says that Our Lady *"is the same ideal that God had in His Heart from all eternity—the Lady whom He calls 'Mother.'"*[87]

This passage above from Matthew 19 powerfully refers to the multifaceted relationship that the Blessed Virgin Mary shared with Her Son, Redeemer, and Lord. In many ways, this original plan for man and woman was a foreshadowing of the perfection of Man and Woman in Jesus and Mary. After Adam and Eve sinned, a great rift appeared not only in their relationship with God, but in their relationship with each other and in the relationship that their mind,

---

[87] Fulton J. Sheen, *The World's First Love, Mary the Mother of God* (San Francisco: Ignatius Press, 1952), 9.

body, and heart had within themselves. *"To the woman he said: I will intensify your toil in childbearing; in pain you shall bring forth children. Yet your urge shall be for your husband, and he shall rule over you"* (Gen 3:16). The original solitude that man and woman had shared with God as a secure womb for their union with Him turned—through sin—into a lonely place where they experienced a separation from God, each other and even within their own hearts. Once again, man and woman were alone.

Looking upon broken creation, the Father foresaw the eternal plan of salvation that included His Son taking on flesh and coming to earth to suffer, die, and then rise to gain eternity for mankind. As the Father contemplated the work of His Son He again said, *"It is not good for the man to be alone. I will make a helper suited to him"* (Gen 2:18). And so, as the *"all-powerful Word from heaven's royal throne leapt into the doomed land"* (Wis 18:15) according to the plan of salvation, He needed flesh from a Mother and a Wife as a Helpmate. And so, the Father fashioned Mary.

Truly, the Word of God left His Father to cling to His Woman/Wife with whom He shared one flesh, and at the moment of the Incarnation Christ exclaimed in His Heart, *"This one, at last, is bone of my bones and flesh of my flesh; This one shall be called 'woman,' for out of man this one has been taken."* And Scripture explains: *"That is why a man leaves his father and mother and clings to his wife, and the two of them become one body"* (Gen 2:23–24). The Virgin Mother and Eternal Son—the new Adam and the new Eve—are knit together as one flesh in the Incarnation. Christ took all of His humanity from Mary—just as *in the beginning* God had created Eve from the side of

Adam. And as they were united as one flesh and in one *fiat* in the Incarnation, so as the plan of God for the redemption of mankind unfolded they were only united more and more deeply as one Heart. For *"what God has joined together, no human being must separate"* (Mt 19:6). Jesus and Mary united as one in the Incarnation were therefore also united as one in the redemption of the world.

Pope St. Pius X explains this in his Encyclical *Ad diem illum* in 1904:

> Will it not appear to all that it is right and proper to affirm that Mary, whom Jesus made **His constant companion** from the house of Nazareth to the place of Calvary, knew, as no other knew, the secrets of His heart, distributes as by a mother's right the treasures of His merits, and is the surest help to the knowledge and love of Christ?[88]

If Jesus and Mary are united so closely as one through love, inherently they also will be united in aspect of that love that is crucified. Later on Pope St. Pius X clearly states that Mary is, "a partaker in the sufferings of Christ and the associate in His Passion."[89]

If Jesus and Mary shared one flesh, how much more did they share one Heart and soul! And if Christ was sent to earth to redeem

---

[88] Pius X, Encyclical Letter *Ad diem illum*, February 2, 1904, § 15, in Calkins, "Mary Coredemptrix in the Papal Magisterium," 56–57, emphasis mine.

[89] Pius X, § 21, in Calkins, 57.

humanity by embracing their suffering in His body, Heart and soul, it follows that Our Lady would mystically endure this suffering right along with Him. But this interior martyrdom is something Our Lady suffered primarily through a union of love. In light of Aquinas' teaching on the compenetration of hearts in love, it is easy to see the depths to which Jesus and Mary shared joys and sorrows.

St. John Eudes beautifully elucidates:

> What a sorrowful sight to see those two Hearts of Jesus and Mary, two Hearts so holy, so innocent, so full of graces and perfections, so enkindled with divine love, so closely united to each other, and compassionate towards each other! The holy Heart of the Mother of Jesus feels most keenly the terrible torments of her Son; the Only Son of Mary is wholly convulsed by the incomparable sufferings of His Mother. Jesus, the innocent Lamb, and Mary, His immaculate Mother, call to each other; the one weeps for the other, receiving no consolation; and the purer and more ardent their mutual love is, the more their sorrows penetrate and pierce....[90]

> What a martyrdom of blood for the Heart of your divine Lamb, the Only Son of God and your Son, in seeing so clearly all the sorrows penetrating your Heart, the desolation in which you are, the anguish necessarily caused by Your absence, and the fact that you can neither speak to Him nor He

---

[90] John Eudes, *The Sacred Heart of Jesus*, trans. Richard Flower (New Hampshire: Loreto Publications, 2011), 66.

to you, because no words can be found capable of appeasing such great sorrows![91]

St. Isaac of Stella explains beautifully the union of Christ's tears with that of the Church –of which Our Lady is the prototype and Queen. He explains how when Jesus took on the flesh of humanity, He did so as a priestly Bridegroom Who then redeemed His beloved Bride through His Passion and Death. Their sorrows were one, but because of this love union, so would be the efficacy of their prayer.

Christ first came as the savior and He redeemed Our Lady just as He redeemed all of humanity. Yet, because the Father desired that His Son would have a spotless home worthy of His Incarnation, He applied the merits of Jesus' redemption to His Mother even before She was born. In this way She was immaculately conceived and sinless from the very beginning.

In the words of St. Isaac of Stella, we read about Christ as the Redeemer going to the greatest extremes of sacrifice in order to save His Beloved. If such words could be spoken about the Church as a whole wedded to Christ on the Cross, how much more profoundly can one specifically apply this analogy to Our Lady. St. Isaac of Stella wrote:

> When the Almighty, the Most High, wedded a bride who was weak and of low estate, He made that maid-servant a queen. He took her from her place behind Him, at His feet, and

---

[91] Eudes, 69.

enthroned her at His side. She had been born from His side, and therefore He betrothed her to Himself. And as all that belongs to the Father belongs also to the Son because by nature they are one, so also the Bridegroom gave all He had to the bride and He shared in all that was hers. He made her one both with Himself and with the Father. Praying for His bride, the Son said to the Father: I want them to be one with us, even as you and I are one.

And so the Bridegroom is one with the Father and one with the bride. Whatever He found in His bride alien to her own nature He took from her and nailed to His Cross when He bore her sins and destroyed them on the tree. He received from her and clothed Himself in what was hers by nature and gave her what belonged to Him as God. He destroyed what was diabolical, took to Himself what was human, and conferred on her what was divine. So all that belonged to the bride was shared in by the Bridegroom, and He who had done no wrong and on whose lips was found no deceit could say: Have pity on me, Lord, for I am weak. Thus, sharing as He did in the bride's weakness, the Bridegroom made His own her cries of distress, and gave His bride all that was His.[92]

As Christ lowered Himself to share in the weakness of humanity, He took all of their suffering upon Himself and, in turn, gave humanity all that was His as the Son of God. Our Lady is the first and

---

[92] Isaac of Stella, *Sermo 11*, in *The Liturgy of the Hours*, 4:246.

fullest receiver of this gift of Christ. First, He lowered Himself to enter Her womb. She shared human flesh with Him along with all of the weakness it encompassed as a result of sin. He took all suffering upon Himself and then, shared with Our Lady and all of humanity the abyss of heavenly treasure.

Our Lady alone because of Her sinlessness could receive the fullness of His gift, for no sin ever blocked the tiniest amount of grace flowing to Her from His Heart. Grace grew exponentially within Her. And, therefore, no one ever received the eternal gifts of divine love that Christ shared with humanity as fully as Our Lady's spotless, open Heart. Yet this gift of divine love came through Christ on earth as a gift of crucified love. Mary never cowered from the tumultuous suffering that accompanied the gift of Her Son's love on Calvary. The Blessed Mother stood with Christ on Golgotha with such bold faithfulness that She is often called the "Tower of Ivory." St. John Henry Newman says:

> When we say a man "towers" over his fellows, we mean to signify that they look small in comparison of him. This quality of greatness is instanced in the Blessed Virgin. Though she suffered more keen and intimate anguish at our Lord's Passion and Crucifixion than any of the Apostles by reason of her being His Mother, yet consider how much more noble she was amid her deep distress than they were. . . . **It is expressly noted of her that she stood by the Cross. She did not grovel in the dust, but stood upright to receive the blows, the stabs, which the long Passion of her Son**

inflicted upon her every moment. In this magnanimity and generosity in suffering she is, as compared with the Apostles, fitly imaged as a Tower.[93]

If we are exploring in this thesis the notion of littleness and pure love being tools that enabled Christ–and then in turn Mary and all of the holy saints that followed Her on Her Son's way of the Cross– to surrender in perfect *fiat* to the Father even unto the Cross, then it is important to pause here to reflect more deeply on Our Lady's specific role in this. Mary was the first and best disciple of Jesus. She was not a redeemer in and of Herself. She was a receiver of Jesus' gift of salvation to mankind. And yet, because She was immaculately conceived, She most perfectly received this gift of redemption all the days of Her life. Her love of God never had sin to obstruct it. She was most little before God, most surrendered, most on fire with love and thus, most profoundly united with Him in His mission that led to Calvary and beyond. Because of this, Mary's union with Jesus was the greatest of all.

Because of Our Lady's pivotal role in giving us the Redeemer through Her *fiat* to the Father, She stands at a special place as the perfect disciple and Mother of all disciples of Her Son. Yet in Herself Our Lady is nothing. She is not the Redeemer. She is simply a receiver of God's presence and love, an obedient Daughter who always fulfilled God's will, a Mother and then, in turn, a Helpmate of the

---

[93] John Henry Newman, *The Mystical Rose*, 117, emphasis mine.

Chapter 5: The Sorrowful Heart of Mary's *Fiat*

Redeemer. But because She accomplished this all so perfectly, She can stand as an example for all the Church.

Rev. Msgr. Arthur B. Calkins in his article *"The Mystery of Mary Co-redemptrix in the Papal Magisterium"* presents a long litany of papal documents explaining Our Lady's role as the new Eve, Helpmate, and Co-redemptrix of Christ the Redeemer. A small few of the most beautiful papal documents from his research are presented here simply to show the deep history of the Church's understanding of Our Lady in this role.

Pope Benedict XV was a firm believer in Our Lady's role as the new Eve who supported and upheld Her Son and spouse Christ on the Cross. He explained:

> But the sufferings of Jesus cannot be separated from the sorrows of Mary. Just as the first Adam had a woman for accomplice in his rebellion against God, so the new Adam wished to have a woman share in His work of re-opening the gates of heaven for men. From the Cross, He addressed His Own Sorrowful Mother as the "woman," and proclaimed Her the new Eve, the Mother of all men, for whom He was dying that they might live.[94]

---

[94] Benedict XV, Homily for the Canonization of St. Gabriel of the Sorrowful Virgin and St. Margaret Mary Alacoque, May 13, 1920, in Calkins, "Mary Coredemptrix in the Papal Magisterium," 52.

Pope Benedict XV starkly proposes Our Lady as Co-redemptrix in a letter he wrote in 1918:

> To such extent did [Mary] suffer and almost die with her suffering and dying Son; to such extent did she surrender her maternal rights over her Son for man's salvation, and immolated Him -insofar as she could – in order to appease the justice of God, that we rightly say **she redeemed the human race together with Christ.**[95]

Venerable Pope Pius XII also boldly proclaimed the union of Mary with Jesus in His work of redemption saying:

> In fact, are not Jesus and Mary ... the new Adam and the new Eve whom the Tree of the Cross unites in pain and love to atone for the sin of our first parents in Eden?[96]

From these considerations we can conclude as follows: in the work of redemption Mary was by God's will joined with Jesus Christ, the cause of salvation, in much the same way as Eve was joined with Adam, the cause of death. Hence it can be said that the work of our salvation was brought about by a

---

[95] Benedict XV, Apostolic Letter *Inter sodalicia*, March 22, 1918, in Miravalle, *With Jesus*, 157–58, emphasis mine.

[96] Pius XII, *L'Osservatore Romano*, April 22–23, 1940, in Calkins, 52.

"restoration" (St. Irenaeus) in which the human race, just as it was doomed to death by a virgin, was saved by a virgin.[97]

Pope Bl. Pius IX (1846–1878) in his Apostolic Constitution *Ineffabilis Deus* published on December 8, 1854 also said:

> Hence, just as Christ, the Mediator between God and man, assumed human nature, blotted the handwriting of the decree that stood against us, and fastened it triumphantly to the cross, so the most holy Virgin, united with Him by a most intimate and indissoluble bond, was, with Him and through Him, eternally at enmity with the evil serpent, and most completely triumphed over him, and thus crushed his head with her immaculate foot.[98]

Pope Leo XIII similarly claimed Mary's association with Jesus in the work of redemption in his rosary Encyclical *Supremi apostolatus* published on September 1, 1883:

> The Blessed Virgin was exempt from the stain of original sin and chosen to be the Mother of God. For this very reason she was associated with Him in the work of man's salvation, and

---

[97] Pius XII, Encyclical Letter *Ad Cæli Reginam*, October 11, 1954, in Calkins, 53.

[98] Pius IX, *Ineffabilis Deus*, December 8, 1854, in Calkins, 55.

enjoys favor and power with her Son greater than any man or angel has ever attained or could attain.[99]

Pius XI builds on the thought of his predecessors explaining how Mary's Immaculate Conception was a necessary preparation for Her role as *"associate in the redemption of mankind."* He said:

> In fact, the august Virgin, conceived without original sin, was chosen to be the Mother of Christ in order to be associated with Him in the Redemption of mankind. For that reason she was adorned with such abundant grace and such great power in her Son's sight that neither human nor angelic nature can ever acquire a like grace or power.[100]

Venerable Pope Pius XII described Mary as the beloved associate of Christ [*alma socia Christi*] affectionately explaining in several papal documents both Her association with Him in His work of redemption along with Her role of Mediatrix of grace:

> He, the Son of God, gave His heavenly Mother a share in His glory, His majesty, His kingship; because, associated as Mother and Minister to the King of martyrs in the ineffable

---

[99] Leo XIII, Encyclical Letter *Supremi apostolatus*, September 1, 1883, § 2, in Calkins, 55.

[100] Pius XI, Letter *Auspicatus profecto*, January 28, 1933, in Calkins, "Mary Coredemptrix in the Papal Magisterium," 57.

Chapter 5: The Sorrowful Heart of Mary's *Fiat*   157

work of man's Redemption, she is likewise associated with Him forever, with power so to speak infinite, in the distribution of the graces which flow from Redemption.[101]

Many other Popes, including Venerable Pope Pius XII, Pope St. John XXIII, Pope St. Paul VI, and Pope John Paul I referred in various documents to Our Lady as the associate or Helpmate of Christ the Redeemer. Pope St. John Paul II built upon his predecessors' love and honor for Our Lady as the Helpmate of Christ in the work of salvation. He took their declarations of Her as the Savior's "associate" and renewed the word "Co-redemptrix" (using it at least six times in published statements).[102]

Pope St. John Paul II explains this title in a longer address in Ecuador on January 31, 1985 referring Our Lady's title of Co-Redemptrix to St. Paul's claim, *"I have been crucified with Christ"* (Gal. 2:20):

> Mary goes before us and accompanies us. The silent journey that begins with her Immaculate Conception and passes through the "yes" of Nazareth, which makes her the Mother of God, finds on Calvary a particularly important moment.

---

[101] Pius XII, Radio Message to Fatima, May 13, 1946, in Calkins, 57–58.

[102] See John Paul II, General Audience, September 8, 1982; Angelus Address, November 4, 1984; Palm Sunday Address, March 31, 1985; Address to Pilgrims, March 24, 1990; and address for the canonization of St. Bridget of Sweden, October 6, 1991.

There also, accepting and assisting at the sacrifice of her Son, Mary is the dawn of Redemption; ... Crucified spiritually with her crucified son (cf. Gal 2:20), she contemplated with heroic love the death of her God, she "lovingly consented to the immolation of this Victim which she herself had brought forth" (*Lumen Gentium*, 58). . . .

In fact, at Calvary she united herself with the sacrifice of her Son that led to the foundation of the Church; her maternal heart shared to the very depths the will of Christ "to gather into one all the dispersed children of God" (Jn 11:52). Having suffered for the Church, Mary deserved to become the Mother of all the disciples of her Son, the Mother of their unity. . . .

The Gospels do not tell us of an appearance of the risen Christ to Mary. Nevertheless, as she was in a special way close to the Cross of her Son, she also had to have a privileged experience of His Resurrection. In fact, Mary's role as Co-Redemptrix did not cease with the glorification of her Son.[103]

In a general audience address of April 9, 1997, the Holy Father explained the difference between every Christian's cooperation with Christ's redeeming work on Calvary and Our Lady's unique role of association:

---

[103] John Paul II, Address at the Marian shrine in Guayaquil, January 31, 1985, in Calkins, "Mary Coredemptrix in the Papal Magisterium," 42–43.

The collaboration of Christians in salvation takes place after the Calvary event, whose fruits they endeavor to spread by prayer and sacrifice. Mary, instead, cooperated during the event itself and in the role of mother; thus, her cooperation embraces the whole of Christ's saving work. She alone was associated in this way with the redemptive sacrifice that merited the salvation of all mankind. In union with Christ and in submission to him, she collaborated in obtaining the grace of salvation for all humanity.

The Blessed Virgin's role as cooperator has its source in her divine motherhood. By giving birth to the One who was destined to achieve man's redemption, by nourishing him, presenting him in the temple and suffering with him as he died on the Cross, "in a wholly singular way she cooperated ... in the work of the Savior" (*Lumen Gentium*, n. 61). Although God's call to cooperate in the work of salvation concerns every human being, the participation of the Savior's mother in humanity's Redemption is a unique and unrepeatable fact.[104]

It is clear from all of these papal teachings that throughout history the Church has clearly understood, as well as promulgated, the important role of Our Lady as a Helpmate, associate and Co-redemptrix with Christ. Yet not only throughout many papacies has the Magisterium explained Our Lady's role as the associate and Co-

---

[104] John Paul II, General Audience, April 9, 1997, in Calkins, 45–46.

redemptrix of Christ, but numerous saints have also understood their heavenly Mother through this title and drawn both comfort and inspiration from Her in Her role as Co-redemptrix. The saints give us insights into truths that move beyond pure theological knowledge or understanding. The wisdom of the saints is imparted to us as a witness and mirror of their love union with God. A knowledge and understanding that comes through love is often a clearer understanding of truth than facts alone. And so, in order to understand best Our Lady's place at the side of Christ the Redeemer (a place that all Christians who make up the body of Christ are called to occupy as well), we must pause to reflect on the insights of the saints on this topic.

The doctor of the Church St. Alphonsus de Liguori explains Our Lady's role and title as Co-redemptrix eloquently. He explains that She, who cooperated through love with Christ in the birth of the Church (by participating in the Incarnation through Her *fiat* consent to the Father), also cooperated through love with Him in its redemption (through Her *fiat* consent to the Father under the Cross):

> She offered to the Eternal Father with so much sorrow of heart the life of her beloved Son for our salvation. Wherefore, St. Augustine asserts that, having then cooperated by her love with Christ in the birth of the faithful to the life of grace, she

became also by this cooperation the spiritual mother of all who are members of our head, Jesus Christ.[105]

But when God saw the great desire of Mary to devote herself also to the salvation of men, he ordained that by the sacrifice and offering of the life of this same Jesus, she might cooperate with him in the work of our salvation, and thus become mother of our souls. And this our Savior signified, when, before expiring, he saw from the cross his mother and the disciple St. John both standing near him, and first spoke to Mary: Behold thy Son . . . as if he said to her: Behold the man who, by the offering thou hast made of my life for his salvation, is already born to grace.[106]

Arnold of Carnotensis says that, at the death of Jesus Christ, she ardently desired to die with her Son for our sake. So that, as St. Ambrose adds, when her Son hung dying on the cross, Mary offered herself to his murderers, that she might give her life for us. . . . Mary suffered the pain of sacrificing the life of her Son Jesus; submitting, for our sake, to see him die before her eyes in cruel torments. By this great offering of Mary we were born to the life of divine grace.[107]

---

[105] Alphonsus de Liguori, *The Glories of Mary*, trans. P. J. Kenedy (Missouri: Aeterna Press, 2015), 18.

[106] Alphonsus de Liguori, 19.

[107] Alphonsus de Liguori, 23–24.

St. Gemma—during recorded ecstasies—spoke of the union of Christ the Victim with His Mother (who also participated in His suffering through a union of compassionate love). She understands Our Lady to be Her own Co-redeeming Mother:

> Oh wicked sinners, stop crucifying Jesus, because at the same time you are also transfixing the Mother. . . . Oh my Mother, where do I find you? Always at the foot of the Cross of Jesus. . . . Oh what pain was yours! . . . I no longer see one sacrifice only, I see two of them: one for Jesus, one for Mary! . . . Oh my Mother, if one were to see you with Jesus he would not be able to say who is the first to expire: is it you or Jesus?
>
> What compassion you show me, oh my Mother, to see you so every Saturday at the foot of the Cross! . . . Oh! I no longer see one Victim only, but there are two.[108]

St. Frances Xavier Cabrini calls the Blessed Virgin the *"New Eve, true Mother of the Living"* who was *"chosen by God to become the Coredemptrix of the human race."*[109] Reflecting on the papal teachings of Pope St. Pius X on Our Lady, Co-Redemptrix, she explains:

---

[108] Gemma Galgani, *Estasi, Diario, Autobiografica, Scritti vari* (Rome: Passionists, 1988), 24 and 34, in Miravale, *With Jesus*, 214–15.

[109] Frances Xavier Cabrini, *Parole sparse della Beata Cabrini*, ed. Giuseppe de Luca (Rome: Istituto Grafico Tiberino, 1938), 164, 169, in Miravalle, 216.

If the glory of giving life to our Redeemer pertained to her, then also, as our Holy Father said so well, the office of guarding and preparing the Sacred Victim of the human race for sacrifice pertained to her as well. Mary was not only the Mother of Jesus in the joys of Bethlehem, but even more so on Calvary, . . . and there she merited to become our most worthy Co-redemptrix.[110]

St. Maximilian Kolbe wrote much on the theology of Our Lady as Co-redemptrix. He once said: *"From that moment (of the Fall) God promised a Redeemer and a Co-redemptrix saying: 'I will place enmities between thee and the Woman, and thy seed and her Seed; She shall crush thy head.'"*[111] He also claimed that:

Clearly, our relationship with Mary Co-redemptrix and Dispensatrix of graces in the economy of Redemption was not understood from the beginning in all its perfection. But in these, our times, faith in the Blessed Virgin Mary's mediation continues to grow more and more each day.[112]

---

[110] Cabrini, 170, in Miravalle, 216–17.

[111] Maximilian Kolbe, *Scritti*, trans. Cristoforo Zambelli (Rome: Militia of Mary Immaculate, 1997), n. 1069, in Miravalle, 217. For other references to Kolbe on this question, see L. Iammorrone, "Il mistero di Maria Corredentrice in san Massimiliano Kolbe," *Maria Corredentrice*, 2:219–56; and H. M. Manteau-Bonamy, *Immaculate Conception and the Holy Spirit*, (San Francisco: Ignatius, 1988), 99–102.

[112] Kolbe, n. 1229, in Miravalle, 217.

St. Leopold Mandic not only referred to Mary as *Co-redemptrix of the human race* thirteen times, but was so dedicated to Her that he wrote a declaration and consecration of his own victimhood to his heavenly Mother under this title:

> I, friar Leopold Mandic Zarevic, firmly believe that the most Blessed Virgin, insofar as she was Co-redemptrix of the human race, is the moral fountain of all grace, since we have received all from her fullness.[113]
>
> In truth, before God and the Blessed Virgin, confirming all by oath, I myself am obliged, in submission to the Co-redemptrix of the human race, to exert all my life's strength, in accord with the obedience I owe my superiors, for the redemption of all dissident Oriental peoples from schism and error.[114]

St. Josemaria Escrivá directly addressed the title of Our Lady as Co-redemptrix. He explains Her powerful role, however subordinate to that of Christ, as such:

> The Supreme Pontiffs have rightly called Mary "Co-redemptrix." At that point, together with her Son who was suffering and dying, she suffered and almost died; at that point

---

[113] Leopold Mandic, *Suo umile servo in Cristo*, ed. P. Tieto, vol. 2, *Scritti* (Padua: Portavoce di San Leopoldo Mandic, 1992) 124, in Miravalle, 220.

[114] Mandic, *Scritti*, 2:97, in Miravalle, 220–21.

she abdicated her maternal rights over her Son for the salvation of humanity and immolated Him, insofar as she was able, in order to placate the justice of God; thus one can rightly say that she redeemed the human race together with Christ. In this fashion we are in a better position to understand that moment of the Lord's Passion which we should never grow tired of meditating upon: "*Stabat iuxta crucem Jesus Mater eius*," "Now there stood by the Cross of Jesus His Mother" (Jn 19:25).[115]

Padre Pio affectionately spoke of Our Lady's interior martyrdom with Christ on the Cross in one of his letters. He unhesitantly referred to Her as Co-redemptrix:

Now I seem to be penetrating what was the martyrdom of our most beloved Mother. . . . Oh, if all people would but penetrate this martyrdom! Who could succeed in suffering with this, yes, our dear Co-redemptrix? Who would refuse her the good title of Queen of Martyrs?[116]

---

[115] Jose Maria Escrivà, *Amici di Dio. Omelie* (Milan: Ares, 1978), 318, in Miravalle, 223–24.

[116] Padre Pio, *Epistolario* (Foggia: San Giovanni Rotondo, 1992), 3:384, in Miravalle, 224.

Bl. James Alberione who founded the Pious Society of St. Paul clarified Mary's inferior role to that of Christ's in the Passion, yet nonetheless explained why Her role was extremely pivotal:

> As Jesus in the Garden of Gethsemani agreed to offer Himself, so too Mary gave her consent to the immolation and, insofar as it stood within her power, she immolated her Son. Her consent was in a different mode, but similar to that given for the Incarnation.... And the union of wills and intentions and sorrows between Mother and Son never came to be interrupted throughout Their lives; and much less was that union broken on Calvary.... As a result of that union of sorrows, wills and intentions between Mary and Jesus Christ, Mary became Reparatrix and our Co-redemptrix and the Dispensatrix of the fruits of the Cross.... The Redeemer is Jesus alone. Jesus is the principal Mediator by office; Mary is the secondary and associated Redemptrix to this great work by the divine will.[117]

St. Mother Teresa also embraced Mary's title of Co-redemptrix as an important designation of Her predilection by the Father. She wrote a letter on August 14, 1993 in which she stated:

---

[117] G. Alberione, *Maria Regina degli Apostoli* (Rome, Edizioni San Paolo, 1948), 110–11, in Miravalle, 227.

Chapter 5: The Sorrowful Heart of Mary's *Fiat*

> Mary is our Co-redemptrix with Jesus. She gave Jesus his body and suffered with him at the foot of the cross.
>
> Mary is the Mediatrix of all grace. She gave Jesus to us, and as our Mother she obtains for us all his graces.
>
> Mary is our Advocate who prays to Jesus for us. It is only through the Heart of Mary that we come to the Eucharistic Heart of Jesus.
>
> The papal definition of Mary as Co-redemptrix, Mediatrix, and Advocate will bring great graces to the Church.[118]

Why is it important for the Church to understand Our Lady's role as Co-redemptrix? It is because each and every Christian is called to imitate Her in this way. Because of Our Lady's Immaculate Conception, She was perfect in this role—and yet each soul little by little as it works with Christ to be transformed by His salvific work is called to become more and more like Mary. Although Christ alone merited and obtained the grace of salvation for each of human being, all are called to participate with Him in the distribution of these redemptive graces through lives of prayer and sacrifice offered for others. In Pope St. John Paul II's writings he often called Christians to co-redeem with Jesus—echoing St. Paul: *"I urge you therefore, brothers, by the mercies of God, to offer your bodies as a living sacrifice, holy and pleasing to God, your spiritual worship"* (Rom 12:1). St. Paul

---

[118] Teresa of Calcutta, "Letter to Vox Populi Mariae Mediatrici," August 14, 1993, Vox Populi Mariae Mediatrici Archives (Hopedale, Ohio), in Miravalle, 229.

strove to imitate Christ Who *"loved us and handed himself over for us as a sacrificial offering to God for a fragrant aroma"* (Eph 5:2). And after patterning his own life on that of Jesus crucified, St. Paul could say, *"Now I rejoice in my sufferings for your sake, and in my flesh I am filling up what is lacking in the afflictions of Christ on behalf of his body, which is the church"* (Col 1:24). What does *"to make up what is lacking in the sufferings of Christ"* mean if not to participate so closely in union with Christ that you help him to Co-redeem?

Jesus Himself called us to help Him in the aiding in the salvation of others. He said, *"But I say to you, love your enemies, and pray for those who persecute you"* (Mt 5:44). If Christ told us to pray for enemies and persecutors, it was because He knew that our prayer would aid in their salvation. In other words, the one praying for his enemy is helping to "co-redeem" him in union with and through Jesus Christ. Our Lady does this in a perfect manner standing under the Cross. As She hears Christ's words, *"Father, forgive them, they know not what they do"* (Lk 23:34), surely Her Heart is united with His sentiments. She, too, prays for the enemies of Christ. Not only with Her lips, but with Her blood pouring from Jesus' Heart.

In this section we read about Our Lady in Her immaculate littleness receiving the fullness of Christ's redemptive grace, which thus united their twin Hearts in perfect love notwithstanding Christ's suffering and death. Now we will explore how this love union transformed Our Lady to join Christ's beautiful role as an Altar, Priest and Victim.

Part 2: Mary as Altar, Priest and Victim with Christ

Our Lady lived out Her co-redemptive role both as a Mother and Wife of Christ. As Jesus offered Himself as the Altar, Priest, and Victim on Calvary, so too Our Lady united with Him also fulfilled this trifold identity as the altar, priest, and victim. She did not do this as the principal eternal high priest. Instead, She did this as the co-redeeming Mother and Helpmate of the Redeemer.

As we stated before, Mary was immaculately conceived because the grace of Christ's redemption was applied to Her earlier in time at the moment of Her conception. Our Lady, like the rest of fallen humanity, needed a Savior. She was not perfect in and of Herself. Her perfection was dependent on the gift of salvation offered by God to humanity through the Passion and death of Jesus Christ. Every moment of Her life Mary perfectly accepted the fullness of God's gift of sanctifying grace won through His redemption of humanity on Cross.

This is an important distinction to make as we enter into this next section of the thesis, more deeply exploring Our Lady's role of Co-redemptrix (Her subordinate, yet full participation in Christ's redemption of mankind), most specifically lived out as a priest, victim and altar along with Him. She was able to do this because She as a weak, little human was gifted a share in His divine life through sanctifying grace. And this participation in God's divine life had an accidental, analogous, physical and formal character.

Like all of humanity, Mary shared in this life of grace accidentally, meaning that Her soul (like all human souls) was created with the divine stamp of the image of God upon it, regardless of Her relationship with Him. All humans have innate dignity simply because God created them and Christ redeemed them -even if they do not know nor accept this gift. Our Lady obviously participated in this accidental aspect of the life of divine grace simply as a woman created and redeemed by God. The gift of sanctifying grace did not change Her into a new creature, instead it perfected Her human weakness, not replacing it. Instead, it was through Our Lady's human 'littleness' and weakness that God's power mysteriously brought Her to perfection.

Our Lady also experienced the analogous aspect of humanity's sharing in divine life through sanctifying grace. This term analogous simply emphasizes the fact that there remains in the life of grace a true harmony and just proportion between redeemed creatures and God. Even Our Lady who reached the greatest apex of grace through the immaculate conception and life of brilliant virtue, was not elevated by such infinite grace to a divine creature beyond that of a human mortal. She always remained a unique, little woman consumed and perfected by God's love and taken up into His life of Redeemer. The closer She drew to Him through a union of grace and love, the more She fully became Herself. Mary's freedom was never annihilated in this process, yet instead the closer She drew to God the more freely She was able to choose Him and His life of love. That is how She was able to participate as a little priest, victim and altar in and with and through Jesus.

Mary's participation with Christ in this life of grace is also physical, meaning that such grace works concretely and intrinsically through the soul's natural powers renewing their very substance. Grace does not impose God upon a human exteriorly like an oppressive dictator, yet instead works with the freedom of man's will entering in to renew his soul so that God Himself can dwell within them. Our Lady participated physically in this life of God through sanctifying grace, meaning that God could animate Her soul infinitely more deeply and fully than She could ever attain by Her own human nature. Human nature does not disappear in this process, rather Our Lady's weak, limited humanity is physically caught up in and transformed by the magnanimity of Christ's divine life shared with Her.

And lastly, we must mention how Our Lady participated in this life of grace in a formal way. This means that the grace comes in a form that is divine. The grace that consumes Our Lady's Heart in union with Christ comes from God and in God, and so, it lifts Mary's entire human nature into the very life of God, thus perfecting this human nature. Through the gift of grace, Our Lady loses nothing of the integrity of Her humanity. Rather, She is lifted higher than anything human nature could naturally reach, to life under the full influence of God's power and love.

These last two aspects of physical and formal participation in divine life through grace speak to every part of a man's existence, whereas everything interior within a human (those aspects unseen and unmeasurable by human science) are so made one with God that nothing exterior could ever separate a soul from Him. And these aspects of the deepest center of one's soul influence all of the powers of one's soul, intrinsically making them holy. In these hidden recesses of Our Lady's Heart Her 'I' is replaced with a 'You' referring to God, allowing Her to praise Him and make sacrifice to Him along with Him.

In regards to our following analysis of Our Lady as priest, victim and altar with Christ, we must keep the above forementioned in mind. She is a priest because She is a member (the greatest and ideal member) of the body of Christ. What She offers is a gift offered through and with Him. She is a victim because She is a member of the body of Christ, and so what She offers is efficacious for souls because it is offered with and through His one sacrifice on Calvary. And Mary is an altar because of Her participation in the life of Christ Who offered His Heart as an Altar of oblation where His love would be crucified and gifted to mankind.

Mary as the Altar of Sacrifice

Our Lady can be presented as the altar of sacrifice upon which Jesus was offered for the salvation of the world in two ways. First, when the angel Gabriel came to Our Lady asking Her to be the Mother of God and She consented with Her *fiat*, Jesus the Redeemer took flesh within Her. The identity of Her Son was the Savior of the world from the beginning. The angel Gabriel announced to both Mary and Joseph that the Son of God to be born of Our Lady was to be named Jesus, meaning "Yahweh saves," or "Savior." And this little Savior of the world was laid by His heavenly Father upon the Heart and in the womb of His Mother—like a little lamb laid on the altar of sacrifice.

Chapter 5: The Sorrowful Heart of Mary's *Fiat*

Our Lady through Her *fiat* not only offered Her body, Her Heart, Her very life as the altar upon which Christ would be laid, but also Mary gave everything to Christ that He substantially needed to be our Savior (that being His flesh and blood). Jesus could not have been the Savior of the world without an incarnated body to suffer with and offer to the Father using it to do His Father's will. The instrument Christ used for salvation was the body and blood He received in the Incarnation. And because the Son of God was conceived by the power of the Holy Spirit, Jesus Christ received all of His flesh and blood from Mary. Her DNA was given to Him completely. In this way, Christ's body is Her body. Just as in Genesis Eve is created from Adam, so in the story of redemption the new Adam is created from the new Eve. And in both cases they can authentically exclaim, *"This one, at last, is bone of my bones and flesh of my flesh"* (Gen 2:23). This is the second way in which Our Lady was an altar—Her flesh given in full to Her Son was the altar upon which His suffering and death and would take place.

Pope St. John Paul II explained the two altars on Calvary—one of Mary's *fiat* in Her Heart and the other Christ's body—and yet, both Her *fiat* and His body found their source in Her:

> A disciple and friend of St. Bernard, Arnold of Chartres, shed light particularly on Mary's offering in the sacrifice of Calvary. He distinguished in the Cross "two altars: one in Mary's heart, the other in Christ's body. Christ sacrificed His flesh, Mary her soul." Mary sacrificed herself spiritually in deep communion with Christ, and implored the world's salvation:

"What the mother asks, the Son approves and the Father grants" (cf. *De septem verbis Domini in cruce*, 3: PL 189, 1694).[119]

It is also important to note that Our Lady's body and soul were the instruments She used to offer not only the sacrifice of Christ, but the sacrifice of Herself as well. Mary's bodily tears were offered to God the sacrifice of Her sorrowful love. Her emotions felt pain and She offered that. Her body was consumed in sorrow and She offered that. Her sensibilities were steeped in darkness at the seeming abandonment of the Father and She offered that. Every experience of pain proper to Our Lady's unique, individual, feminine being before God was offered by Her through the consent of *fiat* love to the Father as a gift-sacrifice to be united to Jesus' sacrifice for the fulfillment of God's plan of salvation for the world. And so, on Calvary, Our Lady was not only a double altar for Christ, but She was also the proper altar upon which Her own personal oblations were sacrificed as the Co-redemptrix with Jesus.

Mary as Priest

This leads us to the role of Mary as priest. The Catholic *Catechism* explains:

---

[119] John Paul II, General Audience, October 25, 1995, in Miravalle, 202.

Chapter 5: The Sorrowful Heart of Mary's *Fiat*

The faithful, who by Baptism are incorporated into Christ and integrated into the People of God, are made sharers in their particular way in the priestly, prophetic, and kingly office of Christ, and have their own part to play in the mission of the whole Christian people in the Church and in the World.[120]

If the faithful of the Church share in the priestly role of Christ, how much more does Our Lady, who is the beginning and prototype of the Church, the spotless *"Wife of Lamb"* (Rev 21:9). Pope St. John Paul II says in *Redemptoris Mater*:

In the liturgy the Church salutes Mary of Nazareth **as the Church's own beginning**, for in the event of the Immaculate Conception the Church sees projected, and anticipated in her most noble member, the saving grace of Easter. And above all, in the Incarnation she encounters Christ and Mary indissolubly joined: he who is the Church's Lord and Head and **she who, uttering the first *fiat* of the New Covenant, prefigures the Church's condition as spouse and mother**.[121]

---

[120] *Catechism*, § 897.

[121] John Paul II, *Redemptoris Mater*, March 25, 1987, § 1, https://www.vatican.va/content/john-paul-ii/en/encyclicals/documents/hf_jp-ii_enc_25031987_redemptoris-mater.html, emphasis mine.

As the beginning and prototype of the Church, Our Lady is the example *par excellence* of how the laity of the Church should live their priestly role in union with Christ. The *Catechism* continues to explain this priestly call saying:

> Hence the laity, dedicated as they are to Christ and anointed by the Holy Spirit, are marvelously called and prepared so that even richer fruits of the Spirit maybe produced in them. For all their works, prayers, and apostolic undertakings, family and married life, daily work, relaxation of mind and body, if they are accomplished in the Spirit—indeed even the hardships of life if patiently born—all these become spiritual sacrifices acceptable to God through Jesus Christ. In the celebration of the Eucharist these may most fittingly be offered to the Father along with the body of the Lord. And so, worshipping everywhere by their holy actions, the laity consecrate the world itself to God, everywhere offering worship by the holiness of their lives.[122]

Who lived this more perfectly than Our Lady? St. Peter Canisius spoke of Her thus:

---

[122] *Catechism*, § 901.

Standing under the cross of her Son, she remained intrepid in her faith, and offered Christ, a true and living Victim, for the expiation of the sins of the world.[123]

St. Lawrence of Brindisi spoke about Mary's priestly role as She shared with Jesus, the "principal Priest," the offering of the one redemptive sacrifice at Calvary:

Did not Mary put her life in danger for us, when she stood by the cross of Christ truly sacrificing Him to God in spirit, as full, abundantly full of the spirit of Abraham, and offering Him in true charity for the salvation of the world? . . . The spirit of Mary was a spiritual priest, as the cross was the altar and Christ the sacrifice; although the spirit of Christ was the principal priest, the spirit of Mary was there together with the spirit of Christ; indeed, it was one spirit with Him as one soul in two bodies. Hence the spirit of Mary together with the spirit of Christ performed the priestly office at the altar of the cross and offered the sacrifice of the cross for the salvation of the world to the Eternal God. . . . For of her, as of God to Whom she was most similar in spirit, we can truly say that she so loved the world as to give her only-begotten Son

---

[123] Peter Canisius, *De Maria Incomparabili Virgine*, 1. 4. c. 26, in Miravalle, *With Jesus*, 109.

so that everyone who believes in Him will not perish, but will have life eternal.[124]

Just as Mary was the altar of sacrifice in a myriad of different ways, so, too, She is the priest offering sacrifice along with Christ in several different manners.

Mary's Offering of Christ, the Victim

The *fiat* that Our Lady prayed in the Annunciation was a *fiat* that accepted the entire mission the Father laid before Her as the Mother of the Redeemer. And this *fiat* to be Jesus' Mother united Her perpetually closer to God eventually blossoming into Her *fiat* standing beneath the Cross. This *fiat* that She prayed with Christ on Calvary—this *"not my will, but yours be done"* (Lk 22:42)—was Her consent to the offering of the sacrifice of Her Son. This *fiat* consent constituted Her own personal gift of Him given back to the Father, crucified to the Father's will. The *fiat* of Jesus and the *fiat* of Mary were individual acts of the will in each person as they consented to Christ's suffering and death—and yet they were full of the compenetrating love of two mutually indwelling Hearts bound as one with the Holy Spirit fastened to the will of the Father. Because these two *fiats* both came from the source of the Holy Spirit praying within them, and because

---

[124] Lawrence of Brindisi, *Opera omnia*, vol. 1, *Mariale* (Patavii: Ex Officina typograhica Seminarii, 1928), 183–84, in Miravalle, 114–15.

both Jesus and Mary were perfectly pure and immaculate, their *fiats* were identical and therefore united together anchoring them to the Heart of God.

Pope Leo XIII beautifully describes the association of these two *fiats* in his Encyclical *Jucunda semper*:

> When she professed herself the handmaid of the Lord for the mother's office, and when, at the foot of the altar, she offered up her whole self with her child Jesus—then and thereafter she took her part in the painful expiation offered by her Son for the sins of the world. It is certain, therefore, that she suffered in the very depths of her soul with His most bitter sufferings and with His torments. Finally, it was before the eyes of Mary that the divine Sacrifice for which she had borne and nurtured the Victim was to be finished. As we contemplate Him in the last and most piteous of these mysteries, we see that "there stood by the cross of Jesus Mary His Mother" (Jn 19:25), who, in a miracle of love, so that she might receive us as her sons, offered generously to Divine Justice her own Son, and in her Heart died with Him, stabbed by the sword of sorrow.[125]

Just as Our Lady presented Jesus as an infant in the Temple to His Father, and then was told that a sword would pierce Her Heart

---

[125] Leo XIII, Encyclical Letter *Iucunda semper*, September 8, 1894, § 3, in Calkins, "Mary Coredemptrix in the Papal Magisterium," 65–66.

(Lk 2:35), so now on Calvary She presents Him again to the Father. And as Christ's hands and feet are pierced open, Her Immaculate Heart is ripped open bleeding mystically as She watches the blood and life She gave Her Jesus through Her *fiat* poured out upon the ground.

Pope St. Pius X speaks of Our Lady's self-immolation through sacrificing Christ thus:

> The most holy Mother of God, accordingly, supplied the "matter for the flesh of the Only-begotten Son of God to be born of human members" (S. Bede Ven. L. Iv. in *Luc.* xl.) so that a Victim for man's salvation might be available. But this is not her only title to our praise. In addition, she was entrusted with the duty of watching over the same Victim, of nourishing Him, and even of offering Him upon the altar at the appointed time.[126]

Many of the Popes have spoken eloquently about Our Lady's offering of Her Son, the Victim, on the Cross. Each sheds light on a different aspect of that offering, and yet each ascertains that it is truly Our Lady's offering of Her Son to the Father that truly makes Her a priest along with Jesus. Pope Benedict XV spoke of Mary's offering as thus:

---

[126] Pius X, *Ad diem illum*, § 12, in Calkins, 66.

Chapter 5: The Sorrowful Heart of Mary's *Fiat*

According to the common teaching of the Doctors it was God's design that the Blessed Virgin Mary, apparently absent from the public life of Jesus, should assist Him when He was dying nailed to the Cross. Mary suffered and, as it were, nearly died with her suffering Son; for the salvation of mankind she renounced her mother's rights and, as far as it depended on her, offered her Son to placate divine justice; so we may well say that she with Christ redeemed mankind.[127]

Pope Pius XI also speaks of Mary's offering, alluding to Her role of reparation:

May the most gracious Mother of God, who gave us Jesus as Redeemer, who reared Him, and at the foot of the Cross offered Him as Victim, who by her mysterious union with Christ and by her matchless grace rightly merits the name Reparatrix, deign to smile upon Our wishes and Our undertakings.[128]

Mary's "priestly" role in offering Christ as the new Eve and 'Mother of the living' was explained by Venerable Pope Pius XII thus:

---

[127] Benedict XV, *Inter sodalicia*, in Calkins, 67.

[128] Pius XI, Encyclical Letter *Miserentissimus Redemptor*, May 8, 1928, § 21, in Calkins, 67–68.

She it was who, immune from all sin, personal or inherited, and ever most closely united with her Son, offered Him on Golgotha to the Eternal Father together with the holocaust of her maternal rights and motherly love, like a new Eve, for all the children of Adam contaminated through this unhappy fall, and thus she, who was the mother of our Head according to the flesh, became by a new title of sorrow and glory the spiritual mother of all His members.[129]

Pope St. John XXIII spoke of Mary's "offering of the Divine Victim" as similar to all of the Catholic faithful of the Church participating in Mass. Of course, Christ is the one Eternal Priest praying *in persona Christi* in the priest at the altar. Yet the lay faithful are co-offerers along with Jesus, the primary Priest. Yet even among the co-offerers praying along with Him, Our Lady stands out as the primary co-offerer of the sacrifice of Jesus along with Himself. He says:

> We trust that, as a result of the homage they have just paid to the Virgin Mary, all Italians will be strengthened in their fervor and veneration of the Blessed Virgin as Mother of the Mystical Body, of which the Eucharist is the symbol and vital center. We trust that they will imitate in her the most perfect model of union with Jesus, our Head; We trust that they will join Mary in her offering of the Divine Victim, and that they

---

[129] Pius XII, Encyclical Letter *Mystici Corporis*, June 29, 1943, § 110, in Calkins, 68–69.

will ask for her motherly mediation to obtain for the Church the gifts of unity, of peace, and especially of a new luxuriant blossoming of religious vocations.[130]

Pope St. Paul VI also described Our Lady's motherly offering of Christ and the importance of Her consent to His immolation:

This union of the Mother and the Son in the work of redemption reaches its climax on Calvary, where Christ "offered himself as the perfect sacrifice to God" (Heb 9:14) and where Mary stood by the cross (cf. Jn 19:25), "suffering grievously with her only-begotten Son. There she united herself with a maternal heart to His sacrifice, and lovingly consented to the immolation of this victim which she herself had brought forth" and also was offering to the eternal Father.[131]

Pope St. John Paul II spoke extensively throughout his pontificate linking Mary's offering of Christ on Calvary with Her offering of Herself—and thus shining forth in this as a model for the Church as

---

[130] John XXIII, Radio Message to Bishops of Italy in Catania on the Occasion of the 16th National Eucharistic Congress and the Consecration of Italy to the Immaculate Heart of Mary, September 13, 1959, in Calkins, 69.

[131] Paul VI, Apostolic Exhortation *Marialis cultus*, February 2, 1974, § 20, in Calkins, 70.

they are called to unite themselves to the priest standing in the place of Christ at Mass:

> Born of the Virgin to be a pure, holy and immaculate oblation, Christ offered on the Cross the one perfect Sacrifice which every Mass, in an unbloody manner, renews and makes present. In that one Sacrifice, Mary, the first redeemed, the Mother of the Church, had an active part. She stood near the Crucified, suffering deeply with her Firstborn; with a motherly heart she associated herself with His Sacrifice; with love she consented to His immolation (cf. *Lumen Gentium*, 58; *Marialis Cultus*, 20): she offered him and she offered herself to the Father. Every Eucharist is a memorial of that Sacrifice and that Passover that restored life to the world; every Mass puts us in intimate communion with her, the Mother, whose sacrifice "becomes present" just as the Sacrifice of her Son "becomes present" at the words of consecration of the bread and wine pronounced by the priest.[132]

Mary as Victim—Mary Offers Herself

Not only does Our Lady offer Christ back to the Father on Calvary but She offers Herself to the Father to be consumed by the same sacrifice of love along with Him. Jesus is crucified physically and Our

---

[132] John Paul II, Angelus for the Feast of Corpus Christi, June 5, 1983, in Calkins, 71.

Chapter 5: The Sorrowful Heart of Mary's *Fiat*   185

Lady is crucified mystically. Yet Her suffering is real and concrete. Mary offers Herself to the Father along with Christ and in this accepts all that it means to be not only the Mother of the Redeemer, but the Mother of the redeemed. Pope Leo XIII speaks of Mary's offering to the Father thus:

> When she professed herself the handmaid of the Lord for the mother's office, and when, at the foot of the altar, she offered up her whole self with her child Jesus—then and thereafter she took her part in the painful expiation offered by her Son for the sins of the world. [133]

Mary did not only suffer on account of Her Son Jesus' suffering, but She felt a double sword in Her Heart: the suffering of Her Son and Her own unique, individual suffering on account of His Passion. These sufferings of Her Heart Our Lady offered to the Father along with the offering of Her Son. St. John Eudes eloquently describes the particular sufferings that the Blessed Mother endured in the Passion. He writes:

> You heard the blows of the hammer as He was being fastened to the Cross: they pierced your Heart. You suffered unspeakable tortures, awaiting that dire hour of the Crucifixion. You saw Him lifted up, while so many shouts and blasphemies were hurled at Him by the evil tongues of the Jews that your

---

[133] Leo XIII, *Iucunda semper*, § 3, in Calkins, 65.

blood congealed in your veins. You spent these sad hours at the foot of the Cross, hearing the awful insults heaped by these wretches upon your Lamb and seeing the frightful tortures which they made Him suffer, until at last you saw Him expire under such obloquy and suffering. . . .

Whereupon they restored Him to your loving arms, that you might wrap His body in a shroud and bury Him and, just as you had given Him at birth the first attentions, you might now perform for Him the last rites; but with sorrows so heavy and anguish so sharp and desolation so penetrating to your Mother's Heart that, if we are to comprehend anything of them, we should have first to comprehend the degree of your well-nigh infinite love for your Son. All things distressed you. Wherever you turned you saw only reasons for sorrow and tears. Your Mother's Heart was rent the more with wounds bleeding and innumerable because your Dear Jesus was also being wounded in Heart and body. It is true that your faith was not diminished and that your obedience kept your Heart perfectly resigned to the divine will, but you did not cease to suffer inconceivable pain, even as your beloved Son, in spite of His most perfect submission to all the commands of His Divine Father. Lastly, no heart with a lesser love than yours will ever be able to comprehend what you suffered at that time.[134]

---

[134] Eudes, *The Sacred Heart of Jesus*, 68–69.

Chapter 5: The Sorrowful Heart of Mary's *Fiat*

These sufferings of Mary are caused by the suffering and death of Her Son, and yet they are personal—they belong to Her sensibilities and Heart and are a gift of Her unique will in union with Jesus to the Father. Pope Benedict XV said that *"the sufferings of Jesus cannot be separated from the sorrows of Mary."*[135] And this offering of Mary of Herself bears fruit in redemptive benefits for the world.

Pope Pius XI similarly expressed:

> By necessity, the Redeemer could not but associate His Mother in His work. For this reason, We invoke her under the title of **Co-redemptrix.** She gave us the Savior, she accompanied Him in the work of Redemption as far as the Cross itself, sharing with Him the sorrows of the agony and of the death in which Jesus consummated the Redemption of mankind.[136]

Venerable Pope Pius XII brilliantly asserts Mary's union with Christ in His redemptive work whereas Her sorrows were joined to His Passion and Death:

---

[135] Benedict XV, Homily for the Canonization of St. Gabriel of the Sorrowful Virgin, in Calkins, "Mary Coredemptrix in the Papal Magisterium," 52.

[136] Pius XI, Address to Pilgrims from Vicenza, October 30, 1933, in Miravalle, *With Jesus*, 158, emphasis mine.

By the will of God, the most Blessed Virgin Mary was inseparably joined with Christ in accomplishing the work of man's redemption, so that <u>our salvation flows from the love of Jesus Christ and His sufferings intimately united with the love and sorrows of His Mother.</u>[137]

And finally, we have Pope St. John Paul II speaking of Our Lady's self-offering in this way:

The Virgin of Nazareth precedes you on your way, the woman made holy by the passover of the Son of God, she who offered herself with Christ for the redemption of all humanity.[138]

The Joint Offering of Jesus and Mary

Although Jesus and Mary uniquely suffered and offered themselves to the Father in *fiat* all of the days of their lives, their oblation was connected due to the intense mutual indwelling love that they shared in and through the Holy Spirit. The *fiats* pronounced by Jesus and Mary throughout their lives and culminating on Calvary were like a dance back and forth, or like two voices singing in harmony

---

[137] Pius XII, Encylical Letter *Haurietis aquas*, May 15, 1956, § 124, in Calkins, "Mary Coredemptrix in the Papal Magisterium," 77.

[138] John Paul II, Speech in Agrigento, Sicily, May 9, 1993, in Calkins, 80.

one song to the Father. If Jesus and Mary were united perfectly in Love, then even if each individually offered themselves along with each other to the Father on Calvary, they also partook in a joint offering of their single, united Heart. Yet, it is important to note that even as they offered a joint offering, Our Lady's offering was a participation through grace in Jesus' offering. Although Mary was united perfectly with Christ in His self-offering to the Father, it must be remembered that Our Lady's role was proportional to Her identity as creature. The harmony of joint self-gift between Jesus and Mary did not elevate Our Lady to an equal with Christ. There was always between the Hearts of Jesus and Mary the due proportion of the woman, Mary, transformed by grace as a Helpmate of the God-Man Jesus Christ.

This is eloquently explained by St. John Eudes, where he emphasizes the union of Jesus and Mary's suffering, while still highlighting the due order that it was Christ the Redeemer Who shared His suffering with His Mother, the creature. St. John Eudes writes:

> O Father of mercies and God of all consolation, what are those two Hearts that You are keeping thus crucified? Why do You not succor Your Only Son and Your loving daughter? Why do You not break the law that You have made that one shall not sacrifice in the same day on Your altar the Lamb and its Mother? And yet here, in one and the same day, at the selfsame hour, on the same Cross and with the same nails, You keep fastened the Only Son of sorrowing Mary and the virgin Heart of His most innocent Mother. Can it be that You care

for the dumb animals, unwilling that the mothers should be sacrificed on the day they suffer the loss of their lambs, more than You do for this most pure Virgin, grieving over the sorrows and the death of her divine Lamb? You will that she should have no other executioner of her martyrdom than her tender love for her Only Son. Nevertheless, in the midst of such cruel tortures, the sight of the sufferings of His most worthy Mother were known to her Beloved Son even as He filled the cup of her affliction and torture. Immortal praise and blessing, O my God, for the incomprehensible love that You have for sinners! Thanksgiving, infinite and eternal, for all the works of that divine love![139]

Pope St. John Paul II also speaks of their union of Hearts as Mary's association with the suffering of Her Son during his catechesis on *Lumen Gentium* in 1997 saying:

With our gaze illumined by the radiance of the Resurrection, we pause to reflect on the Mother's involvement in her Son's redeeming passion, which was completed by her sharing in His suffering. Let us return again, but now in the perspective of the Resurrection, to the foot of the Cross where the Mother endured "with her only-begotten Son the intensity of His suffering, associated herself with His sacrifice in her

---

[139] Eudes, *The Sacred Heart of Jesus*, 69–70.

Mother's heart, and lovingly consented to the immolation of this victim which was born of her" (*Lumen Gentium* #58).[140]

Jesus and Mary were united deeply in the Incarnation (when Christ took flesh from Mary and dwelt within Her), on the Cross (where they were united as one Heart in love and a union of suffering and *fiat* to the Father's will) and in the Eucharist (where Our Lady once again united with Her Son's living body, blood, soul, and divinity under Her Heart). In the Eucharist Our Lady relived this experience of the Incarnation where She offered to Her Son Her body as a tabernacle and altar. In the Eucharist Our Lady united Her daily sufferings to Christ and in their united *fiat* experienced once again His eternal sacrifice on Calvary. Yet our heavenly Mother did not unite as one with Christ on Calvary only for Herself. The new Eve entered the suffering of the Cross with Christ in order to give birth to souls with Him into heaven. The Blessed Mother lived *fiat* and union with Christ as a Helpmate (Wife) and also a *Mother*—for *us*.

Mary as Mediatrix

Pope St. Paul VI spoke of the close relationship between Our Lady was the Co-redemptrix with Christ and the Mediatrix of all graces from Him to Christ's members, the Church:

---

[140] John Paul II, Catechesis, April 2, 1997, in Calkins, "Mary Coredemptrix in the Papal Magisterium," 82.

Joined by a close and indissoluble bond to the mystery of the Incarnation and Redemption, the Blessed Virgin Mary, the Immaculate, was raised body and soul to heavenly glory at the end of her earthly life, and was made like her risen Son in anticipation of the future lot of all the just; and We believe that the Blessed Mother of God, the New Eve, Mother of the Church, continues in heaven her maternal role with regard to Christ's members, cooperating with the birth and growth of divine life in the souls of the redeemed.[141]

St. Edith Stein emphasized that Our Lady was united with Christ as the Co-redemptrix in order to be a conduit of grace for the entire Church. She recognized Our Lady as the new Eve at the side of Christ the new Adam, but she pointed out a difference saying that while Eve was beside Adam for Adam's sake, "Mary is beside Jesus . . . for ours. . . . Her maternal love embraces the whole Mystical Body with Jesus Christ its head."[142]

Pope Leo XIII likewise makes this connection in an Encyclical he wrote about the holy rosary:

> From her heavenly abode, she began, by God's decree, to watch over the Church, to assist and befriend us as our Mother; so that she who was so intimately associated with

---

[141] Paul VI, Apostolic Letter *Solemni hac liturgia (Credo of the People of God)*, § 15, June 30, 1968, in Calkins, 53.

[142] Traflet, *St. Edith Stein: A Spiritual Portrait*, 516–17.

the mystery of human salvation is just as closely associated with the distribution of the graces which from all time will flow from the Redemption.[143]

The union of Our Lady with Christ on the Cross is fruitful in Her role as Mediatrix of grace for Her children. If God made Our Lady the Mother of Jesus Christ—the head of the Church—He naturally at the same time made Her the Mother of the Church—His mystical body. She is joined to Christ in order to bear fruit—giving birth to the souls of all of the faithful into eternal life. Mary is the Mother of the Redeemer, and at the same time the Mother of the redeemed. Our Lady, who did not feel pain upon the birth of the Son of God, wailed in pain within Her Heart as She gave birth to His mystical body under the Cross. The mixing of Our Lady's tears with the blood of Christ on Calvary was fecund to the point of perfection. Just as the Holy Spirit desired to give the Savior to the world through Mary, so He desires to conform souls to Christ through Her help and intercession. No other means to Christ is as fast and efficient as when a soul goes to Him through Mary. She is the instrument chosen by God to be a conduit of His grace to His children.

St. Louis de Montfort, in *True Devotion to Mary*, writes:

> God the Holy Ghost wishes to fashion His chosen ones in and through Mary. He tells Her, "My well-beloved, My

---

[143] Leo XIII, Encyclical Letter *Adiutricem populi*, September 5, 1895, Calkins, "Mary Coredemptrix in the Papal Magisterium," 56.

spouse, let all your virtues take root in My chosen ones that they may grow from strength to strength and from grace to grace. When you were living on earth, practicing the most sublime virtues, I was so pleased with you that I still desire to find you on earth without your ceasing to be in heaven. Reproduce yourself then in My chosen ones, so that I may have the joy of seeing in them the roots of your invincible faith, profound humility, total mortification, sublime prayer, ardent charity, your firm hope and all your virtues. You are always My spouse, as faithful, pure and fruitful as ever. May your faith give Me believers, your purity, virgins; your fruitfulness, elect and living temples." When Mary has taken root in a soul She produces in it wonders of grace which only She can produce: for She alone is the fruitful virgin who never had and never will have Her equal in purity and fruitfulness."[144]

Our Lady does not only exercise Her motherhood in helping souls to reach heaven, but She forms Her children with such attentive love that they become the very greatest saints God has upon the earth. St. Louis de Montfort continues:

Almighty God and His holy Mother are to raise up great saints who will surpass in holiness most other saints as much as the cedars of Lebanon flower above little shrubs.... These

---

[144] Louis de Montfort, *True Devotion to Mary*, 14–15.

great souls filled with grace and zeal will be chosen to oppose the enemies of God who are raging on all sides. They will be exceptionally devoted to the Blessed Virgin. Illumined by Her light, strengthened by Her food, guided by Her spirit, supported by Her arm, sheltered under Her protection, they will fight with one hand and build with the other. With one hand they will give battle, overthrowing and crushing heretics and other heresies, schismatics and their schisms, idolaters and their idolatries sinners and their wickedness. With the other hand they will build the temple of the true Solomon and the mystical city of God, namely, the Blessed Virgin, who is called by the Fathers of the Church the Temple of Solomon and the City of God. By word and example, they will draw all men to a true devotion to Her and though this will make many enemies, it will also bring about many victories and much glory to God alone. . . . This is what was revealed to St. Vincent Ferrer.[145]

St. Bernard of Clairvaux put his absolute trust in Mary's powerful intercession. Venerable Pope Pius XII said, *"So great was his confidence in her most powerful intercession, that he did not hesitate to write: 'It is the will of God that we should have nothing which has not passed through the hands of Mary.' Likewise: 'Such is the will of God,*

---

[145] Louis de Montfort, 18.

Who would have us obtain everything through the hands of Mary.'"[146] St. Bernard says: *"O our mediatrix, O our advocate, reconcile us with thy Son; recommend us to thy Son; present us to thy Son."*[147] *"It is the will of God that we should have everything through Mary."*[148] *"She is full of grace; the overflow is poured out on us."*[149]

In a homily St. Bernard further expressed his love and confidence in Our Lady saying:

> She, I say, is that shining and brilliant star, so much needed, set in place above life's great and spacious sea, glittering with merits, all aglow with examples for our imitation. Oh, whosoever thou art that perceiveth thyself during this mortal existence to be rather drifting in treacherous waters, at the mercy of the winds and the waves, than walking on firm ground, turn not away thine eyes from the splendor of this guiding star, unless thou wish to be submerged by the storm!

---

[146] Pius XII, Encyclical Letter *Doctor mellifluus*, May 24, 1953, § 30, https://www.vatican.va/content/pius-xii/en/encyclicals/documents/hf_p-xii_enc_24051953_doctor-mellifluus.html.

[147] Bernard of Clairvaux, Second Sermon on Advent, no. 5, in Reginald Garrigou-Lagrange, "The Influence of Mary Mediatrix," *The Three Ages of the Interior Life*, vol. 1, trans. M. Timothea Doyle (St. Louis: B. Herder Book Co., 1948), 125, excerpt available at http://www.catholictradition.org/Christ/mediatrix.htm.

[148] Bernard of Clairvaux, Sermon on the Nativity of the Blessed Virgin Mary, no. 7, in Garrigou-Lagrange, 125.

[149] Bernard of Clairvaux, Second Sermon on the Assumption, no. 2, in Garrigou-Lagrange, 125.

When the storms to temptation burst upon thee, when thou seest thyself driven upon the rocks of tribulation, look at the star, call upon Mary. When buffeted by the billows of pride, or ambition, or hatred, or jealousy, look at the star, call upon Mary. Should anger, or avarice, or fleshly desire violently assail the frail vessel of thy soul, look at the star, call upon Mary. If troubled on account of the heinousness of thy sins, distressed at the filthy state of thy conscience, and terrified at the thought of the awful judgment to come, thou art beginning to sink into the bottomless gulf of sadness and to be swallowed in the abyss of despair, then think of Mary. In dangers, in doubts, in difficulties, think of Mary, call upon Mary. Let not her name leave thy lips, never suffer it to leave thy heart. And that thou mayest more surely obtain the assistance of her prayer, see that thou dost walk in her footsteps. With her for guide, thou shalt never go astray; whilst invoking her, thou shalt never lose heart; so long as she is in thy mind, thou shalt not be deceived; whilst she holds thy hand, thou canst not fall; under her protection, thou hast nothing to fear; if she walks before thee, thou shalt not grow weary; if she shows thee favor, thou shalt reach the goal.[150]

---

[150] Bernard of Clairvaux, *Super missus est* 2.17, in Pius XII, *Doctor mellifluus*, § 31.

St. Louis de Montfort similarly encouraged all souls—regardless of how lost and seemingly hopeless—to find their help by hiding in the refuge of Our Lady:

Are you in the miserable state of sin? Then call on the divine Mary and say to her: Ave, which means "I salute thee with the most profound respect, thou who art without sin" and she will deliver you from the evil of your sins.

"Are you groping in the darkness of ignorance and error? Go to Mary and say to her: Hail Mary, which means "Hail thou who are bathed in the light of the Sun of Justice" –and she will give you some of her light.

Have you strayed from the path leading to Heaven? Then call on Mary, for her name means "Star of the Sea, the North Star which guides the ships of our souls during the voyage of this life," and she will guide you to the harbor of eternal salvation.

Are you in sorrow? Turn to Mary, for her name means also "Sea of Bitterness which has been filled with sharp pain in this world but which is now turned into a Sea of the Purest Joy in heaven," and she will turn your sorrow to joy and your afflictions into consolation.

Have you lost the state of grace? Praise and honor the numberless graces with which God has filled the Blessed Virgin and say to her: Thou art full of grace and filled with all the gifts of the Holy Spirit, and she will give you some of these graces.

Are you all alone, having lost God's protection? Pray to Mary, and say: "The Lord is with thee –and this union is far nobler and more intimate than that which He has with saints and the just –because thou art one with Him. He is thy Son and His flesh is thy flesh; thou art united to the Lord because of thy perfect likeness to Him and by your mutual love –for thou art His Mother." And then say to her: "The Three Persons of the Godhead are with thee because thou art the temple of the Most Blessed Trinity," and she will place you once more under the protection and care of Almighty God.

Have you become an outcast and have you been accursed by God? Then say to Our Lady: "Blessed art thou above all women and above all nations, by thy purity and fertility; thou hast turned God's maledictions into blessings for us," and she will bless you.

Do you hunger for the bread of grace and the bread of life? Draw near to her who bore the Living Bread Which came down from heaven, and say to her: "Blessed be the fruit of thy womb Whom thou hast conceived without the slightest loss of thy virginity, Whom thou didst carry without discomfort and to Whom thou didst give birth without pain. Blessed be Jesus Who has redeemed our suffering world when we were in the bondage of sin, Who has healed the world of its sickness, Who has raised the dead to life, brought home the banished, restored sinners to a life of grace and Who has saved men from damnation." Without doubt, your soul will be filled with the bead of grace in this life and of eternal glory in the next. Amen.[151]

As we said at the beginning of this section, Our Lady is not only the Mother of all souls, but also the model disciple that all Christians are to follow in order to be best conformed to Christ. In these past chapters we have thoroughly reflected on Our Lady's littleness, spousal love and *fiat*, which united Her deeply with Her crucified Son, thus making Her the new Eve, His Helpmate, Co-redemptrix, and Mediatrix of all grace. If Mary is the blueprint of how a human creature should best conform themselves to Christ, then it means that Her children who reach perfection (the saints) also should show forth similar characteristics of such holiness. Although each soul is called to a unique participation in Christ's redemptive work and will reflect His saving love within his soul in differing ways, all saints are called to follow a path of holiness mirroring the pattern that Our Lady followed. This road to union with Christ includes aspects of humble littleness, fiery spousal love and a courageous, generous willingness (*fiat*) to endure the Cross with Jesus in order to reach perfect union with Him. This colorful path of the saints is what we will unfold in the following chapters.

---

[151] Louis de Montfort, *Secret of the Rosary*, trans. Mary Barbour (New York: Montfort Publications, 1987), 57–58.

Chapter 6

How Does the Church Live the Cross with Jesus? In *Fiat* through Littleness and Love.

Our Lady is both the Mother and prototype of the Church, which is why She forms Her children to become images of Herself—as She is the perfect reflection of Christ. The more Our Lady is consumed with Christ's love, the more She reflects Him. And thus, as She draws Her spiritual children into this love of Christ helping them become disciples of Christ in their own unique ways, these children also begin to be images of Our Lady in Her reflection of the life of God. In the *Catechism* we read:

> Since the Virgin Mary's role in the mystery of Christ and the Spirit has been treated, it is fitting now to consider her place in the mystery of the Church. "The Virgin Mary ... is acknowledged and honored as being truly the Mother of God and of the Redeemer. ... She is 'clearly the Mother of the members of Christ' ... since she has by her charity joined in bringing about the birth of believers in the Church, who are members of its head." "Mary, Mother of Christ, Mother of the Church."[152]

---

[152] *Catechism*, § 963.

By her complete adherence to the Father's will, to his Son's redemptive work, and to every prompting of the Holy Spirit, the Virgin Mary is the Church's model of faith and charity. Thus, she is a "preeminent and ... wholly unique member of the Church"; indeed, she is the "exemplary realization" (*typus*) of the Church.[153]

After speaking of the Church, her origin, mission, and destiny, we can find no better way to conclude than by looking to Mary. In her we contemplate what the Church already is in her mystery on her own "pilgrimage of faith," and what she will be in the homeland at the end of her journey. There, "in the glory of the Most Holy and Undivided Trinity," "in the communion of all the saints," the Church is awaited by the one she venerates as Mother of her Lord and as her own Mother.

In the meantime the Mother of Jesus, in the glory which she possesses in body and soul in heaven, is the image and beginning of the Church as it is to be perfected in the world to come. Likewise, she shines forth on earth until the day of the Lord shall come, a sign of certain hope and comfort to the pilgrim People of God.[154]

Our Lady is a Mother *par excellence* who, through sharing the divine love and life that has consumed Her entire being making Her

---

[153] *Catechism*, § 967.

[154] *Catechism*, § 972.

'full of grace' with Her children, She draws them close to Christ as little images of Him. Yet She shares Jesus' life with Her children as it flows through Her, marks of Our Lady's maternal love are imbued on their souls as well. As they become unique saints in the life of Christ, they are eternally marked with a motherly connection because this love has entered them through Mary. Pope St. John Paul II reiterated these teachings of the Church on Mary as her prototype and Mother saying:

> The Second Vatican Council ... in the Dogmatic Constitution on the Church, designated the Mother of God as the one who "precedes" the People of God in the pilgrimage of faith, charity and perfect union with Christ. Because of this fact, the whole Church finds a perfect "model" in Mary.
>
> ... Mary brings to the Upper Room at Pentecost the "new motherhood" which became her "part" at the foot of the Cross. This motherhood is to remain in her, and at the same time it is to be transferred from her as a "model" to the whole Church, which will be revealed to the world on the day of the descent of the Holy Spirit, the Paraclete. All those gathered in the Upper Room are aware that from the moment of Christ's return to the Father their life is hid with him in God. Mary lives in this awareness more than anyone else.[155]

---

[155] John Paul II, Letter to Consecrated Persons for the Marian Year, May 22, 1988, § 21, https://www.vatican.va/content/john-paul-ii/en/letters/1988/documents/hf_jp-ii_let_19880522_consecrated-persons.html.

Saints are saints because they conform themselves to Our Lady, who perfectly conformed Herself to Christ. Saints are saints because Jesus' gift of salvation has fully transformed them into the holiest versions of themselves that are possible. Yet, because Our Lady so powerfully reflects Christ in Her union of love with Him, saints who become similar to Christ will innately resemble their spiritual Mother Mary as well. St. Edith Stein explains:

> Since the dispensing of graces is entrusted to the hands of the Queen of Heaven, we will find our way to the goal not only by keeping our eyes raised to her but by maintaining a personal trusting association with her. But the imitation of Mary is not fundamentally different from the imitation of Christ. The imitation of Mary includes the imitation of Christ because Mary is the first Christian to follow Christ, and she is the first and most perfect model of Christ. Indeed, that is why the imitation of Mary is not only relevant to women but to all Christians.[156]

Our Lady imitated Christ by saying *fiat* to the Father's will—even when it presented itself in the form of crucified love. She was able to do that because of the littleness and spousal love She shared with Him. In the same way, Her children the saints are called to wholeheartedly surrender themselves to the will of God even when it

---

[156] Stein, cited in Traflet, *St. Edith Stein: A Spiritual Portrait*, 192.

presents itself through the Cross or crucified love. The saints were able to imitate Our Lady by entering a one-flesh union with Christ through the holy Eucharist (and for some through His wounds taking flesh within their hearts and bodies) because they first imitated Her littleness and spousal love with Him. The littleness of the saints was manifested in their humility, and their spousal love was as pure as Jesus' Own crucified love that came to live in them. As St. Paul claimed, *"I no longer live as I, but Jesus Crucified lives within me"* (Gal 2:20).

Not only was Our Lady called through littleness and spousal love to a perfect union with God culminating in a fusion of Hearts through Her *fiat* to the Cross, but all Christians are called to follow this path laid forth by Her. Every saint of the Church is called to configure himself to Christ and Jesus offers us His Mother to model that for the Church. The Blessed Mother was immaculate, and yet Jesus said to all people, *"Be perfect as my heavenly Father is perfect"* (Mt 5:48). He calls all souls to follow Him saying, *"Whoever wishes to come after me must deny himself, take up his cross, and follow me"* (Mt 16:24). After Christ proposes the Cross to His followers, He continues with an invitation and promise, *"Come to me, all you who labor and are burdened, and I will give you rest. Take my yoke upon you and learn from me, for I am meek and humble of heart; and you will find rest for yourselves. For my yoke is easy, and my burden light"* (Mt 11:28–30). He encourages the saints in the midst of sufferings to unite their sufferings with Him, so that through such dependance on Him they might discover His grace making their burdens light. This only happens because of their stance of littleness before Him and with Him—in meekness and humility.

Great saints are joined to Christ crucified in profound ways. And yet, like Jesus and Mary, they are offered the "tools" to endure such crucifixion (either being literal or mystical) of littleness and deep spousal love for God. In fact, it is not the greatness of saints that makes them saints. It is not their success, their charisms, their popularity, their gifts. No, saints are saints *despite* these things. Saints are saints because of their personal kenosis—their ability to empty out themselves completely upon the altar of Christ's Heart. Jesus said, *"Amen, amen, I say to you, unless a grain of wheat falls to the ground and dies, it remains just a grain of wheat; but if it dies, it produces much fruit"* (Jn 12:24). Christ gave us an example and taught His disciples that it was by lowering oneself even unto death that allowed Him to be lifted up into the glory of God.

Jesus also said, *"Amen, I say to you, unless you turn and become like children, you will not enter the kingdom of heaven"* (Mt 18:3). Saints are saints because of their littleness—that brings along with it innocence, vulnerability before God and a resolute, obedient *fiat* to all that He wills. Saints are saints because they allow themselves to be carried by Christ, the good Shepherd, close to His Heart and to be drenched in the blood flowing from His wounds seeping deep into their souls. Saints are saints because they allow the Lord to recreate them to live authentic, pure, heroic love.

St. Bernard of Clairvaux brilliantly describes the depth of pure love that each soul must embrace in order to be fired as one with Jesus crucified. He said:

Chapter 6: How Does the Church Live the Cross with Jesus?

Love is sufficient of itself, it gives pleasure by itself and because of itself. It is its own merit, its own reward. Love looks for no cause outside itself, no effect beyond itself. Its profit lies in its practice. I love because I love, I love that I may love. Love is a great thing so long as it continually returns to its fountainhead, flows back to its source, always drawing from there the water which constantly replenishes it. Of all the movements, sensations and feelings of the soul, love is the only one in which the creature can respond to the Creator and make some sort of similar return however unequal though it be. For when God loves, all he desires is to be loved in return; the sole purpose of his love is to be loved, in the knowledge that those who love him are made happy by their love of him.[157]

The love that saints embrace with Christ is the purest of loves that seeks truly to only do the Father's will in order to glorify Him. And sharing in such love with Jesus is in itself the only reward that the saints desire. In the end, love will be the measure God uses to both judge and reward the saints. St. John of the Cross taught, *"In the*

---

[157] Bernard of Clairvaux, Sermon 83.4–6, in *The Liturgy of the Hours*, 3:1333.

evening of life, they will examine you on love."[158] And as the saints begin to live this pure love on earth, the entire Church benefits. St. John of the Cross claimed that *"The smallest movement of pure Love is more useful to the Church than all other works put together."*[159]

The love that Jesus places within the saints presses them on to do things that many other people would fear as impossible. St. Teresa of Calcutta lived such love explaining that, *"Intense love does not measure it just gives."* St. Therese of Lisieux similarly said, *"When one loves, one does not calculate."* This love that the saints share with Christ colors all that they do and say—making absolutely everything in their lives a prayer that bears fruit for the Lord. St. Anthony Maria Claret explained:

> Love is the most necessary of all virtues. Love in the person who preaches the word of God is like fire in a musket. If a person were to throw a bullet with his hands, he would hardly make a dent in anything; but if the person takes the same bullet and ignites some gunpowder behind it, it can kill. It is much the same with the word of God. If it is spoken by

---

[158] Guy Gaucher, *John and Therese: Flames of Love: The Influence of St. John of the Cross in the Life and Writings of St. Therese of Lisieux* (New York: Society of St. Paul/Alba House, 1999), 33.

[159] Gaucher, 34.

someone who is filled with the fire of charity—the fire of love of God and neighbor—it will work wonders.[160]

St. Therese of Lisieux in *The Story of a Soul* also explained the all-encompassing power of love behind every vocation:

> Charity gave me the key to my vocation. I understood that the Church being a body composed of different members, the most essential, the most noble of all the organs would not be wanting to her; I understood that the Church has a heart and that this heart is burning with love; that it is love alone which makes the members work, that if love were to die away apostles would no longer preach the Gospel, martyrs would refuse to shed their blood. I understood that love comprises all vocations, that love is everything, that it embraces all times and all places because it is eternal! . . .
>
> You know well enough that Our Lord does not look so much at the greatness of our actions, nor even at their difficulty, but at the love with which we do them.[161]

---

[160] Anthony Mary Claret, *Autobiography and Complementary Writings* (Bangalore, India: Claretian Publications, 2011), 438–39.

[161] Therese of Lisieux, *The Story of a Soul: the Autobiography of St. Therese of Lisieux* B3v, trans. John Clareke (Washington, DC: ICS Publications, 1996), 194.

For the saints it is love that quickly does the work in them of conforming them to Christ and bearing fruit. St. Therese of Lisieux explained how this work of God's love does not need lots of time or energy on the part of the soul striving for sanctity, instead it depends on the depth of their surrender to Him in answering His call of Love. She said: *"The good God does not need years to accomplish His work of love in a soul; one ray from His Heart can, in an instant, make His flower bloom for eternity."*[162] And, *"Love can supply for length of years. Jesus, because He is Eternal, regards not the time but only the love."*[163]

It is a saint's docility before God that allows Him to consume them with His love—which, in turn, carries them through unimaginable sufferings that serve to unite them completely with Christ crucified. Our Lady, the Queen of all Saints, lived this perfectly. But the entire Church is called to follow Her in these bloody footsteps of Her Son—traversing the way of the Cross with Him in order to bear fruit with Him that will last eternally. This is only possible if the saints imitate the littleness and union of love that Jesus and Mary shared. In this next chapter we will explore what kind of littleness saints are called to live. And we will show how through heroically embracing humble, self-emptying littleness, saints are lifted up as great examples for the entire Church.

---

[162] Therese of Lisieux, Letter 103, to her sister Celine, October 20, 1890, excerpt available at https://www.littleflower.org/st-therese/st-therese-quotes/.

[163] Therese of Lisieux, Letter 89, to her sister, Mother Agnes of Jesus, August 1890, excerpt available at https://catholicismpure.wordpress.com/2017/10/03/saint-therese-of-lisieux-on-the-love-of-god/.

Chapter 7

The Saints Call to Littleness in the Church

"The only means of making rapid progress on the way of love is to remain very little."—St. Therese of Lisieux[164]

Jesus is very clear in His instruction to His disciples that in order to reach heaven, one must embrace the littleness of spiritual childhood. He says, *"Amen, I say to you, unless you turn and become like children, you will not enter the kingdom of heaven. Whoever humbles himself like this child is the greatest in the kingdom of heaven"* (Mt 18:3-4). Jesus clarifies this explaining that it is the humility of a child that His followers must emulate, *"Whoever exalts himself will be humbled, but whoever humbles himself will be exalted"* (Mt 23:12). And to further prove His point, Christ offers Himself as an example of such littleness, meekness, and humility saying, *"Take my yoke upon you and learn from me, for I am meek and humble of heart; and you will find rest for yourselves"* (Mt 11:29). Why does Christ absolutely insist on the souls He calls to follow Him embrace an absolute spiritual childhood? It is because the work that Jesus wants to do in His saints is a work that demands utter docility, purity, obedience, trust, and surrender in the souls of His followers in order for them to be transformed by His divine love. Of themselves, the saints could

---

[164] Gaucher, *John and Therese*, 26.

never endure the Passion and Death of Christ that must come to touch their own hearts. Only by total littleness would the saints allow Christ to be "all in all" within them.

As Jesus rested in His Father's will on the Cross, so too all of His followers are called to rest upon His Own Heart as a weaned baby in the arms of their mother:

> LORD, my heart is not proud;
> nor are my eyes haughty.
> I do not busy myself with great matters,
> with things too sublime for me.
> Rather, I have stilled my soul,
> Like a weaned child to its mother,
> weaned is my soul.
> Israel, hope in the LORD,
> now and forever. (Ps 131)

The greatest saintly teacher that the Church has of spiritual childhood is St. Therese of Lisieux. She was named doctor of the Church simply for discovering and teaching so clearly this simple lesson of a soul's need to grow in littleness in order to be conformed to Christ crucified. She said, *"I rejoice to be little, because only children and those who are like them will be admitted to the heavenly banquet."*[165] She further explains:

> My way is entirely one of trust and love. . . . Jesus points out to me the only way which leads to Love's furnace—that way is self-surrender—it is the confidence of the little child who sleeps without fear in its father's arms.
>
> How shall I show my love is proved by deeds? Well—the little child will strew flowers, . . . she will embalm the Divine Throne with their fragrance, will sing with silvery voice the canticle of love.
>
> The Divine Heart's Goodness and Merciful Love are little known! It is true that to enjoy these treasures we must humble ourselves, must confess our nothingness—and here is where many a soul draws back.
>
> How sweet is the way of Love! True, one may fall, one may not be always faithful, but Love, knowing how to draw profit from all, very quickly consumes whatsoever may displease Jesus, leaving naught but humble and profound peace in the innermost soul.[166]

---

[165] Therese of Lisieux, Letter 203, to Fr. Roulland, May 9, 1897, excerpt available at https://biltrix.com/2012/10/01/little-things-done-with-great-love-saint-therese-of-lisieux/.

[166] Therese of Lisieux, *The Story of a Soul,* excerpts taken from https://www.littleflower.org/st-therese/st-therese-quotes/.

St. Therese of Lisieux brilliantly understood that it was in her weakness and dependance on Jesus in littleness that allowed Him to do the greatest work through her. St. Paul similarly expressed this same idea saying:

> *Therefore, that I might not become too elated, a thorn in the flesh was given to me, an angel of Satan, to beat me, to keep me from being too elated. Three times I begged the Lord about this, that it might leave me, but he said to me, "My grace is sufficient for you, for power is made perfect in weakness." I will rather boast most gladly of my weaknesses, in order that the power of Christ may dwell with me. Therefore, I am content with weaknesses, insults, hardships, persecutions, and constraints, for the sake of Christ; for when I am weak, then I am strong.* (2 Cor 12:7–10)

> *Consider your own calling, brothers. Not many of you were wise by human standards, not many were powerful, not many were of noble birth. Rather, God chose the foolish of the world to shame the wise, and God chose the weak of the world to shame the strong, and God chose the lowly and despised of the world, those who count for nothing, to reduce to nothing those who are something, so that no human being might boast before God.* (1 Cor 1:26–29)

St. Paul speaks about his own personal self-emptying kenosis for Christ saying, *"For I am already being poured out like a libation"* (2

Tm 4:6). St. Paul's humble embracing of Christ's path of derision and way of the Cross eventually led to his total conformity with Him, culminating in the wounds of Christ being made visible on His body. *"From now on, let no one make troubles for me; for I bear the marks of Jesus on my body"* (Gal 6:17).

It is by becoming poor in spirit that the kingdom of Christ's love comes to reign in a soul. Humility is truth and the truth of humanity is that all are fallen creatures in need of redemption. Jesus recognizes the weakness of human nature and so He does not require great or impossible things in themselves in order for a soul to reach union with Him. Instead, Jesus came in lowliness—born as a tiny, dependent Infant in a stable—in order to teach us the path of spiritual littleness and childhood. The only great thing that Christ demands of His followers is a fullness of great love. He tells us through St. Paul, *"Let all you do be done with love"* (1 Cor 16:14). St. Josemaria Escriva taught his followers: *"Do everything for love. Thus, there will be no little things: everything will be big. Perseverance in little things for love is heroism."*[167]

Mother Teresa—in following the footsteps of St. Therese of Lisieux—also did not demand great feats from the sisters she formed and the souls entrusted to her. She recognized that it was not the actions themselves but instead the love with which they were done that bore the greatest fruit for heaven. She would say:

---

[167] Jose Maria Escrivà, *The Way*, no. 813 (New York: Scepter Publishers, 1982), 279.

If you can't do great things, do little things with great love. If you can't do them with great love, do them with a little love. If you can't do them with a little love, do them anyway.
Little things are indeed little, but to be faithful in little things is a great thing.

To the good God nothing is little because He is so great and we so small—that is why He stoops down and takes the trouble to make those little things for us—to give us a chance to prove our love for Him. Because He makes them, they are very great. He cannot make anything small; they are infinite. Yes, my dear children, be faithful in little practices of love, of little sacrifices—of the little interior mortification—of the little fidelities to the Rule, which will build in you the life of holiness—make you Christ-like.

Don't look for big things, just do small things with great love. The smaller the thing, the greater must be our love.[168]

St. Francis Xavier challenged those around him to *"Be great in little things."*[169] He explained that when one is aware of his own smallness and weakness, working along with God's grace to do little things

---

[168] Teresa of Calcutta, *Come Be My Light: The Private Writings of the "Saint of Calcutta,"* ed. Brian Kolodiejchuk (New York: M.C. Doubleday, 2007), 34.

[169] Famous motto of Francis Xavier, available at https://www.christianitytoday.com/history/people/missionaries/francis-xavier.html.

well, then God's grace will powerfully uphold him and work through him. He told his missionaries:

> For this reason, it is right that those who have a desire to serve God should take great pains in little matters, and lower themselves and empty themselves as much as possible, so that they may have an utter distrust of themselves, and an immense trust in God, and thus they may become accustomed, when great dangers of life or death or great trials present themselves, to have great hope in the goodness and mercy of God. And this they will gain, if they conquer themselves in things, however little they may be, to which they have an aversion, and if they devote themselves altogether to the study of Christian humility, and so are entirely free from self-confidence, while they raise up their hearts to placing the very highest confidence in God. For in truth no man is really timid and weak who knowingly leans upon the assistance of God.[170]

---

[170] Francis Xavier, as cited in Henry James Coleridge, *The Life and Letters of St. Francis Xavier*, vol. 2, bk. 6, p. 231, (London: Burns Oates & Washbourne, 1921), available at https://www.google.com/books/edition/The_Life_and_Letters_of_St_Francis_Xavie/MUoAAAAAMAAJ?hl=en&gbpv=1&bsq=%20great%20little%20things.

St. Augustine similarly taught, *"That which is least, then, is very little; but to be faithful in that which is least is great."*[171]

Jesus continually urged St. Faustina along the path of spiritual childhood by demanding great trust of her. A small child naturally trusts—even without knowing it at first. When one is little, he experiences a natural dependance on others for basic needs. Jesus led St. Faustina along the path of spiritual littleness so that her trust in Him would grow to be a great fire that would set the world ablaze with confidence in His holy love, provision, and mercy. Jesus told St. Faustina, *"Your great trust in Me forces me to continuously grant you graces. You have great and incomprehensible rights over My Heart, for you are a daughter of complete trust."*[172] He also lamented to her about the great pain caused to His Sacred Heart when the souls He loved and died for refuse to trust Him. *"[Jesus says;] Distrust on the part of souls is tearing at My insides. The distrust of a chosen soul causes Me even greater pain; despite My inexhaustible love for them they do not trust Me. Even My death is not enough for them. Woe to the soul that abuses these gifts."*[173]

Another aspect of littleness is silence and hiddenness. In His Incarnation Christ, Who was the Word, was silent at first as a Baby. And He came as God hidden in human flesh, the King of the

---

[171] Augustine, *De doctrina Christiana* 4.35, https://www.newadvent.org/fathers/12024.htm.

[172] Maria Faustina Kowalska, *Divine Mercy in My Soul*, no. 718 (Stockbridge: Marians of the Immaculate Conception, 2001).

[173] Kowalska, *Divine Mercy in My Soul*, no. 50.

universe hidden in a lowly stable. Our Lady also was the silent one - with only a few words of Hers recorded in all of scripture. So much of Her Heart and life remain hidden in God as a mysterious marvel in His sight alone—existing for His love alone. To become a child means to grow silent and hidden in humility in order to allow Christ the Word to speak through you. This is done so that all that others witness in one's hidden presence is Jesus' immense love.

St. Teresa Margaret Redi burned with a holy desire for hiddenness and God heard the prayer of her heart. In her biography Margaret Rowe wrote:

> The cornerstone of her spirituality was to remain hidden, to appear just like everyone else in spite of her heroic virtue. To our loss, she has remained very much hidden even after her death. Fr. Gabriel of St. Mary Magdalen comments that "This is an odd fact, for we do not hesitate to rank her among the primary figures who represent the glory of Carmel—among Teresa of Jesus, John of the Cross, and Therese of the Child Jesus."[174]

St. Teresa Margaret Redi did not see this hiddenness as simply remaining concealed in a Carmel, but extended into everything she did—especially embracing silence as the cocoon that would keep her

---

[174] Margaret Rowe, *God is Love: St. Teresa Margaret Redi: Her Life* (Washington, DC: ICS Publications Institute of Carmelite Studies, 2003), back cover.

as a secret to God. She said that she desired to *"hide herself in the Sacred Heart as in a desert."* And she did this by embracing the littleness of silence. She said, *"She who is silent everywhere finds peace."* And *"she who desires peace must see, suffer and be silent."*[175]

St. Edith Stein wrote of the Christ Child as being the One Who espouses a soul—encouraging her to join Him in His littleness. She said, *"The Divine Child offers us His hand to renew our bridal bond. Let us hurry to clasp this hand. The Lord is my light and my salvation—of whom shall I be afraid?"*[176] She continues speaking of the holy innocents, *"Those who want to belong entirely to Him (the Divine Child) must deliver themselves to Him in complete self-renunciation, surrender to the divine decision like these children."*[177] She further explains:

> The love of the Cross in no way contradicts being a joyful child of God. Helping Christ carry His Cross fills one with a strong and pure joy, and those who may and can do so, the builders of God's kingdom, are the most authentic children of God . . .
>
> To suffer and to be happy although suffering, to have one's feet on the earth, to walk on the dirty and rough paths

---

[175] Rowe, 118.

[176] Edith Stein, *The Collected Works of Edith Stein*, vol. 4, *The Hidden Life: Essays, Meditations and Spiritual Texts*, trans. Waltraut Stein (Washington DC: ICS Publications, 1992). 115.

[177] Stein, 4:114.

Chapter 7: The Saints Call to Littleness in the Church

of this earth and yet to be enthroned with Christ at the Father's right hand, to laugh and cry with the children of this world and ceaselessly sing the praises of God with the choirs of angels—this is the life of the Christian until the morning of eternity breaks forth.[178]

In another place St. Edith Stein draws out the foundation of "littleness" as lived in the ordinariness and hiddenness of a Carmelite vocation as necessary to a Carmelite's ascent to union with Christ:

> Carmelites can repay God's love by their everyday lives in no other way than by carrying out their daily duties faithfully in every respect—all the little sacrifices ... letting no opportunity go by for serving others in love. Finally, crowning this is the personal sacrifice that the Lord may impose on the individual soul. This is the 'little way' a bouquet of insignificant little blossoms that are daily placed before the Almighty—perhaps a silent, life-long martyrdom that no one suspects and that is at the same time a source of deep peace and hearty joyousness and a fountain of grace that bubbles over everything—we do not know where it goes, and the people whom it reaches do not know from whence it comes.[179]

---

[178] Stein, 4:93.
[179] Stein, 4:6.

St. Paul of the Cross spent his entire vocation preaching about the Passion of Christ and trying to conform the souls entrusted to his spiritual care into the image of Jesus crucified. St. Paul of the Cross innately understood that before a soul could ascent Mt. Calvary with Jesus, she first had to lower herself into the abyss of her own littleness and nothingness. It was only then that Jesus could set her on fire with His love, thus uniting her to Himself on the Cross. As will be shown later, often the Lord appeared as the Divine Child to the great mystics in order to espouse them to Himself—and unite them to His wounds. The Lord, Who came to earth as a tiny little one, insists that the souls united with Him in grace traverse the same path of humility and poverty of spirit as He did. St. Paul of the Cross taught:

> God delights in those who make themselves little and become as little children; he keeps them near His person, and nourishes them with the milk of divine love, in order to prepare them for the sweet wine of holy love, which inebriates those who drinks it. . . . Let us make ourselves as children with Jesus, hiding ourselves in our nothingness; let us be humble and simple as children by an exact obedience, by purity of heart, by love of holy poverty, by a love of sufferings, and, above all, by childlike simplicity in the faithful observance of our rules and constitutions. . . . Contemplate the divine Child, trembling with cold, which He suffered that He might enkindle in our hearts the flames of divine love. . . . Model your hearts on that of the divine Infant that He may

vivify you, encourage you, inflame you, sanctify you, render you capable of doing great things for the glory of God. . . . O Jesus, life of my life, joy of my soul, God of my heart, accept my heart as an altar on which I will sacrifice to Thee the gold of ardent charity, the incense of continual, humble and fervent prayer, and the myrrh of constant mortification![180]

St. Paul of the Cross, like St. Teresa Margaret Redi, recognized that silence was a great virtue that comes from humility—and that a heart made little by silence is easily set aflame by the gifts of divine love. He said, *"Love speaks little. The language of divine love is a burning heart; no words can express its ardors; they make of the loving soul a victim of love, a holocaust, consumed and reduced to ashes in the divine fire of charity."*[181]

He also understood that the purpose of this personal kenosis of the saints, which causes them to dive full force into the humble littleness of the Word made flesh, is so that they can be filled with the flames of divine love that make of them priests, victims, and altars along with Christ. He said, *"When you attain true humility of heart and self-contempt ask leave of Jesus to enter His divine Heart, and you will at once obtain it. Place yourself as a victim on that altar, where the*

---

[180] Paul of the Cross, *Flowers of the Passion: Thoughts of St. Paul of the Cross*, trans. Ella A. Mulligan (New York: Benziger Brothers, 1893), 38–41.

[181] Paul of the Cross, 54–55.

fire of divine love is ever burning. Let this sacred flame burn you to the marrow of your bones."[182]

St. Paul of the Cross recognized the immense importance of turning to Our Lady not only as a model, but also as a Motherly intercessor who desires to help all of Her children:

> Take flight into the Immaculate Heart of Mary.... Ask grace to live always immersed in that immense ocean of divine love whence springs that other ocean of the sufferings of Jesus and the dolors of Mary. Let us be pierced through by those sufferings and these dolors; and let the sword be well tempered, that the wound of love may be the deeper; for the deeper it is, the sooner will the captive soul escape from her prison.... Unite the sufferings of Jesus with those of the holy Virgin, and, bowing yourself beneath their weight, make of yourself a holocaust of love and sorrow.[183]

One of the early Church Fathers, the great Cappadocian, Gregory of Nyssa, writing in the fourth century, tells us that by imitating Our Lady in humility and pure love, Christ can take flesh and be born as a child in each soul surrendered to Him:

> What happened in the stainless Mary when the fullness of the God-head which was in Christ shone out through her,

---

[182] Paul of the Cross, 172.

[183] Paul of the Cross, 44–45.

that happens in every soul that leads by rule the virgin life. No longer indeed does the Master come with bodily presence; "we know Christ no longer according to the flesh"; but, spiritually, He dwells in us and brings His Father with Him, as the Gospel somewhere tells.[184]

He teaches that in this way the child Jesus is born in each one of us.

Lastly, we present the teachings of St. Clare of Assisi to St. Agnes where she describes this same process that St. Paul of the Cross proposed of meditating on and imitating the humility of the Infant Christ in order for the soul longing to be His bride to be capable of receiving His nuptial love. She writes:

> Behold his poverty even as he was laid in the manger and wrapped in swaddling clothes. What wondrous humility, what marvelous poverty! The King of angels, the Lord of heaven and earth resting in a manger! Look more deeply into the mirror and meditate on his humility, or simply on his poverty. Behold the many labors and sufferings he endured to redeem the human race. Then, in the depths of this very mirror, ponder his unspeakable love which caused him to suffer on the wood of the cross and to endure the most

---

[184] Gregory of Nyssa, *On Virginity* 2, trans. William Moore and Henry Austin Wilson (New York: Aeterna Press, 2016), 4–5.

shameful kind of death. The mirror himself, from his position on the cross, warned passersby to weigh carefully this act, as he said: *All of you who pass by this way, behold and see if there is any sorrow like mine.* Let us answer his cries and lamentations with one voice and one spirit; *I will be mindful and remember, and my soul will be consumed within me.* In this way, queen of the king of heaven, your love will burn with an ever brighter flame.[185]

Although it is fundamental that Christians follow Christ on the path of littleness in order to grow in holiness, it is important to note that there is a paradox in this path: in that the littler one grows in the spiritual life, the greater they are before the eyes of God, and also often the brighter they shine before the eyes of others in the world. Authentic littleness put at the service of God is filled with the might and powerful, transforming love of His divinity. In this, miserable little sinners who recognize their need for the Lord and who docilely open themselves up to His great abyss of grace, actually become witnesses of His glory and powerful conduits of His grace to others. For the saints, the wisdom that leads them to recognize their own weak littleness at the same time grants them the genius of partaking in the life of God's love. And this is perceived by others around them as a

---

[185] Clare of Assisi, Letter to Blessed Agnes of Prague, *Escritos de Santa Clara*, 339–41 (Madrid 1970), in *The Liturgy of the Hours*, 3:1311.

monumental feat. As is evident in the lives of the saints, to the degree one grows in littleness before God is the degree that He can then consume them with the passionate love of His Heart. And so, to the degree a saint is humble and little, is the degree that God's love will possess them. In this next chapter we will look at how a soul grows in God's love to the point of a mystical marital union with Him.

Chapter 8

The Church and Each Soul Within Her as the "Bride, the Wife of the Lamb"

What does it mean for a child of God to become the bride, the wife of the lamb? Not only did Jesus Christ embrace a deep kenosis and fiery love union with the Trinity in order to endure His Passion and Death to save us, but He calls each and every soul saved by His blood to enter into that same littleness and spousal love union with Him—just as His Mother Mary perfectly did. Souls ravished by love of Jesus naturally burn with a desire to be made one with Him, regardless of the cost. The spousal love they share with Jesus not only drives them forward to desire an even deeper union with Him—one that carries them through the Cross—but it is also this powerful love that they share which upholds such souls in their life of crucifixion. Ultimately, it is this nuptial love with Christ that consumes them whole making of them a priest, altar, and victim along with Him, allowing them to "co-redeem" and bear fruit of eternal life for souls.

Let us begin with a taste of what this bridal love of Christ looks like as is described by St. Clare in her letter to St. Agnes:

> Happy indeed is she who is granted a place at the divine banquet, for she may cling with her inmost heart to him whose beauty eternally awes the blessed hosts of heaven; to him whose love inspires love, whose contemplation refreshes, whose generosity satisfies, whose gentleness delights, whose

memory shines sweetly as the dawn; to him whose fragrance revives the dead, and whose glorious vision will bless all the citizens of that heavenly Jerusalem. For his is the splendor of eternal glory, the brightness of eternal light, and the mirror without cloud.

Queen and bride of Jesus Christ, look into that mirror daily and study well your reflection, that you may adorn yourself, mind and body, with an enveloping garment of every virtue, and thus find yourself attired in flowers and gowns befitting the daughter and most chaste bride of the king on high. In this mirror blessed poverty, holy humility and ineffable love are also reflected. With the grace of God the whole mirror will be your source of contemplation.[186]

In this passage St. Clare speaks of the powerful love of Christ that consumes a soul totally given over to Him. She explains how such a soul will come to resemble her Beloved Lord in all virtues, but most especially the virtues of humility and love. These two virtues are paramount for a soul who will ultimately be lifted to the Cross with Christ.

As will be seen in this section, souls united with Jesus in the mystical marriage inevitably are united with Him on the Cross. The deepest love that Christ shared with humanity to save them was a love that was crucified. In the lives of countless mystics and saints,

---

[186] Clare of Assisi, Letter to Blessed Agnes of Prague, in *The Liturgy of the Hours*, 3:1310–11.

the closer the soul grows in union with Christ, the deeper He imprints His sufferings upon their lives. Often a mystical marriage will culminate with a heart wound or the stigmata appearing on the flesh of the saintly victim. In those united closest to Christ there awakens an unquenchable thirst to suffer with Him, recognizing the merit of such pure love for the good of others.

A beautiful example of this process through littleness and spousal love culminating in a union on the Cross with Christ is dear St. Agatha. We see very clearly in an ancient homily by St. Methodius of Sicily on the martyrdom of St. Agatha, that St. Agatha even in her littleness was made the "wife of Jesus" through her suffering and martyrdom with Him. He states:

> The woman who invites us to this banquet is both a wife and virgin. To use the analogy of Paul, she is the bride who has been betrothed to one husband, Christ. A true virgin, she wore the glow of pure conscience and the crimson of the Lamb's blood for her cosmetics. Again and again, she meditated on the death of her eager lover. For her, Christ's death was recent, his blood was still moist. Her robe is the mark of her faithful witness to Christ. It bears the indelible marks of his crimson blood and the shining threads of her eloquence. She offers to all who come after her these treasures of her eloquent confession.[187]

---

[187] Methodius of Sicily, Homily on Saint Agatha (Analecta Bollandiana 68:76–78), in *The Liturgy of the Hours*, 2:1661–62.

Hundreds of years later another young virgin would be willing to sacrifice her life as she knew it in order to follow Christ. Although St. Kateri Tekakwitha was not a physical martyr, she left her people and embraced a life of lowliness and interior suffering in order to follow Jesus, claiming that she was His wife. According to Fr. Pierre Cholenec, a Jesuit priest who was a mentor, Kateri said, *"I have deliberated enough. For a long time my decision on what I will do has been made. I have consecrated myself entirely to Jesus, son of Mary, I have chosen Him for husband and He alone will take me for wife."*[188]

In both of these accounts of St. Agatha and St. Kateri, we see the unabashed claim these two saints had relying on their spousalship with Christ as His "wife" to carry them through their own personal sharings in His Cross. By living out their call as the "wife of the Lamb that was slain," no suffering intimidated them from drinking the full cup that Christ offered them from the Cross. Both Kateri and Agatha did this in imitation of their Blessed Mother the "Woman of Sorrows."

St. Agnes similarly models for us the power of Christ's spousal love consuming a little soul committed to Him even through the most terrible martyrdom. St. Ambrose marveled at the example of this little virgin bride in the face of her torture and martyrdom suffered on behalf of her crucified Husband. He writes:

---

[188] Kateri Tekakwitha, as cited in "Witness to Freedom: St. Kateri Tekakwitha," United States Conference of Catholic Bishops, https://www.usccb.org/issues-and-action/religious-liberty/fortnight-for-freedom/upload/Kateri-Tekakwitha-Fortnight-2016.pdf.

She is said to have suffered martyrdom when twelve years old. The more hateful was the cruelty, which spared not so tender an age, the greater in truth was the power of faith which found evidence even in that age. Was there room for a wound in that small body? And she who had no room for the blow of the steel had that wherewith to conquer the steel. But maidens of that age are unable to bear even the angry looks of parents, and are wont to cry at the pricks of a needle as though they were wounds. She was fearless under the cruel hands of the executioners, she was unmoved by the heavy weight of the creaking chains, offering her whole body to the sword of the raging soldier, as yet ignorant of death, but ready for it. Or if she were unwillingly hurried to the altars, she was ready to stretch forth her hands to Christ at the sacrificial fires, and at the sacrilegious altars themselves, to make the sign of the Lord the Conqueror, or again to place her neck and both her hands in the iron bands, but no band could enclose such slender limbs.

A new kind of martyrdom! Not yet of fit age for punishment but already ripe for victory, difficult to contend with but easy to be crowned, she filled the office of teaching valor while having the disadvantage of youth. She would not as a bride so hasten to the couch, as being a virgin, she joyfully went to the place of punishment with hurrying step, her head not adorned with plaited hair, but with Christ. All wept, she alone was without a tear. All wondered that she was so readily prodigal of her life, which she had not yet enjoyed, and now gave up as though she had gone through it. Everyone was astounded that there was now one to bear witness to the Godhead, who as yet could not, because of her age, dispose of herself. And she brought it to pass that she should be believed concerning God, whose evidence concerning man would not be accepted. For that which is beyond nature is from the Author of nature.

What threats the executioner used to make her fear him, what allurements to persuade her, how many desired that she would come to them in marriage! But she answered: "It would be an injury to my spouse to look on any one as likely to please me. He Who chose me first for Himself shall receive me. Why are you delaying, executioner? Let this body perish which can be loved by eyes which I would not." She stood, she prayed, she bent down her neck. You could see the executioner tremble, as though he himself had been condemned, and his right hand shake, his face grow pale, as he feared the peril of another, while the maiden feared not for her own. You have then in one victim a twofold martyrdom, of modesty and of religion. She both remained a virgin and she obtained martyrdom.[189]

---

[189] Ambrose, *On Virgins* 1.2, 5,7–9 (Migne PL 16, 189–91), in *The Liturgy of the Hours,* 3:1311–12.

Here St. Ambrose highlights the beauty of St. Agnes' littleness put at the service of love for Jesus her Bridegroom that gives her strength and courage to suffer joyfully with Him and for Him. It is St. Agnes' littleness and spousal love that fuse her so closely with Christ crucified and which, in turn, make her a little bridal priest, victim and altar with Him. This is a beautiful example of what a saintly soul undergoes interiorly when they experience a mystical marriage with Jesus. Jesus' greatness humbles a soul exposing the reality of her littleness before God, while at the same time consuming her with a fiery love that unites them as one—albeit in a union disproportionate as the infinite love of Jesus Christ the divine Bridegroom lifts the small human creature into the center of His Heart. The soul and God are not made one as two hearts side by side are equalized through love, but rather the soul is immersed in the Godhead through grace and made one with Him as He comes to possess her in full. This consummation mysteriously makes the soul a more perfect version of her unique self, while at the same time shining forth her Beloved's divine light, life and love. And the little, saintly soul set on fire with God's love thus makes Christ's sufferings her own and offers all pain that she encounters in and through Christ along with His one offering as Priest, Victim and Altar on Calvary.

There are numerous ways that Christ takes a soul from the abyss of her misery, purifying her and eventually consummating His union with her through a mystical marriage. Yet for all souls united with Christ in this complete way, the "two become one flesh" in a very real way, manifesting differently in the soul depending on her specific vocation and charism. Regardless of how this takes place, some similarities are found. In the *The Spiritual Canticle*, St. John of the Cross describes the mystical marriage as such:

> The spiritual marriage is incomparably greater than the spiritual espousal, for it is a total transformation in the beloved in which each surrenders the entire possession of self to the other with a certain consummation of the union of love. The soul thereby becomes divine, becomes God through participation, insofar as is possible in this life. And thus, I think that this state never occurs without the soul's being confirmed in grace, for the faith of both is confirmed when God's faith in the soul is here confirmed. It is accordingly the highest state attainable in this life.
>
> Just as in the consummation of carnal marriage there are two in one flesh, as Sacred Scripture points out [Gn 2:24], so all when the spiritual marriage between God and the soul is consummated, there are two natures in one spirit and love, as St. Paul says in making this same comparison: *whoever is joined to the Lord is one spirit with Him* [1 Cor 6:17]. This union resembles the union of the light of a star or candle with the light of the sun, for what then sheds light is not the star or the candle, but the sun, which has absorbed the other lights into its own . . .
>
> This is like saying: She has been transformed into her God, here referred to as 'the sweet garden,' because of the sweet and pleasant dwelling she finds in him . . . For after the soul has been for some time the betrothed of the Son of God

in gentle and complete love, God calls her and places her in His flowering garden to consummate this most joyful state of marriage with Him. The union wrought between the two natures and the communication of the divine to the human in this state is such that even though neither changes its being, both appear to be God. Yet in this life the union cannot be perfect, although it is beyond words and thought.[190]

St. John of the Cross here beautifully speaks of a soul being absorbed into God—not losing her own identity, yet His identity radiating so brightly from her that she seems to have been transformed into His very Being. St. John of the Cross speaks of this as a joyful state of marriage of the soul to God, yet this union is not one without pain. Instead, the love of the soul for Christ is so powerful that it finds more joy in union with Him than sorrow over the sufferings caused by that union. Somehow the saints who live a deep mystical marriage with Christ radiate joy and peace from their union with Jesus, even when He shares His body's and Heart's deep wounds with them.

St. John of the Cross continues to describe the effects of divine union in his writing *The Living Flame of Love*. Here we read how the soul, finally united with her beloved Jesus, experiences not only the sublimity of the fullness of His divine love, but also the wounds of

---

[190] John of the Cross, *The Spiritual Canticle* 22.3-4, in *Selected Writings*, ed. Kieran Kavanaugh (New York: Paulist Press, 1987), 257–58.

His crucified love within her own heart, life, and body. St. John poetically describes it:

> O flame of living love, most tenderly, didst wound my soul in deepest center—since you are no longer full of pain, perfect, if it be your will! Tear through the veil of this sweet encounter!
>
> O cautery so sweet! O wound full of delight! O soft hand! O gentle touch! Taste of eternal life you give and pay off every debt! By slaying, you change death to life.
>
> O luminous lamps of fire in whose resplendent rays the caves of sense—profound abyss—which once were dark, bereft of sight, with rarest beauty unite in gift for the Beloved warmth and light.
>
> How gently, filled with love, you awake in my inmost heart where secretly you swell, alone: with your breath so delicious, replete with good and glory, how delicately you enamor me![191]

Here it is clear that the cautery of the wounds caused by a soul's union with divine love is something that enflames the soul with joy and longing. As a soul unites with God and her heart meets His Heart, her wounds meet His Wounds, and they are united as one,

---

[191] John of the Cross, *The Living Flame of Love,* st. 1–4, translation in Stein, *The Science of the Cross,* trans. Josephine Koeppel (Washington, DC: ICS Publications, 2002), 185–86.

heaven seems to be poured out within the creature's soul. Such a deep fusion of love makes the saint's offering as priest, victim and altar with and in Christ something easy and delightful. The love that the soul shares with Christ overshadows the pain experienced on account of that love. And it expresses itself naturally in an act of praise and adoration of God simply by this pain and love being offered to Him. The crucified love of Christ shared with a soul in a mystical marriage naturally draws her up into His Own offering as the Eternal High Priest, Victim and Altar. And the soul through saying *fiat* to all that the Bridegroom asks of her finds joy in these wounds of love. In the next chapter we will read how the saints experienced a mystical marriage with Christ through uniting with Him crucified. It is clear from all of the unique accounts of their mystical encounters with Him that for a saint to love is to suffer and to suffer is to love.

Chapter 9

The Saints Experience Nuptial Union with Christ on the Cross—Crucified Love is Marital Love

The degree that a soul loves Christ is the degree that she will suffer with Him. Mystical marital union with Christ does not mean one is preserved from pain, rather the closer a soul is united to Jesus the more His Passion and Death come to live in her. Mother Teresa's experience of mystical union with Jesus crucified precisely echoed this notion. She wrote to a spiritual father, *"No, Father, I am not alone. I have His darkness—I have His pain—I have the terrible longing for God—to love and not to be loved. I know I have Jesus—in that unbroken union—for my mind is fixed on Him and in Him alone, in my will."*[192]

St. Edith Stein in *The Science of the Cross* explains this phenomenon:

> Through the mutual surrender of the two, a union results that comes close to the hypostatic one. It opens the soul for the reception of divine life and makes it possible for the Lord, through the entire subjection of the individual's will to the divine will, to make disposition of these persons as of

---

[192] Teresa of Calcultta, *Come Be My Light*, 223.

members of His body. They no longer live their life, but the life of Christ; they no longer suffer their own pain, but rather the passion of Christ.[193]

The hypostatic union is the union of Christ's two natures of God and Man mutually and fully present in the person of Jesus. A soul that enters a mystical marriage with Christ is united as one with Him with His human nature uniting with the soul and His divine nature growing forth life from within her. And yet, although the union of a mystical marriage with Christ comes close to a hypostatic one (as St. Edith Stein asserts), it is not the same thing. Christ has both the divine nature and human nature in their full essence united within His one being. He Himself is the source of these two natures united perfectly within Him. In a mystical marriage, Christ shares His divinity with the soul that He has taken to Himself in a nuptial embrace, yet that soul will never have a divine nature as its own source or in its full essence within herself. She will always be a human creature perfected *by* God and *taken up* into the presence of God. The mystical marriage unites two beings as one, yet the creature is always still subordinate to the Godhead in the hierarchy of grace. In such a union, the human soul is always the vessel from which Christ's life and Passion pour forth upon the world (and never vise-versa). And in this manner, the union is not the making equal of two beings, but instead the perfecting of the human creature to become the perfect tabernacle of God's presence and love.

---

[193] Stein, *Science of the Cross*, 261.

St. Edith Stein writes about the bridal union of a soul with God taking place *"under the tree of the Cross"*—where the soul mystically married to Jesus "co-suffers" crucified love with Christ even unto death.[194] She explains, *"The bridal union of the soul with God is the goal for which she was crated, purchased through the Cross, consummated on the Cross and sealed for all eternity with the Cross."*[195] She echoes St. John of the Cross' sentiment that Jesus, *"imposes suffering on us according to the measure of our love."*[196] The closer a soul draws to Christ in a mystical marriage, the more silent she becomes. The Word of God takes the place of her own voice in many ways, and she in all littleness spends her time like the Magdalene, sitting at the feet of Jesus listening to Him. *"She had a sister named Mary [who] sat beside the Lord at his feet listening to him speak. . . . [Jesus said,] 'There is need of only one thing. Mary has chosen the better part and it will not be taken from her'"* (Lk 10:39, 42).

As the soul draws close to Jesus in a mystical marriage—in a silent union of hearts—the more profoundly she shares in His sufferings. His wounds break forth upon the soul's own life, heart, and body. In each account of a saint drawing close to Christ, the process is identical to the example that Jesus Himself gave us, as well as set forth in His Mother who allowed God to make Her the perfect vessel of Christ both God and man. In Our Lady's union with Christ, the hypostatic union of Jesus as both God and Man affects the mystical

---

[194] Stein, 260.
[195] Stein, 273.
[196] Stein, 277.

union of His Heart with the soul of His Mother fusing them as one. Yet all the while, Christ alone is the principal cause of this mystical marriage and Mary simply responds fully to His gift of grace.

A similar process happens with each saint made perfect in Christ. First, there is a growth in littleness—a purification resulting in great humility and purity, in addition to a great obedience to all that the Father asks. There is also a self-emptying to make room for Christ's life to reign in full. Secondly, the soul is set on fire with a passionate love for Jesus—desiring because of this Love to relieve His suffering by sharing it in herself. As the soul draws closer to Jesus, His sufferings become more pronounced. Jesus is the crucified Husband of the soul who unites with Him on the Cross. Sometimes this mystical marriage with Christ manifests itself in His physical wounds appearing on the bodies of the saints. At other times there is a mystical piercing or marking of hearts, which after death is verified. Some unite so closely with Christ in divine love that they seem to die of love itself. For example, the spiritual director of St. Teresa Margaret Redi—in reflecting on her death—said, *"She could not have lived very much longer, so great was the strength of the love of God in her."*[197]

St. John of the Cross wrote about a soul being so consumed with divine love that, in some, it indeed caused their death. St. Therese of Lisieux treasured this teaching of his and hoped that one day this would be made real in her own life. She quoted St. John of the Cross:

> The death of such persons is very gentle and very sweet, sweeter and more gentle than was their whole spiritual life

---

[197] Rowe, *God is Love,* back cover.

on earth. For they die with the most sublime impulses and delightful encounters of love, resembling the swan whose song is much sweeter at the moment of death.[198]

St. Therese of Lisieux recognized that being a spouse of Christ meant being crucified—both in her own life and death. She said *"her Spouse is not a Spouse who will lead her to festivals, but up the hill of Calvary."*[199] She saw her sickness as a concrete mystical marriage. For example, when she coughed up blood one night she embraced it as a betrothal from Jesus—a promise that He would soon come for her. She wrote:

God granted me, last year, the consolation of observing the fast during Lent in all its rigor. Never had I felt so strong and this strength remained with me until Easter. On Good Friday, however, Jesus wished to give me the hope of going to see Him soon in heaven. Oh! How sweet this memory really is! After remaining at the Tomb until midnight, I returned to our cell, but I had scarcely laid my head upon the pillow when I felt something like a bubbling stream mounting to my lips. I didn't know what it was, but I thought that perhaps I was going to die and my soul was flooded with joy. However,

---

[198] John of the Cross, *The Living Flame of Love*, trans. K. Kavanaugh and O. Rodriquesz (Washington, DC: ICS Publications, 1973), 592.

[199] Guy Gaucher, *The Passion of St. Therese of Lisieux* (New York: The Crossroad Publishing Company, 1999), 225.

as our lamp was extinguished, I told myself I would have to wait until the morning to be certain of my good fortune, for it seemed to me that it was blood I had coughed up. The morning was not long in coming; upon awakening, I thought immediately of the joyful thing that I had to learn and so I went over to the window. I was able to see that I was not mistaken. Ah! My soul was filled with a great consolation; I was interiorly persuaded that Jesus, on the anniversary of His own death, wanted to have me hear His first call. It was like a sweet and distant murmur that announced the Bridegroom's arrival.[200]

Ultimately Therese recognized that her union with Christ crucified would be one leading to death. As His love in her increased, so would His Passion. In speaking of her own death and desire for union with Christ she said, *"I no longer rely on sickness, it is too slow a guide. I now rely only on love."*[201]

She later expanded on this desire as she reflected on St. John of the Cross. She said:

"Tear through the veil of this sweet encounter!" I've always applied these words to the death of love that I desire. Love will not wear out the veil of my life. It will tear it suddenly.

---

[200] Therese of Lisieux, *Story of a Soul* C4v, p. 210–11.

[201] Therese of Lisieux, "To Live for Love," in Gaucher, *Passion of St. Therese*, 221–22.

With what longing and what consolation I have repeated from the beginning of my religious life these other words of St. John of the Cross: "It is of the highest importance that the soul practice love very much."

... Ah! It is incredible how all my hopes have been fulfilled. When I used to read St. John of the Cross, I begged God to accomplish in me what he wrote, that is, even if I were to live to be very old, to consume me rapidly in Love, and I have been answered![202]

St. Teresa Margaret Redi was another daughter of Carmel who lived a great littleness, experienced a great spousal union with Christ and therefore longed to suffer with Him. Margaret Rowe describes St. Teresa Margaret Redi thus:

Of the soul transformed by love, St. John of the Cross writes: "when it is so far transformed and perfected interiorly in the fire of love, (the soul) is not only united with this fire, but it has now become one living flame within it. Such the soul feels itself to be." St. Teresa, describing this state of the Sixth Mansion, uses words which well describe Teresa Margaret's interior state: "The soul has been wounded with love for the Spouse, and seeks more opportunity of being alone, trying so

---

[202] Gaucher, *Passion of St. Therese*, 222.

far as is possible to one in its state, to renounce everything which can disturb it in this its solitude.[203]

This living flame of Christ's love impels the soul forward with courage to unite ever more deeply with her wounded Savior on Golgotha. St. Therese Margaret Redi herself said:

> In all things I shall be content, knowing that the route I travel leads to Calvary. The thornier the path, the heavier the cross, the more consoled I shall be, because I desire to love you with a suffering love, a selfless love, an active love, with a firm, undivided, persevering love. ... I have promised you many things, but in no wise do I depend upon my own indolent spirit. You have enlightened me as to what I must do; now help me to execute it. All this I hope of your infinite mercy.[204]

Commenting on this, Fr. Gabriel of St. Mary Magdalene, O.C.D. said, *"At the foot of the Cross, suffering becomes more a proof of love than a punishment."*[205]

St. Elizabeth of Trinity, another great Carmelite mystic, also expressed her desire to be united to her heavenly crucified Spouse in His Passion even unto death. She writes in her notes:

---

[203] Rowe, *God is Love*, 220.

[204] Rowe, 219.

[205] Rowe, 221.

I want to leave all, I long to give You my life and to share Your agony. May I die crucified.[206]

Also, in one of St. Elizabeth of the Trinity's prayers, we not only hear her great desire to suffer with Christ, but we see the exact movements of her heart that lead to this desire. In the first stanza of her prayer, she prays that she can empty herself (kenosis) and therefore become a tabernacle of His presence. She prays for silence (which stems from littleness) that leads to His Word taking flesh within her. Next, she asks to be crucified in love with Him. She clearly identifies her spousal relationship with Him as something that occurs in the fires of His crucified love. And finally, she speaks of listening to Him and gazing upon His light until His presence consumes her. She desires to be lifted up and absorbed into His presence. As Christ became flesh in Our Lady, St. Elizabeth of the Trinity desires for Him to be buried within her even as she is buried in Him and consumed in whole by His love. She prays:

> O my God, Trinity Whom I adore; help me to forget myself entirely that I may be established in You as still and as peaceful as if my soul were already in eternity. May nothing trouble my peace or make me leave you, O my Unchanging One, but may each minute carry me further into the depths of Your

---

[206] Elizabeth of the Trinity, *Poems*, September 1897, in Penny Hickey, *Drink of the Stream: Prayers of Carmelites* (San Francisco: Ignatius Press, 2002), 296.

mystery. Give peace to my soul, make it Your heaven, Your beloved dwelling and Your resting place. May I never leave You there alone but be wholly present, my faith wholly vigilant wholly adoring and wholly surrendered to Your creative action.

O My beloved Christ, crucified by love, I wish to be a bride for Your Heart; I wish to cover You with glory; I wish to love You . . . even unto death! But I feel my weakness, and I ask You to "clothe me with yourself," to identify my soul with all the movements of Your Soul, to overwhelm me, to possess me, to substitute Yourself for me that my life may be but a radiance of Your Life. Come into me as Adorer, as Restorer, as Savior.

Eternal Word, Word of my God, I want to spend my life in listening to You, to become wholly teachable that I may learn all from You. Then, through all nights, all voids, all helplessness, I want to gaze on You and always remain in Your great light. O my beloved Star, so fascinate me that I may not withdraw from Your radiance.

Consuming Fire, Spirit of Love, "come upon me," and create in my soul a kind of incarnation of the Word: that I may be another humanity for Him in which He can renew His whole Mystery. And You, O Father, bend lovingly over Your poor little creature; "cover her with your shadow," seeing in her only the "Beloved in whom You are well pleased."

My Three, my All, my Beatitude infinite Solitude, Immensity in which I lose myself, I surrender myself to You as

Your prey. Bury Yourself in me that I may bury myself in You until I depart to contemplate in Your light the abyss of Your greatness.[207]

St. Edith Stein also clearly saw her religious vows as a Carmelite bride of Christ in light of Jesus crucified. To Edith, to be united to Jesus Christ maritally in Carmel, meant to be crucified. This did not only mean a conquering of oneself through embracing a life of poverty, chastity and obedience. She profoundly understood that the cause of such pain was also partly due to the resistance of the spirit of the antichrist that opposes those who seek to become one with Jesus. St. Edith Stein sees a spiritual battle as part of the suffering one endures on her path to mystical union with Jesus. She herself suffered a great spiritual war ending with her own martyrdom, yet she drew strength from her love union with Christ to suffer well the hostility thrown against her. She never experienced the mystical marriage or stigmata in a supernatural way, but she ended up so conformed to Christ that she bravely went forth to suffer and die with her Jewish people as a martyr in Auschwitz. She beautifully wrote about this with her pen before the Lord asked her to write about it with her life and blood:

The Savior today looks at us, solemnly probing us, and asks each one of us: Will you remain faithful to the Crucified?

---

[207] Elizabeth of the Trinity, *Personal Notes* 15, November 21, 1904, in Marian Murphy, *Always Believe in Love: Selected Writings of Elizabeth of the Trinity* (Washington, D.C.: ICS Publications, 2017), 127-8.

Consider carefully! The world is in flames, the battle between Christ and the Antichrist has broken into the open. If you decide for Christ, it could cost you your life. . . . Before you hangs the Savior on the Cross, because he became obedient unto death on the Cross. He came into the world not to do His own will, but His Father's will. If you intend to be the bride of the Crucified, you too must completely renounce your own will and no longer have any desire except to fulfill God's will. He speaks to you in the holy Rule and the Constitutions of the Order. He speaks to you through the mouth of your superiors. He speaks to you by the gentle breath of the Holy Spirit in the depths of your heart. To remain true to your vow of obedience, you must listen to this voice day and night and follow its orders. However, this means daily and hourly crucifying your self-will and self-love.

The Savior hangs naked and destitute before you the Cross because he has chosen poverty. . . . The Savior hangs before you with a pierced heart. He has spilled His heart's blood to win your heart. If you want to follow him in holy purity, your heart must be free of every earthly desire. Jesus, the Crucified, is to be the only object of your longings, your wishes, your thoughts.

The arms of the Crucified are spread out to draw you to His heart. He wants your life in order to give you His.[208]

---

[208] Stein, *Collected Works*, 4:94–95.

St. Edith Stein saw the natural result of such a nuptial union of the soul with Christ crucified as a means of saving other souls. Like her heavenly Mother, who she referred to as Our Lady, Co-redemptrix, Edith strives to a union with Christ crucified ultimately to help Him in the salvation of souls in the world. She understood her vocation as the bride of Jesus crucified in Carmel as a means of helping souls all over the world. And she specifically saw the sacrifice of her life with Christ in Carmel as a means of bringing grace to her own Jewish people. She continues:

> The world is in flames. The conflagration can also reach our house. But high above all flames towers the Cross. They cannot consume it. It is the path from earth to heaven. It will lift one who embraces it in faith, love, and hope into the bosom of the Trinity.
>
> The world is in flames. Are you impelled to put them out? Look at the Cross. From the open heart gushes the blood of the Savior. This extinguishes the flames of hell. Make your heart free by the faithful fulfilment of your vows; then the flood of divine love will be poured into your heart until it overflows and becomes fruitful to all the ends of the earth. Do you hear the groans of the wounded on the battlefields in the west and the east? You are not a physician and not a nurse and cannot bind up the wounds. You are enclosed in a cell and cannot get to them. Do you hear the anguish of the dying? You would like to be a priest and comfort them. Does the lament of the widows and orphans distress you? You

would like to be an angel of mercy and help them. Look at the Crucified. If you are nuptially bound to him by the faithful observance of your holy vows, your being is precious blood. Bound to him, you are omnipresent as he is. . . . You can be at all fronts, wherever there is grief, in the power of the Cross. Your compassionate love takes you everywhere, this love from the divine heart.[209]

Here we see how St. Edith Stein clearly sees her mystical marriage with Christ draws her into Christ's very work of atonement. She sees herself—as well as all souls called to such intimate union with Christ the Bridegroom—mandated to show forth the face of divine love in the midst of human hostility and suffering. She claims that the world is in flames over the violence of sin consuming it. And she calls to all souls who love Christ to put those flames out by allowing His divine love to pour forth freely and fully through them. The answer to such suffering and evil is declared to be love alone. And love in the face of such depravity is a participation in Christ's crucified love—which in itself atones for man's sin.

St. Catherine of Alexandria was another saint who was mystically married to Christ and went forth to unite with Him on the Cross through martyrdom. There are many varied stories about her conversion, mystical marriage and eventual death. In one, the Christ Child took a ring from the young John the Baptist, with His other hand He took Catherine's hand to receive it. Another tells the story

---

[209] Stein, *Collected Works*, 4:95–96.

differently. It is said that she was a daughter of the king of Alexandria and one day met an old hermit who gave her an icon of Our Lady with Baby Jesus—this image caused Catherine to fall deeply in love with Christ and desire to marry Him alone. Not long afterwards she had a dream where the hermit led her to Our Lady who led her to Christ Who told her that she was not "fair enough" for Him. Upon waking she visited the hermit and asked what this meant. He instructed her in the faith and baptized her along with her mother. After this she had a second dream where she was presented to Jesus as His mystical wife and He accepted her and placed a ring on her finger. When she awoke it said that this ring was on her hand! After this she was determined to never marry any other earthly husband. Because she was a princess of prominence, when she was eighteen she was presented to the Roman Emperor to be married. She took this opportunity to fiercely criticize his cruel persecution of Christians and she argued with him through logic as to how silly and wrong it was to worship pagan gods. When he called in learned people to argue with her, she converted them all, along with the emperor's wife, and for this she was put to death.[210] In Catherine of Alexandria we see a soul who lowered herself from a high earthly position in imitation of Christ. After embracing a life of "littleness" with Him, she was mystically married to Him through a dream and eventually was

---

[210] "The Mystical Marriage of St. Catherine of Alexandria," *The Madonna, the Magdalene, and the Muse: Women in Religious Art* (blog), https://madonnamagdalenemuse.wordpress.com/christian-saints/the-mystical-marriage-of-st-catherine-of-alexandria-by-pinturicchio/.

called to the consummation of this marriage through a terrible martyrdom. In this St. Catherine of Alexandria fully lived what it meant to be Jesus' "little wife crucified."

Often when a soul is united with Jesus in a mystical marriage, it is consummated by a sharing of His wounds in that soul's life, heart, and body. It is most often the Christ Child Who approaches His beloved—encouraging her in this form to little herself before the great God—in order to receive the divine grace of mystical marriage to Him. For St. Teresa of Avila, the elements of littleness, spousal love, and the Cross were all very present in her experience of the mystical marriage. The experience began at Mass, when at Communion St. John of the Cross had broken the Host before giving it to her; St. Teresa humbled by this gesture wondered if St. John was trying to mortify her. But then the Lord spoke to her:

"Do not fear, daughter, for no one will be a party to separating you from Me," making me understand that what just happened didn't matter. Then He appeared to me in an imaginative vision, as at other times, very interiorly, and He gave me His right hand and said:

"Behold this nail; it is a sign you will be My bride from today on. Until now, you have not merited this; from now on not only will you look after My honor as being the honor of your Creator, King, and God, but you will look after it as My true bride. My honor is yours, and yours Mine."

This favor produced such an effect in me I couldn't contain myself, and I remained as though entranced. I asked the

Lord either to raise me from my lowliness or not grant me such a favor.[211]

Later the Lord explained to her the new power that her prayer had before the throne of the Father because of this mystical marriage:

> You already know of the espousal between you and Me. Because of this espousal, whatever I have is yours. So I give you all the trials and sufferings I underwent, and by these means, as with something belonging to you, you can make requests of my Father.[212]

This was not to be the last experience of St. Teresa with the suffering Lord. Not long later she experienced the transverberation of her heart—a consummation of her love with Christ that physically left a wound on her heart the rest of her life. St. Teresa describes the experience in the Book of her Life:

> I saw an angel beside me toward the left side, in bodily form. He was not very large, but small, very beautiful, his face so blazing with light that he seemed to be one of the very highest angels, who appear all on fire. They must be those they call

---

[211] Teresa of Avila, *Collected Works of St. Teresa of Avila*, trans. Kieran Kavanaugh and Otilio Rodriguez (Washington, D.C.: ICS Publications, 1987), 1:402.

[212] Teresa of Avila, 1:412.

Cherubim. . . . I saw in his hands a long dart of gold, and at the end of the iron there seemed to me to be a little fire. This I thought he thrust through my heart several times, and that it reached my very entrails. As he withdrew it, I thought it brought them with it, and left me all burning with a great love of God. So great was the pain, that it made me give those moans; and so utter the sweetness that this sharpest of pains gave me, that there was no wanting it to stop, nor is there any contenting of the soul with less than God. [213]

Although St. Teresa experienced this all in a spiritual realm, upon her death her heart was removed from her body and it was discovered that there was an actual wound on her heart from the angel's spear. Her heart remains incorrupt and many people claim they can see this heart wound.

St. John of the Cross writes about different ways that God wounds the heart that He marries with love. He says that *"The cautery is the Holy Spirit; the hand is the Father; and the touch is the Son."* He goes on to explain the way of wounding that St. Teresa experienced:

> It will happen that while the soul is inflamed with the Love of God, it will feel that a seraph is assailing it by means of an arrow or dart which is all afire with love. And the seraph pierces and in an instant cauterizes this soul, which, like a

---

[213] Teresa of Avila, 1:389.

red-hot coal, or better a flame, is already enkindled. And then in this cauterization, when the soul is transpierced with that dart, the flame gushes forth, vehemently and with sudden ascent, like the fire in a furnace or an oven when someone uses a poker or bellows to stir and excite it. And being wounded by this fiery dart, the soul feels the wound with unsurpassable delight. Besides being fully stirred in greater sweetness by the blowing or impetuous motion of the seraph, in which it feels in its intense ardor to be dissolving in love.... Who can fittingly speak of this intimate point of the wound, which seems to be in the middle of the heart of the spirit.... The soul feels its ardor strengthen and increase and its love become so refined in this ardor that seemingly there are seas of loving fire within it, reaching to the heights and depths of the earthly and heavenly spheres, imbuing all with love. It seems to it that the entire universe is a sea of love in which it is engulfed, for, conscious of the living point or center of love within itself, it is unable to catch sight of the boundaries of this love.... The soul is converted into an immense fire of Love. Few persons have reached these heights.[214]

St. Catherine of Siena also profoundly understood that the mystical marriage leads to a deep "one flesh union" with Christ crucified. In fact, she claimed that the very ring that the Lord offered to her in

---

[214] John of the Cross, *The Living Flame of Love* 2:9–12, in *Selected Writings* (New York: Paulist Press, 1987), 303–5.

her marriage was made of His flesh, although her spiritual director said that to others it shone as gold. Most likely, the flesh of the resurrected Lord taking her to Himself was itself brilliant gold. After receiving this ring from the Lord, Catherine would also receive the honor of His sacred wounds on her body. In a letter to Sister Bartolomea della Seta she explains the soul's one-flesh union with Christ her beloved in such a way:

> Now what greater joy can the bride have than to be conformed to her Bridegroom, and clothed with similar garments? So, since Christ crucified in His life chose nothing but the Cross and pain, and clothed Himself in this raiment, His bride holds herself blessed when she is clothed in this same garment; and because she sees that the Bridegroom has loved her so beyond measure, she loves and receives Him with such love and desire as no tongue can suffice to tell . . . Bathe yourself in the Blood of Christ crucified, and so live, as is my will, that you neither seek nor will anything but the Crucified, like a true bride, bought with the Blood of Christ crucified. Know well that you are a bride, and that He has wedded you and every creature, not with a ring of silver, but with the ring of His flesh. O depth and height of Love unspeakable, how did You love this bride, the human race! . . . [You] have wedded it with Your flesh. You have given Your Blood for a pledge,

and at the last, sacrificing Your body, You have made the payment.[215]

Here St. Catherine speaks of a soul being bathed and baptized in the blood of Jesus—and thus, becoming His bride. This imagery is powerful in its illustration of what it means for a soul to be nuptially united to Christ. It means, in essence, to be completely crucified with and for Him. Jesus' flesh and blood poured out upon a soul purifies her and unites her to Himself. As a man and wife become one in the marital act, so too Christ and a soul wedded to Him become one in the mutual gift of one's body and soul to each other. A soul offers Christ her body and soul and Jesus takes what is depraved in her upon Himself and pours out upon and within her His divine life and crucified love through His flesh on the Cross and in the Eucharist. St. Catherine herself would be mystically married to Christ and this mystical union would be consummated by the gift of His wounds appearing in blood upon her own flesh.

St. Catherine's spiritual director, St. Raymond of Capua described her mystical marriage:

> One day, at the approach of the holy season of Lent, when Christians celebrate the Carnival. ... Catharine withdrew into her cell there to enjoy her Spouse more intimately by

---

[215] Catherine of Siena, *The Letters of Saint Catherine of Siena*, trans. and ed. Vida D. Scudder (1905), ed. Darrell Write (2016) (Scotts Valley, CA: CreateSpace Independent Publishing Platform, 2016), 119 and 122.

fasting and prayer; she reiterated her petition with more fervor than ever, and our Lord answered her "Because thou hast shunned the vanities of the world and forbidden pleasure, and hast fixed on me alone all the desires of thy heart, I intend, whilst thy family are rejoicing in profane feasts and festivals, to celebrate the wedding which is to unite me to thy soul. I am going, according to my promise, to espouse thee in faith." Jesus Christ then spoke more, when the Blessed Virgin appeared; and with his glorious Mother, St. John the Evangelist, the apostle St. Paul, St. Dominic, founder of her Order, and with them the prophet David who drew from his harp tones of heavenly sweetness. The Mother of God took in Her holy hand the right hand of Catharine, in order to present it to Her Son, asking Him to deign to espouse her in Faith. The Savior consented to it with love, and offered her a golden ring, set with four precious stones, in the center of which blazed a magnificent diamond. He placed it Himself on Catharine's finger, saying to her "There! I marry you to me in faith, to me, your Creator and Savior. Keep this faith unspotted until you come to me in heaven and celebrate the marriage that has no end. From this time forward, daughter, act firmly and decisively in everything that in my Providence I shall ask you to do. Armed as you are with the strength of faith, you will overcome all your enemies and be happy." The vision disappeared, and the ring remained on the finger of Catharine. She saw it, but it was invisible to others![216]

In this mystical marriage, Jesus offered St. Catherine a physical token of His flesh in the form of a ring that He placed upon her finger. As she received this ring, she was agreeing to enter into His redemptive work of priest, victim and altar with Him. Her flesh, too, would be lacerated with wounds. Later on, Christ shared His flesh with Catherine in a new way as she received the stigmata. This occurred at Mass after receiving Communion. Suddenly red rays shot out from the crucifix and pierced her. St. Catherine begged the Lord to keep her wounds invisible until after her death—a request that He granted.

St. Rita had been a married woman, a mother, a widow, and then eventually embraced the religious life. Knowing well what it meant to be married, she put the ferocity of her love at the service of her crucified Husband and Lord. After taking her to Himself as His bride, Jesus also shared the wound from His crown of thorns with St. Rita. One day she heard a sermon on the sufferings of Christ—specifically on the great sufferings caused by the crown of thorns. She was beside herself with compassion—overwhelmed with grief at His suffering—and when she returned home and went to the chapel to pray, she prostrated herself before the crucifix.

---

[216] Raymond of Capua, *The Life of St. Catherine of Siena*, trans. George Lamb (Charlotte, North Carolina: Tan Books, 2011), 81–83.

With the desire to suffer some of the pain her divine Spouse suffered, she asked Jesus to give her, at least, one of the many thorns of the crown of thorns that tormented His sacred head, saying to Him: "O my God and crucified Lord! O You who were innocent and without sin or crime! O You who have suffered so much for love of me! You have suffered arrest, buffeting, insults, a scourging, a crown of thorns and finally a cruel death on the Cross. Why do You wish that I, Your unworthy servant, who was the cause of Your sufferings and Your pains, should have no share in Your sufferings? Make me, O my sweet Jesus, a participant if not all of all of Your Passion, at least of a part of it. Recognizing my indignity and my unworthiness, I do not ask You to imprint on my body, as you did in the hearts of St. Augustine and St. Francis, the wounds that You still preserve as precious rubies in Heaven. I do not ask You to stamp Your holy Cross as You did in the heart of St. Monica. Nor do I ask You to form in my heart the instruments of Your Passion, as You did in the heart of my holy sister St. Clare of Montefalco. I only ask You for one of the seventy-two thorns which pierced Your head and caused You so much pain, so that I may feel a part of the pain You felt. O my loving Savior! Do not refuse me this favor. Do not deny me this grace. I will not leave here consoled, if You send me away without so desired a pledge of Your love."

When St. Rita concluded her prayerful petition, her divine Spouse, not wishing to resist any longer the desire of His faithful bride, granted her request. Making of His crown of thorns, so to speak, a bow, and of one of the thorns, an arrow, Jesus fired it at the forehead of St. Rita with such impetus and force that it penetrated the flesh and bone, and remained fixed in the middle of the forehead, leaving a wound that lasted all of her life—and even to this day, the scar of the wound remains plainly visible.[217]

Here we see another brilliant example of Christ giving Himself in the flesh in full to the human creature mystically married to Him. Love unites the soul with Jesus and this love actually transforms the bride into another image of Christ crucified. For St. Catherine of Siena, Christ shared His flesh intimately with her in the form of a ring around her finger and His wounds upon her hands. With St. Rita He answered her thirst for union with His crucified love by sharing a ring around her forehead in the form of the crown of thorns, one of which pierced her flesh open to bleed along with her beloved. Each saint is granted a different sharing in the sufferings of Christ through their union with Him, dependent upon their unique personality and vocation and spirituality in the Church. And yet, each saint is touched not only by divine love in their nuptial union with Christ, but also experiences Christ's flesh being made one with their own.

---

[217] Joseph Sicardo, *St. Rita of Cascia: Saint of the Impossible (Wife, Mother, Widow, Nun 1381–1457)* (Rockford, Illinois: Tan Books and Publishers, Inc., 1990), 110–11.

Christ lives His Passion concretely in different, unique ways with each soul He draws to Himself in love.

St. Angela of Foligno also was led by Christ on the path of union with Him as His crucified bride. Jesus began to impress on her the image of His crucified life, filled her with the drink of His wounds, and finally united with her in a mystical marriage culminating in the stigmata:

> During an "illumination" while the Eucharist was being celebrated Angela was drawn and absorbed into the "fathomless abysses of God." Under the impact of this vision the crucified God and man appeared to her and bestowed upon her soul, in a perfect manner, "the double state of his own life": the total absorption in the experience of the sweetness of the uncreated God and the cruel death pangs of his crucifixion.[218]

Here we note, once again, the relationship between Christ's hypostatic union and the mystical union He draws a soul into with Himself. St. Angela speaks of Christ as both God and Man sharing the double state of His Own life with her. And yet, as we spoke of before, this is not done in an identical way in a human creature as it was present within Christ Himself. In a mystical marriage, Christ shares *His* humanity and divinity with His beloved. And all of the soul's being is consumed by His presence of both God and man. Yet although

---

[218] Angela of Foligno, *Passionate Mystic of the Double Abyss: Selected Writings*, ed. Paul Lachance (New York: New City Press, 2006), 21.

the soul has a taste and experience of His divinity as she is absorbed into Him, she does not become God herself. She is always in human form experiencing the divine life through grace given to her from Jesus Christ. In this union Christ truly shares His flesh with her as He shared a ring of flesh with St. Catherine and a crown of thorns that tore the flesh of St. Rita. As we will read here—after bathing St. Angela in His precious blood (similar to what St. Catherine described)—He offers her a ring as a physical sign of His union with her as well. St. Angela explains:

> ... While I was standing in prayer, Christ on the cross appeared more clearly to me.... He then called me to place my mouth to the wound in his side. It seemed to me that I saw and drank the blood which was freshly flowing from his side. His intention was to make me understand that by this blood he would cleanse me. And at this I began to experience a great joy, although when I thought about the passion I was still filled with sadness.[219]
>
> I see the God-man. He draws my soul with great gentleness and he sometimes says to me: "You are I and I am you." I see then, those eyes and that face so gracious and attractive as he leans to embrace me. In short, what proceeds from those eyes and that face is what I said that I saw in that previous darkness which comes from within, and which delights me so that I can say nothing about it. When I am in the God-

---

[219] Angela of Foligno, 40.

man my soul is alive. And I am in the God-man much more than in the other vision of seeing God with darkness. The soul is alive in that vision concerning the God-man. The vision with darkness, however, draws me so much more that there is no comparison. On the other hand, I am in the God-man almost continually. It began in this continual fashion on a certain occasion when I was given the assurance that there was no intermediary between God and myself. Since that time there has not been a day or night in which I did not continually experience this joy of the humanity of Christ.[220]

The Lord returned to Angela much later and renewed this mystical marriage with the gift of a ring. She writes, "*The angels added: "Prepare yourself to receive the one who has espoused you with the ring of his love. This union with him has already been realized. Now, he wishes to renew it.*"[221]

Bl. Osanna of Mantua was very young—only six years old—when she had a vision of Christ wearing His crown of thorns and carrying His Cross. This vision convicted Osanna to give her entire life to Jesus, not only with a willingness to endure the sufferings life brought her way, but actively asking to share more in His Passion. She prayed, "O, my only Love! Must the thorns then be for Thee alone; for Thee alone the nails and the cross; and for me sweetness and consolation?

---

[220] Angela of Foligno, 74.

[221] Angela of Foligno, 106.

Ah! not so. I will not share Thy glory unless Thou make me also share Thy pains."[222]

When Bl. Osanna was 18, she experienced a mystical marriage to Jesus. When she was 30 years old, He fully conformed her to His crucified state, causing the stigmata to appear on her head, her side, and her feet. The wound on her side was caused by a long nail of Christ. He also at times allowed her to suffer the sacred wounds of His crowning with thorns. She endured the wounds without blood. St. Osanna tried to hide these wounds, although the wounds on her feet made it difficult for her to walk. Yet, even with the great mystical sufferings she endured, she (like St. Catherine of Siena) never forgot about Christ suffering in His body, the Church. Through everything she continued to be a spiritual guide to the poorest of the poor and the beggars for whom she cared. Much of her inheritance she gave to the needy.

St. Veronica Guiliani was another soul that Jesus took to Himself in a life of littleness, spousal love, and the Cross. Jesus did not spare this great saint ordinary suffering in this life, but her heart was continually fired with an increasing desire to unite more and more with Him on the Cross. St. Veronica Guiliani's mystical marriage with Christ was deeply united to her one-flesh union with His wounds. It

---

[222] Ossana of Mantua, as cited in Larry Peterson, "This Saint Didn't Want Sweetness if Jesus Had Nails and Thorns," *Aletheia*, June 19, 2020, https://aleteia.org/2020/06/19/this-saint-didnt-want-sweetness-if-jesus-had-thorns-and-nails/.

began by Jesus showing her a ring in His wounded Heart that would unite her to Him and explains:

> Know then, My beloved, that thou hast afforded Me this gratification by thy sufferings of the last two days. Every time that thou didst repeat the declaration that thou hadst no other will but Mine, and every time that thine act of resignation was renewed, thou didst give beauty to My holy Wounds; and of all thy sufferings together I have formed this jewel, which I keep in My Side, and on which I look with the greatest pleasure. Never shall I cease to behold it, and with loving eyes I shall see it grow constantly more and more beautiful. Now thou mayest indeed comprehend how dear to Me is thy suffering![223]

After seeing this ring, Veronica experienced the gift of the crowning with thorns, followed by a mystical marriage to Christ and the transverberation of her heart, which left permanent markings of His Passion upon her physical heart. Finally, she received the stigmata. She describes these all here:

> On Good Friday, I seemed to have a vision. . . . The Lord showed himself to me all wounded and crowned with thorns. . . . I felt the sorrow of sorrows that the Lord felt and at the

---

[223] Filippo Maria Salvatori, *The Life of St. Veronica Giuliani, Capuchin Nun* (Potosi, WI: St. Athanasius Press, 2014), 94.

same time I felt a deep sorrow for my sins and the offenses that I had committed. . . . He put this crown on my head and I seemed to have felt the thorns pierce through into the inside of my mouth, ears, all my head, my eyes, my temples, and my brain. It was so much suffering; I fell on the ground as if dead. The Lord lifted me up and told me: "**You will feel these pains as long as you are alive, more or less according to my wish.**" Again, I fell down and the Lord lifted me. I fell for a third time. Oh God! I cannot describe what the Lord communicated to me about His sufferings: I know very well that in a certain way he left an imprint of His Passion in my heart that I have never forgotten.[224]

Her experiences continued a few days later on Easter Sunday:

When she went to receive Holy Communion, she could hear the choirs of angels singing, "Come, spouse of Christ." Soon after she went into ecstasy and saw Jesus in all His glory with His Holy Wounds all resplendent. Jesus was seated on a throne made of gold with precious stones and there was another throne next to him made of alabaster and precious stones. This was the throne of the Virgin Mary. . . . Veronica could not explain how but she felt she was being dressed and adorned with precious stones and white lace. Then, she saw

---

[224] Veronica Giuliani, *The Diary of St. Veronica Giuliani,* trans. Bret Thoman (Georgia: Icona Press, 2023), 80–81.

Jesus like this, "He was so beautiful that I cannot describe it. ... His hands, feet and side, that is, His Wounds, were so resplendent that it seems to me that instead of wounds, they were beautiful precious stones. Only the wound of the side seemed to be open and from it came out rays of sun. ... It seems that inside this holy wound was the ring that I was to wear. At this time it seems that the Lord raised His right hand as if to bless me and said: **"Come spouse of Christ."** The Virgin Mary, together with all who were present said, **"Accept the crown which God prepared for you from all eternity."**

Then St. Catherine started undressing her and Jesus asked the Virgin Mary to redress her. The Virgin Mary took St. Catherine's cloak and put it on Veronica. This cloak was covered with precious stones that seemed to change colors, which symbolized the virtues. Then, Jesus took the ring from His side wound and placed it on the Virgin Mary's hand. The ring seemed to be made out of gold and covered by enamel which formed the name of Jesus on the precious stone. When Jesus put the ring on her finger, she felt a greater union with Him.[225]

The transverberaton happened on Christmas Eve, 1696:

---

[225] Angelica Avcikurt, "St. Veronica Giuliani: An Extraordinary Mystic and Victim Soul," *Mystics of the Church*, https://www.mysticsofthechurch.com/2015/07/st-veronica-giuliani-extraordinary.html.

I only remember that the child Jesus had like a bow and arrow in his hands, and it seemed that He sent it to my heart. I felt great pain. When I came back to my senses, I saw that my heart had been wounded and it was bleeding. I cannot express in writing or with words what the Lord communicated to me at that moment. I only remember that I experienced an intimate union with Him and He made me understand that this wound was nothing compared to the wound He would inflict on me soon." This wound would remain open and bleeding for several days and then it would close. She describes that she felt pain all the time and like a flame inside the wound. The wound would reopen at times and stay open for several days again. She would offer the pain of this wound in union to the sufferings and wounds of Jesus for the conversion of sinners.

The wound Jesus "would inflict on her soon" took place on March 8, 1697 before a crucifix: "Being in front of Him, very close, it seemed that He detached His right arm and with that great nail that He held in His hand, He wounded my heart. I felt great pain, and quickly returned to myself.[226]

Upon her death, the images of the Passion were found to be imprinted onto the heart of St. Veronica Giuliani in this manner:

---

[226] Avcikurt, "Extraordinary Mystic."

On Good Friday, April 5, 1697, St. Veronica Giuliani received the stigmata. She had a vision of Jesus crucified and the Virgin Mary, as Our Lady of Sorrows. She explains:

> The Lord drew this soul to Himself, to a loving union with Him, and such a desire came to me to be crucified with the Lord! Thus turned to the Most Holy Virgin, I said to her, "O Mother of Piety, of Mercy, implore me this grace of being crucified with my crucified Spouse!" And turning to her Son, she said to Him, "Hurry, quickly; crucify this soul," And the Lord said, "She shall have the grace."
>
> ... In an instant, I saw five resplendent rays come out of His Most Holy Wounds, and they all came toward me. And I saw the said rays become like little flames. In four, there were the nails, and in one, there was the spear, as of gold, all enflamed. And it passed through my heart from side to side,

---

[227] The image is taken from the handwritten journal of St. Veronica Giuliani and can be found at https://catholicmagazine.news/st-veronica-giuliani-the-passion-of-christ-in-veronica.

and the nails passed through my hands and feet. I felt great pain, but in the same pain, I saw myself and felt myself completely transformed into God. Right away, I was wounded. Those flames became again resplendent rays, and I saw them settle on the hands, feet and side of the Crucifix. The Lord confirmed me as His bride; He delivered me to His Mother; He dedicated me forever under her custody.[228]

In this we see a perfect example of a soul united with Jesus crucified, conformed to Our Lady of Sorrows, through littleness (humility), spousal love (mystical marriage) the Cross (victim soul). There was no part of St. Veronica's body that did not suffer with Christ. And yet, she explains how this pain somehow mystically transformed her in God. She was lifted out of herself in the midst of sharing Jesus' crucified love to also experience a union with His divinity. In this she could offer with Him as a priest, victim and altar suffering in atonement for sin. This led St. Veronica Guiliani to also be a mediatrix of grace for sinners, as she claimed that she placed herself as a victim between Christ and sinners.[229]

St. Mechthild also experienced a mystical marriage with Christ. He not only conformed her little by little to Himself—sharing His wounds within her heart, but allowed her to draw close to Him in order to drink directly from His side as St. Angela of Foligno did. By drinking of Christ's blood and love mystically pouring forth from

---

[228] Giuliani, *Diary*, 119–20.
[229] Salvatori, *Life of St. Veronica Giuliani*, 125.

His side, these saints were filled with both His human suffering and divine life simultaneously. In her writings St. Mechthild describes:

> While she wondered and waited in great desire, the Lord beckoned to her with his hand. Then Love took the soul and brought her to the Lord. She bent down to the wound in her only Savior's honey-flowing heart, quaffing from it a beverage filled with every sweetness and delight. There all her bitterness was turned into sweetness, all her fear into confidence. There too she ate from the honeyed Heart of Christ the sweetest fruit, which she took from God's heart and put in her mouth.[230]

Not long after, she was united with Jesus in a mystical marriage:

> While she was praying fervently and desiring the Beloved of her soul, suddenly a divine force drew her soul to itself so powerfully that she seemed to be sitting at the Lord's side. Pressing the soul against his heart in a sweet embrace, the Lord suffused and filled her so abundantly with his grace that it felt as if her whole body were flowing like a river into all the saints, suffusing them with new and special joy. They held their hearts in their hands like shining lamps, filled with the

---

[230] Mechthild of Hackeborn, *Mechthild of Hackeborn and the Nuns of Helfta,* trans. Barbara Newman (New York: Paulist Press, 2017), 128–29.

gift that God had infused into the soul, and thanked the Lord for that soul with deep gratitude and gladness.

Then Love spoke to the soul "Enter into the joy of your Lord" (Mt 25:21). At these words the soul was totally rapt into God. Just as a drop of water infused into wine is changed wholly into wine, so this blessed soul passed into God and became one spirit with him (1 Cor 6:17). In this union, the soul was annihilated in herself. But God strengthened her and said, "I will pour into you everything that a human being can ever grasp, and I will multiply my gifts in you as much as it is possible for mortals to bear." And Love said, "Rest here in the heart of your Lover, lest you be troubled in prosperous times. Rest there in remembrance of your Beloved's gifts, lest you be troubled in difficult times."[231]

Here we see clearly how the sufferings of Christ shared with His beloved bride became the source of her greatest joy, peace, strength and confident contentment.

St. Mary Magdalene de' Pazzi also experienced being united with Jesus in a mystical marriage that culminated in the sharing in His Passion. As we read her mystical experiences, we cannot help but think of how clearly she imitated Our Lady in docile littleness and fiery love, which allowed crucified Jesus to unite so closely to her that the Word was made flesh within her own body and soul in the form of the sacred stigmata. The height of her experiences being thus:

---

[231] Mechthild of Hackeborn, 129–30.

In Lent of 1585, the extraordinary phenomena reached their apex and on March 25, she felt the words "*Et Verbum caro factum est*" being engraved on her chest. On Monday of Holy Week, she received the holy stigmata of Christ in an invisible form.

On Holy Thursday, Sister Mary Magdalene became wrapt in an ecstasy that lasted twenty-six hours. Throughout the entire time in which the Passion of the Divine Redeemer was commemorated, she felt within herself, physically, the same sufferings, the same anguish and the same torments as Jesus. In astonishment, the other sisters saw her making her way through the rooms of the monastery, accompanying the Divine Master in his agony, at his judgement, and during his painful crowning with thorns. Finally, they saw her enter the chapter room with a cross on her shoulders. She prostrated on the ground to be nailed to the wood, then, with her back to the wall and arms open, she repeated the seven last words of Jesus Crucified.[232]

It is beautiful to read in this experience of St. Mary Magdalene de' Pazzi how Christ shared the experience of the Incarnation with her through sharing His Suffering. As He wrote *"And the Word*

---

[232] Sr. Clara Isabel Morazzani, "St. Mary Magdalene de Pazzi: God Is Love, and Is Not Loved!" *Heralds of the Gospel Magazine* 43 (May 2011), https://catholicmagazine.news/st-mary-magdalene-de-pazzi-god-is-love-and-is-not-loved/.

became flesh" upon her chest, He truly enfleshed Himself within her heart in the invisible stigmata. The deeper their union grew, the more profoundly she experienced the Passion. His wounds and blood were the pen that wrote His presence upon her heart and within her entire being. And this she bore valiantly because of the deep nuptial union of love that she shared with Him. Mystical union with Jesus crucified was the source of her pain, and yet also the source of her desire and strength to bear it.

Jesus Himself told St. Faustina that to be His bride she would have to be crucified with Him. The beloved always comes to resembled the lover. She is another great example of a saint who followed the path of littleness, humility and self-emptying, spousal love and the Cross. St. Faustina profoundly lived as Jesus' "little wife crucified." She explained:

> Jesus was suddenly standing before me, stripped of His clothes, His body completely covered with wounds, His eyes flooded with tears and blood, His face disfigured and covered with spittle. The Lord then said to me, "The bride must resemble her Betrothed." I understood these words to the very depth. There is no room for doubt here. My likeness to Jesus must be through suffering and humility. "See what love of human souls has done to Me. My daughter, in your heart I find everything that so great a number of souls refuses Me.

Your heart is My repose. I often wait with great graces until towards the end of prayer.[233]

St. Faustina understood that her bridal union with Christ would be through uniting first with His humility and then with His crucified love.

St. Lutgarde also followed Christ's pattern of spiritual transformation beginning with littleness and culminating in her soul's union with His crucified spousal love. It was actually St. Lutgarde's great love for the littleness and martyrdom of St. Agnes that catapulted her into a mystical marriage with Christ which led to her receiving His wounds in the stigmata:

> She had a tremendous desire to prove her love for Christ by suffering martyrdom for His sake. . . . One night, then, she had gone to the dormitory and was praying by her bed before retiring, when the thought of martyrdom came to her. She remembered St. Agnes, and was filled with so powerful and so burning a desire to die for Christ, like the Roman virgin martyr, that the might of her love became almost strong enough to kill her outright. Then suddenly a vein near her heart burst, and through a wide-open wound in her side, blood began to pour forth, soaking her robe and cowl. As she lost her senses and sank to the floor, Christ appeared to her, in glory, His face radiant with joy, and said to her: "Because

---

[233] Kowalska, *Diary*, no. 268.

Chapter 9: The Saints Experience Nuptial Union with Christ

of the great and fervent desire of martyrdom with which thou hast now shed thy blood, know that thou shalt receive the same reward in heaven as the most blessed Agnes received, in the severing of her head for My faith: because by thy desire even unto the shedding of blood, though hast equaled her martyrdom." Thus wounded once, with a wound like the spear wound in Christ's Heart, Lutgarde was never wounded again: but she kept the scar until the end of her life. This occurred in her twenty-ninth year.[234]

Another Carmelite, St. Miriam the little Arab, was the epitome of humility—and for that reason she is always referred to as the *little Arab*. And yet, St. Miriam's profound simplicity and humility propelled her into such a profound spousal union with Christ that she not only suffered the stigmata, but repeatedly suffered the entire Passion of Christ as well as other unimaginable sufferings. This prodigy, even while yet young, was resolute to become married only to Christ. Her faith was tested greatly when a Muslim servant of her uncle (her legal guardian after the death of her parents) threatened her with death if she would not apostatize the faith. Refusing, he slit her throat and threw her in a ditch to die. Yet the Blessed Mother appeared to her, stitched her throat and nursed her back to health eventually

---

[234] "St. Lutgarde of Aywières: The First Known Woman with the Stigmata," *Mystics of the Church*, https://www.mysticsofthechurch.com/2015/09/st-lutgarde-of-aywieres-first-known.html. This experience is described in greater length in Thomas Merton, *What are These Wounds?* (Mansfield Centre, CT: Martino Publishing, 2014), 127.

leading her to safety in a church where a priest helped her sneak away from her uncle and the servant. She embraced the life of a servant and nanny, which eventually led her to France and joining the Carmel. As if a living martyrdom was not enough of a consummation of her heart's stalwart faith and union with Christ, she continued on the path of living martyrdom by suffering His Passion with Him. St. Miriam, the little Arab, also was truly a "little wife crucified" of Christ, suffering in imitation of Our Lady and baring in her body the wounds that Mary bore within her soul:

> The stigmata of the heart was the first to be manifested. She was twenty years of age, and it happened in August, 1866 at Marseille. She was praying in the chapel one evening, when, in the tabernacle she saw Jesus, who appeared to her with His five wounds and the crown of thorns. It seemed to her she saw coals of wrath in His hands. She heard Jesus say to His Mother prostrate at His feet: "Oh, how My Father is offended!" The little postulant then sprang toward Jesus, she put her hand on the wound of His Heart, exclaiming: "My God, give me, please, all these sufferings, but have mercy on sinners." Coming out of the ecstasy, she saw her hand covered with blood, and she experienced a severe pain in her left side: the latter would bleed every Friday.
>
> On March 27, 1867, the other stigmata appeared. The privileged one of the Crucified confided to the mistress of novices:

"It seemed to me that I was gathering roses to decorate Mary's altar: these roses appeared to have thorns on both sides, and the thorns were thrust in my hands and into my feet. When I came to myself, my mouth was very bitter, my feet and hands swollen: in the middle of my hands and on my feet there were black bumps." The following day, Thursday, the sufferings continued to increase until Friday. It was the Feast of the five wounds of Christ. In the morning, about ten o'clock, the black scabs fell off, the crown of thorns appeared on her forehead, blood flowed from her head and feet. The prodigy was renewed during the months of April and the first two weeks of May. It ceased upon an order of the mistress of novices. This latter, in order to put an end to the rumors that were circulating in the community, asked the postulant to obtain from God that nothing would appear exteriorly. To the great joy of the stigmatist, the wounds closed and healed up.[235]

St. Clare of Montefalco had an incredible experience upon becoming united with Christ as His "little wife crucified." Similar to St. Veronica Giuliani, she accepted an offer from Jesus for Him to plant His Cross within her heart. St. Clare of Montefalco came to so resemble her crucified Husband that upon her death a literal crucifix

---

[235] "Saint Mariam Baouardy, the Little Arab and Lily of Palestine," *Mystics of the Church*, https://www.mysticsofthechurch.com/2010/07/blessed-mariam-baouardy-little-arab-and.html.

along with images of the scourging, crown of thorns, and instruments of His Passion were found imprinted upon her heart:

> Clare reported having a vision in which she saw herself being judged in front of God. Clare also reported having a vision of Jesus dressed as a poor traveler. She described His countenance as being overwhelmed by the weight of the cross, and His body as showing signs of fatigue. Clare knelt in front of Him, and trying to stop Him asked, "My Lord, where are you going"? Jesus answered her, "I have looked all over the world for a strong place where to plant this cross firmly, and I have not found any." After she reached the cross, making known her desire to help Him carry it, He said to her, "Clare, I have found a place for My cross here. I have finally found someone to whom I can trust mine cross," and He implanted it in her heart. The intense pain that she felt in all her being, upon receiving the cross in her heart, remained with her. The rest of her years were spent in pain and suffering, and yet she continued to joyfully serve her fellow Nuns as their Abbess.

She often told the sisters in her Order, "If you seek the Cross of Christ, take my heart, there you will find the suffering Lord." After her death, the Sisters remembered her words and had her heart extracted. The larger than average heart when opened revealed astonishing symbols of the Lord's Passion, all composed of cardiac tissue.²³⁶

²³⁷

St. Gemma Galgani likewise through her encounters with Jesus came to imitate Him in His littleness and as the fire of His love consumed her, she underwent a mystical marriage culminating in a one-flesh union with Him in the stigmata. Her spiritual director recorded her experience of this as thus (these are her words that he wrote down):

> Oh love, oh infinite love! . . . See: Your love, oh Lord, Your love penetrates even to my body, with too much fury. When, when will I unite with You, oh Lord, Who with such force of

---

²³⁶ "Mysterious Heart of Saint Clare of Montefalco," *Anointing Fire Catholic Ministries*, August 11, 2019, https://www.afcmmedia.org/Mystical-07.html.

²³⁷ Rye Evangelista, *Heart of St. Clare of Montefalco*, Flickr, June 26, 2008, https://flic.kr/p/4Z1yJW.

love keeps me in union here on earth? . . . Do it, do it! . . . Let me die, and die of love! . . . What a beautiful death, oh Lord, to die a victim of love . . . a victim for You! Calm down, calm down oh Jesus; if not, Your love will end up burning me to ashes! . . . Oh love, oh infinite love! . . . Oh love of my Jesus! . . . Let Your love penetrate my all; from You I want nothing else. My God, my God, I love You! . . .

Jesus, You ask only love from me; and I, in order to love You, ask much love also, for I have not enough. . . . When, Jesus, will You become my Heavenly Spouse?"

You are on fire Oh Lord, and I burn. Oh pain, oh infinitely happy love! Oh sweet fire! Oh sweet flames! And would You wish my heart to become a flame? Oh, I have found the flame that destroys and reduces to ashes! Cease, cease, I cannot withdraw my heart from so much fire. What am I saying? No; rather come Jesus! I will open my heart to You; put Thy Divine fire into it. You are a flame, and let my heart be turned into a flame! . . . Come then, Oh Jesus! Your heart is a flame and you wish mine to be turned into a flame as well. . . . Jesus, I feel I must die when you are throbbing so in my heart.[238]

After being enflamed with the fires of Christ's love and a longing for deeper union with Him, St. Gemma was gifted a one-flesh union

---

[238] "St. Gemma Galgani, the Lover of Jesus," *Mystics of the Church*, https://www.mysticsofthechurch.com/2009/12/st-gemma-galgani-lover-of-jesus.html.

with Jesus through His wounds bursting forth from her own body. Her experience of the stigmata was described in such a way:

> The Blessed Mother appeared to her, along with her guardian Angel. The Blessed Virgin told her: "Jesus my Son loves you very much and He wishes to give you a grace. Do you know how to make yourself worthy of it?" In my misery I did not know what to answer. She continued "I will be your Mother. Will you be a true daughter?" She then spread her mantle and covered me with it. At that moment Jesus appeared with all His wounds open, but blood no longer came out of those wounds. Rather, flames of fire issued forth from them and in an instant these flames came to touch my hands, my feet and my heart. I felt as if I would die. I fell to the floor, but my Mother supported me, keeping me covered in her mantle. I had to remain several hours in that position. Finally she kissed me on my forehead, and all vanished, and I found myself kneeling on the floor. But I still felt an intense pain in my hands, feet and heart. I arose to go to bed, and I then noticed that blood was flowing from those parts where I felt pain. I covered them as well as I could, and then with the help of my angel, I was able to go to bed. These sufferings and pains, although they afflicted me, filled me with perfect peace. The next morning I was able to go to Communion only with great difficulty, and I put on a pair of gloves in order to hide my hands. I could hardly stand on my feet, and I thought I would

die at any minute. The sufferings continued until 3pm on Friday afternoon, the solemnity of the Sacred Heart of Jesus.[239]

St. Rose of Lima said, *"Apart from the cross, there is no other ladder by which we may get to heaven."*[240] She deeply understood that to be the bride of Christ meant to be crowned with thorns and united with Him. As a child, her family tried to adorn her with pretty clothes and a wreath of roses. At first, she resisted such pomp, but then she realized that she could use the wreath of roses to hide a crown of thorns that she wore upon her head as penance. She endured great sufferings that included the persecution of her beloved Indians, personal illness of asthma and arthritis, and interior disturbances through dreams. Her only spiritual support came from her close Dominican friend, St. Martin de Porres,

> who assured her that her visions and spiritual aridity were signs of the highest friendship with God. Other religious, through jealousy, had Rose examined by the Inquisition. The inquisitors found her to be enjoying God's highest favor in the midst of her suffering and desolation. During this time, Rose received the grace of mystical marriage with Christ and had a ring engraved with the words He spoke to her: "Rose

---

[239] "St. Gemma Galgani, the Lover of Jesus."

[240] Rose of Lima: *Vita mirabilis*, ed. P. Hansen (Louvain, 1668), in *Catechism*, § 618.

of My Heart, be My spouse." Not long after, she died of a terrible fever and paralysis at age 31.[241]

St. Catherine del Ricci also was made into a "little wife crucified" of Christ. At a young age she suffered great illness that humbled her greatly, but also protected her from the arranged marriage her father had ordered. He succumbed to her request to enter a convent only because of her illness, which immediately disappeared upon her entrance. St. Catherine del Ricci felt that she could not love Christ as she ought with her own weak, little heart and so she begged Jesus to give her a new one. One day in ecstasy Jesus granted her request in a greater way than she imagined by giving her the Heart of His Mother so that she could love Him as Our Lady did. Not long afterwards she was mystically married to Him. In a vision He took a ring off of His finger and put it on her hand saying, *"My daughter, receive this ring as pledge and proof that thou dost now, and ever shalt, belong to Me."*[242] This ring was visible to many of her sisters, leaving a permanent red mark on her finger and looking as if it was hidden underneath her flesh. A year after becoming Christ's little spouse, her marriage was consummated on the Cross:

---

[241] "St. Rose of Lima," Dominican Sisters of Saint Cecilia, https://www.nashvilledominican.org/community/our-dominican-heritage/our-saints-and-blesseds/st-rose-lima/.

[242] "Saint Catherine de' Ricci," in Bob and Penny Lord, *Visions of Heaven, Hell and Purgatory* (Morrilton, AR: Journeys of Faith Publishing, 2009), 9.

She went into a long ecstasy which lasted twenty-eight hours! She saw a beautiful Angel approach her with the arrows of the Passion, and felt the pains shoot into her hands, feet and side.... Her stigmata ... was manifested in different ways to different people. Some saw what is considered the traditional Stigmata, that is the hands, feet and side pierced and bleeding. Others saw a brilliant light coming from the wounds, so dazzling they had to look away. Then there were those who saw healed wounds, with just the red puffiness and swelling of wounds that had healed, black spots appearing in the center (of the wounds.) In these instances, the blood under the skin appeared to be flowing in a circular movement around the black center.[243]

Catherine (also) received the crown of thorns. One day, our Blessed Mother appeared to Catherine. She was holding crowns and offered them to Catherine: one of the thorns and one of silver. She already had the stigmata and was experiencing great pain; weak, she asked for the crown of silver. Our Lady said: "Catherine which crown did our spouse wear?" Catherine replied: "Then Mother Mary, place on my head the one my Lord wore.[244]

St. Gertrude was also deeply united with the littleness, spousal love and the Cross of Christ. One day she began to pray, *"O most*

---

[243] "Saint Catherine de' Ricci," in Lord, 10.
[244] "Saint Catherine de' Ricci," in Lord, 12.

merciful Lord, engrave Thy Wounds upon my heart with Thy most precious Blood, that I may read in them both Thy grief and Thy love; and that the memory of Thy Wounds may ever remain in my inmost heart, to excite my compassion for Thy sufferings and to increase in me Thy love."[245] Shortly thereafter she wrote, "I perceived in spirit that Thou hadst imprinted in the depth of my heart the adorable marks of Thy sacred Wounds, even as they are on Thy Body, that Thou hadst cured my soul, in imprinting these Wounds on it, and that, to satisfy its thirst, Thou hadst given it the precious beverage of thy love."[246]

Seven years later St. Gertrude received the piercing of the heart in such a manner. One day after Communion—recollecting herself deeply in prayer—"it seemed to me that I saw a ray of light like an arrow coming forth from the Wound of the right side of the crucifix, which was in an elevated place, and it continued, as it were, to advance and retire for some time, sweetly attracting my cold affections."[247] The following Wednesday she said, "Thou camest suddenly before me, and didst imprint a wound in my heart."[248]

It was only after imprinting His crucified love upon St. Gertrude's heart that the child Jesus came to unite most intimately with her in full. She recalled that this Christmas grace as such:

---

[245] Gertrude the Great, *The Life and Revelations of St. Gertrude the Great*, trans. Poor Clares of Kenmare, NC (Gastonia: Tan, 2002), 77.

[246] Gertrude the Great, 78.

[247] Gertrude the Great, 80.

[248] Gertrude the Great, 80.

I say, my soul beheld before it suddenly a delicate Child, but just born, in whom were concealed the greatest gifts of perfection. I imagined that I perceived this precious deposit in my bosom with the tenderest affection. As I possessed it within me, it seemed to me that all at once I was changed into the color of this Divine Infant, if we may be permitted to call "color" that which cannot be compared to anything visible. ... My soul which was enriched by the presence of my Beloved, soon knew, by its transports of joy, that it possessed the presence of its Spouse. Then it received these words with exceeding avidity, which were presented as a delicious beverage to satisfy the ardor of its thirst: "As I am the figure of the substance of God, My Father, in His Divinity, so also you shall be the figure of My substance in My Humanity, receiving in your deified soul the infusions of My Divinity, as the air receives the brightness of the solar rays, that these rays may penetrate you so intimately as to prepare you for the closest union with Me."[249]

These are only a few examples of the numerous graces that St. Gertrude received in order to become Jesus Christ's little wife crucified.

One more saint who followed Jesus in littleness and fiery divine love that united her to the Cross with him was Venerable Antonetta Meo. She was a beautiful example of littleness simply because she

---

[249] Gertrude the Great, 82–83.

only lived to six years of age. Preserved in deep innocence, she accepted the powerful divine love of her beloved Jesus into her heart and this love drew forth a great desire in her heart to suffer with Him. Her crucifixion came through the form of cancer that eventually claimed her young life. And yet she offered to Jesus all of her suffering for the salvation of souls. She often would write letters to Christ and we see her profound spirituality in these letters:

> Dear Jesus the Crucified, I love You so much. I love You so I want to stay with You on the Calvary and I suffer with joy because I know I'm on Calvary. Dear Jesus, I thank You for having sent me this illness because it is a means to get to Paradise. Dear Jesus tell God the Father that I love Him, too. Dear Jesus I want to be Your lamp and Your lily dear Jesus. Dear Jesus, give me the strength to bear this pain that I offer to You for sinners. Dear Jesus tell the Holy Spirit to enlighten me with love and fill me with its seven gifts. Dear Jesus tell sweet Virgin Mary that I love Her so much and I want to stay with Her on Calvary because I want to be Your victim of love dear Jesus. Dear Jesus, I entrust my father confessor to You and grant him every necessary favor. Dear Jesus I entrust my parents and my sister Margherita to You. Dear Jesus, greetings and kisses.—Antonietta of Jesus[250]

---

[250] Antonietta Meo, Letter 162, June 2, 1937, in *Lamp & Lily*, trans. Becket Ghioto (self-pub., 2018), 217–18.

Many other female mystics and saints—most particularly St. Margaret of Cortona and St. Hildegard—similarly experienced the nuptials of Christ on the tree of the Cross. In this they were first led on a path of self-abnegation where they embraced a great littleness before Christ, then being mystically espoused and married to Him and thus, were called to share in His Passion with Him bearing His sacred wounds on their own bodies to the world.

Jesus Christ not only calls female souls to a mystical marriage on the Cross with Him, but as we have seen glimpses in the writing of St. John of the Cross already, He calls all souls to this union of divine love which transcends our human experience of gender and love. The mystical marriage of a man to Christ resembles a soul marrying their God, a child resting on the heart of their beloved Father, or as Bl. Henry Suzo experienced, a marriage to Christ through the Holy Spirit Who he called Eternal Wisdom.

St. John of the Cross underwent a profound purgation where he was stripped to the very core of humble littleness both by experiencing a dark night of the soul while simultaneously being imprisoned by his Carmelite brothers. The profound suffering he endured not only conformed him to the little, meek, and humble Savior, but imprinted upon the heart of St. John of the Cross the interior wounds that Jesus suffered on the Cross, which in turn united him as one with Christ in a mystical marriage. Similar to St. Mother Teresa who suffered the Passion with Christ through sharing in His darkness, feelings of abandonment, rejection, fear, and thirst, St. John of the Cross valiantly accepted a great interior martyrdom with Jesus eventually leading to a complete union with Him. We are blessed to have an account of this through the poem he wrote while suffering interiorly while imprisoned where he describes what it was like to rest his head on the Heart of his beloved as St. John the apostle did. Yet the Heart he rested upon was the Heart of love crucified. He describes this experience thus in his poems *The Dark Night of the Soul* and *Living Flame of Love*. In the first, he describes the process of being made little and emptied out through darkness, solitude, and thirst. In the second he unites with his Beloved, yet through a flame of love that wounds him—cauterizes him—one with Christ. In this way, he greatly resembles Our Lady of Sorrows with the seven swords in Her Heart under the Cross. In *Dark Night of the Soul* we read:

> In this night so full of chance; in secrecy, since none caught sight of me; since, too, I was aware of naught and without light or guide save that which in my heart was burning.
>
> And this conducted me far surer than the light of brightest day; thence, where for me eagerly was waiting He whom I know so well, aside, there were no one could part us.
>
> O night that was a guide! O night, more lovely than the rosy dawn! O night, you that united the most beloved with her lover, transforming the beloved into her lover.[251]

He later additionally writes in *The Living Flame of Love*:

---

[251] John of the Cross, *Dark Night of the Soul*, st. 3–5, in Stein, *Science of the Cross*, 43.

O flame of living love, most tenderly, didst wound my soul in deepest center—since you are no longer full of pain, perfect, if it be your will! Tear through the veil of this sweet encounter!

O cautery so sweet! O wound full of delight! O soft hand! O gentle touch! Taste of eternal life you give and pay off every debt! By slaying, you change death to life.

O luminous lamps of fire in whose resplendent rays the caves of sense—profound abyss—which once were dark, bereft of sight, with rarest beauty unite in gift for the Beloved warmth and light.

How gently, filled with love, you awake in my inmost heart where secretly you swell, alone: with your breath so delicious, replete with good and glory, how delicately you enamor me![252]

Another male mystic who profoundly experienced a mystical marriage with Christ was Bl. Bernard de Hoyos, SJ, an eighteenth-century Spanish Jesuit. Like St. Veronica Giuliani he experienced a nuptial union with Christ as a Child, and like St. John the Evangelist he rested on Jesus' chest like the beloved. He had a vision of the mystical marriage of his soul to God and was given a ring to confirm this grace, similar to the experiences of St. Catherine of Siena, St. Angela of Foligno and St. Veronica Giuliani. He described his experience as thus:

---

[252] John of the Cross, *Living Flame of Love*, st. 1–4, in Stein, 6:185–86.

After I went to Communion on Assumption Day, I heard the angels singing: "Behold the bridegroom who cometh. Go ye forth to meet him!" (Mt 25:6). My soul composed itself and in an imaginative vision I saw all that follows. I felt myself robed by unknown hands with a white garment adorned with precious stones—the wedding garments, a symbol of purity and of the other virtues. Immediately there appeared on the one hand St. Michael, St. Therese, our father St. Ignatius and St. Francis de Sales, the former vested as a priest and the latter as a bishop; on the other, my holy angel, St. Mary Magdalen of Pazzi, Venerable Father Padial and St. Francis Xavier also as a priest. In imaginative vision could be seen, beyond the two rows of saints, three beautiful thrones, one vacant and smaller, another occupied by the Most Blessed Virgin Mary, to the right hand of Christ, who occupied the third, wholly of gold with three steps. In an intellectual vision I also contemplated the Most Blessed Trinity, and this mystery I grasped still more clearly than ever before as well as that of the God-Man who presently, as a divine lodestone, attracted to Himself all the affections of my soul.

Clad in white as told, I approached the degrees of Jesus' throne, to whom I was presented by the Most Blessed Virgin Mary. I kissed with great joy the sacred wounds of His feet, and then He asked if my soul desired to be His spouse, for He wished to be its Spouse. Lost in its nothingness and in His love, my soul gave I know not what answer, but it meant: "Behold the handmaid of the Lord," (Lk 1:38). Then rising from the throne, He had me mount to its topmost step, and, His divine right hand clasping mine, He said, "I, in the name of My Divinity and of My Humanity in My quality of Sovereign Priest with My divine and human natures, am plighting troth with you, O cherished soul, an eternal union of love. Be seated now on the throne of My spouses and experience what you are to possess eternally."

Always holding my right hand, the Lord had me occupy the empty throne; then He fitted on my finger a gold ring set with a sparkling gem which I did not recognize. "May this ring," He said to me, "be an earnest of our love. You are Mine, and I am yours. You may call yourself and sign Bernard of Jesus, thus, as I said to my spouse, St. Theresa, you are Bernard of Jesus and I am Jesus of Bernard. My honor is yours; your honor Mine. Consider My glory that of your Spouse; I will consider yours that of My spouse. All Mine is yours and all yours is Mine. What I am by nature you share by grace. You and I are one!"

These and other very tender words Jesus spoke to my soul. The ring on my middle finger I confided to the Most Blessed Virgin Mary as to the Keeper of so great a token.[253]

Well-known is the experience of St. Francis of Assisi who embraced such a great kenosis and shrinking of his ego that he became

---

[253] Henri Béchard, *The Visions of Bernard Francis de Hoyos, S. J.* (New York: Vantage Press, 1959), 89–91.

the very icon of poverty lived both on a physical plane as well as interiorly. He was so little of heart before the Lord that he did not shy away from becoming the poorest man on earth—giving away all of his riches—and humbling himself to the point of embracing and kissing a leper. It was precisely because he imitated Christ's Own humility that he was granted such a great love for our Savior and that he eventually was imprinted with His very wounds on his body. His experience is described thus:

> On September 14, 1224—feast of the Exultation of the Holy Cross—while making a retreat in the mountains of La Verna, a seraph visited St. Francis of Assisi during his prayer. The saint was asking how to better please God, so he opened the Bible several times to read God's Word. Repeatedly he opened to the account of our Lord's crucifixion. He sensed that it was Christ's crucifixion that best pleased God.
>
> St Francis prayed: "O Lord Jesus Christ, before I die I ask you for two graces; first, that in my lifetime I may feel, as far as possible, both in my soul and body, that pain which you, sweet Lord, endured in the hour of your most bitter Passion; second, that I may feel in my heart as far as possible that excess of love which moved you, O Son of God, to suffer so cruel a Passion for us sinners."
>
> As he prayed an angelic seraph appeared descending from heaven. The angel had six fiery and shining wings. Seraphim (or seraphs) are those angels who are closest to God, in constant praise and worship of his majesty, singing "Holy,

holy, holy." Between the seraph's wings appeared a figure of a man whose hands and feet were fastened to a cross. Two wings floated above the head of the man, two extended outward for flight, and two covered his body.

Upon seeing this, St. Francis was flooded with emotions of both joy and sorrow: the tender and affectionate look of Christ towards him as he was carried by the seraph filled St. Francis with joy; yet the pain of being nailed to the cross caused St. Francis to experience great sorrow. This led to a wonderful dialogue of flaming love.

When the vision ended, St. Francis realized that he had received the stigmata, the miraculous impressions in his own flesh of the wounds of Jesus Christ: the nail prints appeared in his hands and feet with the nails and a wound piercing his side from which flowed blood. These wounds caused St. Francis constant pain, and would last two years until his death. The wounds helped him identify himself with the totality of Christ's salvific love, a merciful love with an intensity that was blinding, like looking into the sun.[254]

Thomas of Celano wrote about this experience a few years after St. Francis' death:

---

[254] "St. Francis of Assisi Receives Stigmata from Seraphs," Saint Mary of the Angels, https://www.sma-church.org/st-francis-of-assisi-receives-stigmata-from-seraphs/.

The marks of nails began to appear in his hands and feet, just as he had seen them slightly earlier in the crucified man above him. His wrists and feet seemed to be pierced by nails, with the heads of the nails appearing on his wrists and on the upper sides of his feet, the points appearing on the other side. The marks were round on the palm of each hand but elongated on the other side, and small pieces of flesh jutting out from the rest took on the appearance of the nail-ends, bent and driven back. In the same way the marks of nails were impressed on his feet and projected beyond the rest of the flesh. Moreover, his right side had a large wound as if it had been pierced with a spear, and it often bled so that his tunic and trousers were soaked with his sacred blood.[255]

St. Charles de Foucauld also embraced a life of deep littleness with Christ—so much so that his followers are called "little sisters" and "little brothers." Embracing a life of deep poverty, humility, simplicity, and self-sacrifice, he went to live as a hermit alone in a Muslim region in Algeria. He fell so in love with Christ that he arranged the affairs of his day in synch with the heartbeat of Jesus in Nazareth—always striving to imitate His great humility and poverty. This powerful love of Christ that drove him into the pagan desert also claimed his life. Desiring union with Christ crucified, he eventually

---

[255] "The Stigmata of Saint Francis of Assisi," Sacred Heart Catholic Church, https://sacredheartfla.org/about-us/being-franciscan/fraciscan-feast-days/the-feast-of-the-stigmata-of-st-francis-of-assisi/.

was given to drink of the cup of martyrdom and was killed by a Muslim for his love of Jesus. Although his spirituality differed from other mystics with great visions of espousals with Christ, St. Charles de Foucauld followed the same path these others did (in littleness, spousal love and the Cross)—yet he lived it out in the midst of ordinary and often hidden suffering.

Perhaps the most well-known stigmatist of our time is St. Padre Pio. He also very well fits the diagram Christ set forth for all souls (desiring to follow Him) to conform to His littleness, spousal love, and the Cross. Padre Pio was humbled from the very time he was a child and permitted by the Lord to suffer terribly at the hands of the evil one. In continually lowering himself before the hand of the Almighty, God was able to continually fill his soul with His Own passionate fiery love—and eventually this love imprinted the sacred wounds of Christ on his body. St. Padre Pio bore these wounds heroically for 50 years, after which they disappeared as miraculously as they first had come. The physical wounds of Christ on St. Padre Pio's hands, feet, side, and shoulder were not enough to satiate his incredible longing to partake in Christ's Passion with Him, in order to save souls. St. Padre Pio understood suffering not only as the needle that sewed his heart one with the Lord's, but also as the instrument he needed to use in order to snatch souls heading towards perdition. His writing powerfully expresses both his love union with Christ in suffering, as well as his respect for its power to plead for sinners before the throne of God. These great graces would pour out upon this son of St. Francis without hindering his ever-growing stance of weakness and humility before both God and man. He explained:

When Jesus wants me to understand that He loves me, He allows me to savor the wounds, the thorns, the agonies of His passion.... When He wants to delight me, He fills my heart with that spirit which is all fire; He speaks to me of His delights. But when He wants to be delighted, He speaks to me of His sorrows, He invites me—with a voice full of both supplication and authority—to affix my body [to the cross] in order to alleviate His suffering. Who can resist Him? I realize how much my miseries have caused Him to suffer, how much I have offended Him. I desire no other than Jesus alone, I want nothing more than His pains (because this is what Jesus wishes). Let me say—since no one can hear me—I am disposed to remain forever deprived of the sweetness Jesus allows me to feel. I am ready to suffer Jesus hiding His beautiful eyes from me, so long as He does not hide His love from me, because then I would die. But I do not feel I can be deprived of suffering—for this I lack strength.... Perhaps I have not yet expressed myself clearly with regards to the secret of this suffering. Jesus, the Man of Sorrows, wants all Christians to imitate Him; He has offered this chalice to me yet again, and I have accepted it. That is why He does not spare me. My humble sufferings are worth nothing, but Jesus delights in them because He loved [suffering] on earth. ... Now shouldn't this alone be enough to humiliate me, to make me seek to be hidden from the eyes of men, since I was made worthy of suffering with Jesus and as Jesus? Ah, my father! I feel too keenly my ingratitude toward God's majesty.

O what precious moments these are. It is a happiness that the Lord gives me to relish almost always in moments of affliction. At these moments, more than ever, when the whole world troubles and weighs on me, I desire nothing other than to love and to suffer. Yes, my father, even in the midst of so much suffering I am happy because it seems as if my heart is beating with Jesus' heart.[256]

I want nobody but Jesus alone; I desire nothing else than suffering from Him (which is Jesus' Own desire). ... I am ready to suffer Jesus' hiding of His beautiful eyes from me, as long as He doesn't hide His love, which would kill me. But to be deprived of suffering, I am not able, I do not have the strength.[257]

He [God] chooses some souls. From among these, despite all my faults, He has also chosen my soul to help Him in the great project of saving humanity. The more these chosen souls suffer without any comfort, the more the sufferings of our good Jesus are lightened.[258]

---

[256] Pio of Pietrelcina, *Secrets of a Soul: Padre Pio's Letters to His Spiritual Directors,* trans. Elvira G. DiFabio (Boston: Pauline Books and Media, 2002), 44–45.

[257] Pio of Pietrelcina, *Inspiration from the Letters of Padre Pio: Words of Light,* no. 335, trans. Andrew Tulloch, comp. Raniero Cantalamessa (Brewster, Massachusetts: Paraclete Press, 2000), 68.

[258] Pio of Pietrelcina, *Letters of Padre Pio,* no. 304, p. 70.

"My son," said Jesus, "I need victims to calm the just, divine, anger of my Father; renew the sacrifice of your entire self to me, and do it without any reservation."[259]

Alas, I feel that sharp pain within my spirit, the thorn that agonizes me day and night! What bitter pain I experience in my extremities and in my heart! All these pains keep me in a continual swoon, and however sweet this swoon may be, it is equally painful and sharp.[260]

St. Padre Pio on several occasions was demanded in obedience to recount how he received the stigmata from Christ. In a more detailed account that he gave to his spiritual director he wrote about both this experience, as well as the experience of his heart being wounded by love:

> I saw before me a mysterious person, similar to the one I saw on the fifth of August, different only in that he had hands, feet and side which were pouring with blood.
>
> The sight of him terrified me. I would not know how to tell you what I felt in that instant. I felt myself dying, and I would be dead if the Lord hadn't kept my heart going, which I felt leaping about in my chest.
>
> The vision of this person withdrew, and I noticed that my hands, feet and side were pierced and pouring with blood.

---

[259] Pio of Pietrelcina, no. 343, p. 72.
[260] Pio of Pietrelcina, no. 1103, p. 72.

Imagine the agony that I felt then, and that I continue to feel almost every day.

The wound of the heart poured constantly with blood, especially from Thursday evening until Saturday. My Father, I am dying of the pain because of this agony and the ensuing shame that I feel deep in my soul. I fear that I will die for loss of blood if the Lord does not listen to the groans of my poor heart, and to my call for an end to what's happening to me.[261]

I had stayed in church to make my thanksgiving for the mass, when all of a sudden, I felt my heart wounded by a dart of fire so living and burning that I thought I would die of it. I cannot find the right words to help you understand the intensity of this flame. I am completely powerless to express myself? Would you believe it? The soul, victim of these consolations, has become mute. . . . What a beautiful thing it is to become a victim of love. . . . My dear Father, at present Jesus has withdrawn His lance of fire, but the wound is mortal.[262]

The spirituality of St. Padre Pio is an exact identification of Our Lord in His littleness, fiery spousal love and crucifixion. He explains:

First of all, I must confess that for me it is a great disgrace not to know how to describe this volcano, which is constantly

---

[261] Pio of Pietrelcina, no. 1093, p. 76.
[262] Pio of Pietrelcina, 114.

burning and which burns me. Jesus put it in this tiny heart of mine, and I can neither describe it nor quench it. The explanation is simple: I am devoured by the love of God and the love of neighbor. God is always fixed in my mind and imprinted on my heart. I never lose sight of Him; I admire His beauty, His smiles and the troubles He gives, His mercy, His vengeance, or better, the rigors of His justice.[263]

There are other male saints who, after undergoing a great personal kenosis with Christ, experienced a physical manifestation of Christ's crucified, spousal love and presence uniting with them. There was St. Philip Neri, whose heart was physically enlarged with Love. There was St. Charles Borromeo, whose heart is preserved incorrupt—a sign that the Holy Spirit completely consumed it with heavenly grace. There was St. Edmund Campion, whose heart was cruelly torn from his body in his martyrdom—the Lord thus using a natural means to emphasize to the world the special love of this great martyr for Christ willing to withstand the greatest of tortures for Him. St. Thomas Aquinas was so humble that he was named "the dumb ox" and was united so fully with the pure love of Christ that while suffering imprisonment in his family's dungeon and overcoming the advances of a prostitute sent to lead him to sin, was granted with a grace of such preservation in purity of heart that he was never again tempted by this sin. In icons of St. Thomas Aquinas one can always see a sunburst on his breast– representing the purity of his

---

[263] Pio of Pietrelcina, no. 1047, p. 112.

love and the radiance of Christ—Truth Incarnate—Who came to live fully in him. St. Anthony Maria Claret was so deeply united with Jesus that he carried the Eucharistic presence perpetually in his own heart—depicted in icons of him as a light hovering upon his breast.

The ways of God's love are manifold and unique, always dependent on the creative artistry of God as well as the character of the soul He unites to Himself. And yet, while the means of achieving union with Christ crucified as the Divine Bridegroom vary greatly in each unique individual, the result is always the conformity of a soul to Christ first in His littleness, and then in His spousal love consuming them in and through the Cross. Once a soul is united with Jesus crucified, she begins to live fully as a priest, victim and altar with Him. It is a soul's union with Christ in this way that her suffering becomes enormously efficacious for others and in this imitates Our Lady in co-redeeming with Him. This is what we will explore deeper in the next chapter.

Chapter 10

The Saints' Call to the Cross and Co-redeeming Love—Priests, Altars and Victims with Christ

St. Teresa Margaret Redi said, *"The mirror we have to consult to arrive at divine union is the Sacred Heart of Jesus crucified."*[264] Just as Our Lady was called to be a perfect reflection of Jesus Christ—Priest, Altar, and Victim—by becoming His Helpmate, so too the entire Church is called to follow Her example of this discipleship. All souls are called to be co-redeemers with Christ. Pope St. John Paul II explained:

> Each one is also called to share in that suffering through which the Redemption was accomplished. He is called to share in that suffering through which all human suffering has also been redeemed. In bringing about the Redemption through suffering, Christ has also raised human suffering to the level of the Redemption. Thus, each man, in his suffering, can also become a sharer in the redemptive suffering of Christ.[265]

---

[264] Rowe, *God is Love*, 113.

[265] John Paul II, Apostolic Letter *Salvifici doloris*, February 11, 1984, § 19, https://www.vatican.va/content/john-paul-ii/en/apost_letters/1984/documents/hf_jp-ii_apl_11021984_salvifici-doloris.html.

In addressing the sick at the Hospital of the Brothers of St. John of God on April 5, 1981, Pope St. John Paul II encouraged them saying:

> Is it necessary to remind all of you, sorely tried by suffering, who are listening to me, that your pain unites you more and more with the Lamb of God, who "takes away the sin of the world" through His Passion (Jn 1:29)? And that therefore you, too, associated with him in suffering, can be **co-redeemers** of mankind? You know these shining truths. Never tire of offering your sufferings for the Church, that all her children may be consistent with their faith, persevering in prayer and fervent in hope.[266]

On January 13, 1982 after giving his general audience address the Pope addressed himself to the sick saying:

> To the sick who are present and to those who are in hospital wards, in nursing homes and in families I say: never feel alone, because the Lord is with you and will never abandon you. Be courageous and strong: unite your pains and

---

[266] John Paul II, Address to the Sick in Fatebenefratelli on Rome's Tiber Island, April 5, 1981, in Calkins, "Mary Coredemptrix in the Papal Magisterium," 46.

sufferings to those of the Crucified and you will become **co-redeemers** of humanity, together with Christ.[267]

Not only did St. Pope John Paul II understand the importance of souls offering their suffering in union with Christ to help aid the salvation of others, but many other saints have understood the importance of this co-redeeming work as well. Offering up one's suffering with Jesus for the salvation of others is not a vocation for only a few, special souls in the Church. Rather, it is the call of all Christians. Many saints have deeply encouraged all souls to embrace suffering both as a place of union with Jesus, as well as a means to aid other souls on their path to heaven. St. Josemaria Escriva is one saint who understood the call of all souls to partake in the Cross with Christ. He said:

> When you see a poor wooden Cross, alone, uncared-for, and of no value ... and without its Crucified, don't forget that that Cross is your Cross: the Cross of each day, the hidden Cross, without splendor or consolation ... , the Cross which is awaiting the Crucified it lacks: and that Crucified must be you.[268]

The saints are brilliant co-redeemers with Christ each in their own unique way. As the soul grows in the gown of Christ's humility,

---

[267] John Paul II, General Audience, January 13, 1982, in Calkins, 46.
[268] Escriva, *The Way*, no. 178, p. 58.

kenosis, and littleness and is seared one in a mystical marriage of union through divine love with Him, she innately comes to not only identify with and compassion His great sufferings on the Cross, but desires profusely to take them upon herself as well. Saints see suffering as the greatest jewels and proof of God's love for them. St. Ignatius of Loyola explains:

> If God gives you an abundant harvest of trials, it is a sign of great holiness which He desires you to attain. Do you want to become a great saint? Ask God to send you many sufferings. The flame of Divine Love never rises higher than when fed with the wood of the Cross, which the infinite charity of the Savior used to finish His sacrifice. All the pleasures of the world are nothing compared with the sweetness found in the gall and vinegar offered to Jesus Christ. That is, hard and painful things endured for Jesus Christ and with Jesus Christ.[269]

Congruent with the saints growing desire to be dressed in the wounds of their beloved Jesus crucified, is a self-knowledge of their own ineptitude and human limit in facing such a great feat. Yet it is Jesus Christ Crucified's Own love that is transforming their souls who upholds them in this process—accepting their offerings as

---

[269] Ignatius of Loyola, as cited in Ray Sullivan, "Saints' Quotes on Redemptive Suffering," *Catholic Stand,* April 20, 2023, https://catholicstand.com/saints-quotes-on-redemptive-suffering/.

priests, their own sufferings as victims and their hearts as the altars on which He Himself is immolated. In the end it is love that humbles, transforms, unites and consumes a soul. Love does all of the work. St. Teresa Margaret Redi expresses this in her prayer, *"But how confused I am, my God, when I see what a worthless victim I am, and how unfitting is this sacrifice I ask you to accept. Yet I am confident that all will be accomplished by the fire of divine love."*[270] St. Therese similarly said:

> When one casts oneself headlong into the furnace of divine love, how can one fail to be consumed? ... Always love knows how to make the best of everything; whatever offends our Lord is burnt up in its fire, and nothing is left but a humble, absorbing peace, deep down in the heart.[271]

Bl. Conchita of Mexico said, *"I want to live on love, but on a love which crucified me. My soul constantly enters into the abyss of Love."*[272]

This work of becoming little priests, victims, and altars with Christ not only has the purpose of purifying and making up for one's own faults, or of simply uniting a saint's soul with that of her

---

[270] Rowe, *God is Love*, 218.

[271] Therese of Lisieux, *Story of a Soul* A83r—84r, translation as found at https://arewethereyet-davisfarmmom.blogspot.com/2012/10/on-feast-of-little-flower.html.

[272] Conchita, *Conchita: A Mother's Spiritual Diary*, ed. M.M. Philipon, trans. Aloysius J. Owen (New York: Society of St. Paul, 2007), 141.

Redeemer. It also has a sanctifying purpose for the good of all souls within the Church. In this way, we clearly see the call of every Christian to answer the command of Jesus, Who said, *"If you are to be my disciples take up your cross and follow me"* (Mt 16:24), calling all souls to *"remain in me, as I remain in you. Just as a branch cannot bear fruit on its own unless it remains on the vine, so neither can you unless you remain in me. I am the vine, you are the branches. Whoever remains in me and I in him will bear much fruit, because without me you can do nothing"* (Jn 15:4–5). The fruit of remaining in Christ crucified is that the saints who obey this directive become "co-redeemers" with Him. St. Paul said, *"Now I rejoice in my sufferings for your sake, and in my flesh I am filling up what is lacking in the afflictions of Christ on behalf of his body, which is the church"* (Col 1:24).

Each of the saints who we have reflected upon has undergone a transforming process of being made "little" by God, united to Him in divine spousal love and then crucified with Him for their own good and the good of all souls. The saints have often taught that the highest form of prayer and love is not found in ecstasy or sublime consolation, but in suffering. Fr. Marie-Eugene taught, *"St. John of the Cross says that even in transforming union, when the soul enjoys peace, it knows suffering, a suffering that is no longer purifying (directed towards herself) but a suffering of radiance (for others, a suffering of the apostolate.)"*[273] This suffering with Christ for souls not only makes the Cross and Christ's wounds visible in the heart of the saints in varying ways, but unites them to Him Eucharistically. This is why

---

[273] Gaucher, John and Therese, 90.

in some saints Christ became one flesh with them through His wounds; in others He manifested images of His Passion or a Cross in their hearts; in others, they radiated the Eucharistic presence; in others, people found His glance of love in their eyes—coming from His radiant presence glowing in their hearts. Whether visibly or more hiddenly, Jesus Christ crucified came to live and die in the saints who allowed Him to draw them close to Himself.

St. Thomas Aquinas explains that the Eucharist produces in man the same effect as the Passion: sanctifying grace.[274] And it is in the Passion living in the body and soul of a saint that radiates the body, blood, soul, and divinity of Christ in a similar—although not exact—way as the Eucharist. At Mass, Christ humbles Himself becoming bread and wine not for the sake of these accidents of bread and wine, but in order to sneak into human hearts and transform them into Himself. As we have seen, the saints allow Him to do this in full. St. Edith Stein explains, *"To die on the cross with Christ in order to be resurrected with him becomes a reality for every Christian. . . . For those who, with living faith, offer or participate in the Mass the same things happens in and for them that happened on Golgotha."*[275] St. Therese also saw herself as having become a living tabernacle. In her act of oblation, she says: *"Remain in me as in a tabernacle and never separate yourself from your little host."* [276]

---

[274] Aquinas, *Summa theologica*, III q. 79, a. 1.
[275] Stein, *Science of the Cross*, 22.
[276] Gaucher, *John and Therese*, 110.

As saints enter into the Mass—and into a daily living out of the Mass through union with Jesus crucified as Priest, Victim, and Altar—a profusion of grace flows out of them that begins to draw in hundreds and thousands of souls to Christ. This happens because of their suffering united to that of Christ's suffering on Calvary on every altar at every Mass offered in the world. In a letter of September 1919, St. Teresa of the Andes said, *"We [religious] are co-redeemers of the world. And souls are not redeemed without the cross."*[277] Jesus told St. Catherine of Siena to persistently offer prayers, sacrifices, sweat, and tears on behalf of His Bride the Church. He promised that He would use that to wash her and to save souls. He also said to St. Catherine, *"I beg you to pray to me for [sinners]. I ask for your tears and sweat on their behalf so that they may receive mercy from me."*[278]

St. Faustina was often shown by Jesus His desire that she suffer and pray for souls with Him. Later He would show her the fruit of such sacred work with Him:

> Jesus says; "My daughter, I want to instruct you on how you are to rescue souls through sacrifice and prayer. You will save more souls through prayer and suffering than will a missionary through his teachings and sermons alone. I want to see you as a sacrifice of living love, which only then carries weight before Me. ... And great will be your power for

---

[277] John Paul II, Homily for Canonization of St. Teresa de los Andes, March 21, 1993, https://teresadelosandes.org/1english/saint-textesjp2.php.

[278] Catherine of Sienna, *The Dialogue* (India: Tan Books, 2010), 44.

whomever you intercede. Outwardly, your sacrifice must look like this: silent, hidden, permeated with love, imbued with prayer.[279]

On the First Friday of the month, before Communion, I saw a large ciborium filled with sacred hosts. A hand placed the ciborium in front of me, and I took it in my hands. There were a thousand living hosts inside. Then I heard a voice, "These are hosts which have been received by the souls for whom you have obtained the grace of true conversion during this Lent."[280]

Jesus also showed St. Faustina how daily sacrifices made by religious communities sustain the world in existence, acting as a shield blunting the sword of God's justice upon the world. She recorded it thus:

During the renewal of the vows, I saw the Lord Jesus on the Epistle side (of the altar), wearing a white garment with a golden belt and holding a terrible sword in His hand. This lasted until the moment when the sisters began to renew their vows. Then I saw a resplendence beyond compare and, in front of this brilliance, a white cloud in the shape of a scale. Then Jesus approached and put the sword on one side of the scale, and it fell heavily towards the ground until it was about

---

[279] Kowalska, *Divine Mercy in My Soul*, no. 1767, p. 627.
[280] Kowalska, no. 640, p. 266.

to touch it. Just then the sisters finished renewing their vows. Then I saw Angels who took something from each of the sisters and placed it in a golden vessel on the other side of the scale, it immediately outweighed and raised up the side on which the sword had been laid. At that moment, a flame issued forth from the thurible, and it reached all the way to the brilliance. Then I heard a voice coming from the brilliance: "Put the sword back in its place; the sacrifice is greater.[281]

Jesus to St. Faustina:

For the sake of your love, I withhold the just chastisements, which mankind has deserved. A single act of pure love pleases Me more than a thousand imperfect prayers. One of your sighs of love atones for many offenses with which the godless overwhelm Me. The smallest act of virtue has unlimited value in My eyes because of your great love for Me. In a soul that lives on My love alone, I reign as in heaven. I watch over it day and night. In it I find My happiness; My ear is attentive to each request of its heart; often I anticipate its requests. O child, especially beloved by Me, apple of My eye, rest a moment near My Heart and taste of the love in which you will delight for all eternity. But child, you are not yet in your homeland; so go, fortified by My grace, and fight for My kingdom in human souls; fight as a king's child would; and

---

[281] Kowalska, no. 394, p. 176.

remember that the days of your exile will pass quickly, and with them the possibility of earning merit for heaven. I expect from you, My child, a great number of souls who will glorify My mercy for all eternity. My child, that you may answer My call worthily, receive Me daily in Holy Communion. It will give you strength.[282]

Perhaps no saint has written so much on this mystery of the soul transformed into Christ being called to participate with Him in the Eucharistic sacrifice of Calvary as Blessed Conchita from Mexico (otherwise known as Bl. Maria Concepcion Cabrera de Armida). Jesus not only called her into a mystical priesthood with Him, but explained to her through many revelations what it meant to be His priest, victim, and altar with Him. He said:

> The Church is one, one only Altar, one only Victim. . . . All souls, victims, should offer themselves in union with this great Victim.[283]
> Here is your priesthood: to be a victim with the Victim.[284]
> You are at once altar and priest, since you possess the most holy Victim of Calvary and of the Eucharist and since you have the power of offering Him constantly for the salvation of the world. It is the most precious fruit of the great

---

[282] Kowalska, no. 1489, p. 533.
[283] Conchita, *Spiritual Diary*, June 20, 1898, p. 125.
[284] Conchita, *Spiritual Diary*, July 17, 1906, p. 125.

favor of My mystical incarnation in your heart. . . . You are My altar and at the same time you will be My victim. Offer yourself in union with Me. Offer Me at every instant to the eternal Father, with the sublime intent of saving souls and of glorifying Him. Forget all and especially yourself. Let this be your constant concern. You have received a sublime mission. As you see, it is not for yourself alone, but universal, obliging you with all purity possible to be at the same time altar and victim consumed in holocaust with the other Victim, the Unique Host, pleasing to God and able to save the world.[285]

Jesus said, "You will enkindle in a multitude of hearts the fire of the Holy Spirit, you will bless them with the sacred wood of the Cross."[286]

The Word became flesh and becomes flesh again in souls only to be crucified. It is the purpose of all mystical incarnations. . . . Your Word has just become flesh mystically in your heart . . . in order to be constantly sacrificed there not only an altar of stone, but in a living temple of the Holy Spirit, by a priest and a victim, who, by an inconceivable grace, received the power to participate in the love of the Father. In fact, the Father wishes that I Myself, united to your soul as victim, have you sacrifice Me and immolate Me with the same love of the Father on behalf of a world which has need

---

[285] Conchita, *Spiritual Diary*, June 21, 1906, pp. 125–26.
[286] Conchita, *Spiritual Diary*, 141.

of this spiritual shock and of a grace of this nature in order to be converted. Embrace the Cross and be saved.[287]

There are souls who have been consecrated through priestly unction, but there are likewise, in the world, priestly souls, who, although they have neither the dignity nor are consecrated as priests, have a priestly mission, and they offer themselves to the Father in union with Me, to immolate themselves as He desires. These souls mightily aid the Church on the spiritual plane.[288]

Here we read about the soul's role as priest, altar and victim lived in union with Christ through suffering. And yet, Jesus' words have an incarnational tone to them. He speaks to Bl. Conchita about how He, the Word, will take flesh within her in order to make her a priest, altar and victim with Him. In these words, one sees how suffering is not something imposed harshly upon her from outside, but rather through her reception of Jesus' presence into her heart His sufferings take root within her. Christ's words to her emphasize the importance of her free self-gift to Him as she responds to His invitation of love and willingly offers herself (and all of the sufferings of her life) back to Him and with Him to the Father. Jesus also makes an important distinction between a soul living Christ's priesthood with Him through offering her sufferings in union with Him, as opposed to the work of the priest offering the Eucharistic sacrifice at Mass. Jesus

---

[287] Conchita, *Spiritual Diary*, October, 22, 1907, p. 159.
[288] Conchita, *Spiritual Diary*, January 8, 1928, pp. 188–89.

beautifully spoke to her about the ministerial priesthood versus the mystical priesthood that all souls are called to partake in, and that saints accomplish fully:

> When I pronounced these words: "Do this in memory of Me," I was not addressing Myself only to priests. Of course, they alone have the power to change the substance of bread into My most holy Body and the substance of wine into My Blood. But the power to unite in one single oblation all oblations belongs to all Christians. It belongs to all Christians, members of one single Body, to become one with the Victim on the altar by faith and works, offering Me as Host in propriation to My eternal Father.[289]

Once again in all of this we see how each soul created by God progresses along the path of littleness consumed with the fullness of divine love in the mystical marriage, which then incarnates the presence of Jesus crucified within them in varying ways, leading them to completing His call to be priests, victims, and altars with Him for the salvation of the world.

---

[289] Conchita, *Spiritual Diary*, June 7, 1916, p. 189.

The Saints' Vocation to a Complete Fiat to God's Will as Jesus and Mary Lived

St. John of the Cross taught that *"one act of pure love is worth more to the Church than all other acts combined."*[290] St. Faustina similarly prayed:

> O my Jesus, I know that, in order to be useful to souls, one has to strive for the closest possible union with You, who are Eternal Love.[291]
>
> I can be wholly useful to the Church by my personal sanctity, which throbs with life in the whole Church, for we all make up one organism in Jesus.[292]

Love is the elevator that lifts one into union with Christ. Love is the glue that adheres one's soul to the will of God. In all that has been reflected upon here, it is easy to conclude that it is love—synonymous with *fiat*—that brings about perfect holiness. Love as shown forth in Christ is the self-emptying gift of oneself for the good of the beloved. When a soul says *fiat* to God, in essence that soul is saying *'I want to forget myself and offer all that I am and have to you, Father, for the fulfillment of your will.'* For a soul that loves, no sacrifice is too

---

[290] John of the Cross, *Spiritual Canticle* 28, note 2, in *Selected Writings*, 270.

[291] Kowalska, *Divine Mercy in My Soul*, no. 1595, p. 567.

[292] Kowalska, no. 1364, p. 488.

great a cost for the good of the beloved. Authentic love is always generous. It does not give half of oneself. True love always is willing to give all of oneself to the end. Christ is an example of that in His love for humanity that stooped down to take upon His shoulders their fallen humanity and sin in order to redeem it, transform it, and lift them up to union with His Father through surrendering in *fiat* to His will. Love for Christ united Our Lady's Heart with His in the Passion. Only love was the measure of the depth of suffering She endured in union with Him—not only to take some of it upon Her back and into Her Heart, but also in order to offer it to Her children (all souls in the Church) to save them from hell. Love is what draws each saint into the abasement of humble littleness and self-emptying with Christ, allowing Him not only to transform them but to also consume them on the altar of the Cross in union with His Own Passion, suffering, and death. Love conforms the hearts of each saint to unite their wills to that of God's in perfect surrender. This love enlightens their path and strengthens their hearts to complete His will in their lives in totality.

Conclusion

In the midst of a world that seeks to be big, powerful, wealthy, popular, self-gratifying and comfortable, the example that Jesus painted with His life is a powerful portal of grace for the souls called to follow Him. Jesus, Who was God incarnate, emptied Himself completely before the Father taking the form of a human slave in order to save men. This embracing of littleness and humility was the conduit of salvation for all of creation. Jesus did not stop at simply lowering Himself as God made Man, but even allowed the immense love of His self-gift to be rejected, mocked and denied by man culminating in His Own Passion and Death, which He offered back for the salvation of the world. It was Christ's passionate love both of the Father in heaven and of His creation on earth which held Him firm in a faithful *fiat* to the Cross. By laying down His life for the salvation of humanity, Jesus was the new Adam and the faithful High Priest, Victim and Altar through which eternal life was won for mankind.

Our Lady centered Her life around the Word incarnate. She was preserved for Him from birth, longed for Him in prayer, accepted His flesh into Her Own womb through saying *fiat*, served and glorified Him throughout His life and mystically died in union with Him on Calvary for the salvation of all souls entrusted to Her. Mary was united to Christ's work of salvation in a subordinate, and yet perfect way, all of the days of Her life. She was created to be Jesus' Mother and is glorified in heaven as our Mother because of Her role as His Helpmate in His work of redemption. Like Jesus Who She adored and served Her entire life long, it was Mary's fiery love of God as well as a sharing in God's love for man that pushed Her forth in Her *fiat* to do His will all the days of Her life. This perfect self-gift in *fiat* to the Father was tested in the crucible of Jesus' suffering and death on Calvary. Through Our Lady's faithfulness to Christ in all things, never counting the cost to Herself, She fulfilled the role of His Helpmate and the new Eve in the work of redemption. Mary fully shared with Jesus in His suffering. She was not equal to Him and yet Her gift to Him was complete. In this She lived as a bridal priest, victim and altar along with Him on the Cross. And in this She won the grace to be Co-redemptrix, as well as the Mediatrix of all grace to Her spiritual children on earth.

Not only have we seen how it was Jesus and Mary's littleness and fiery spousal love that drew them to the Cross and nailed them fast upon it in *fiat*, but we have also seen how this is the path upon which all saints have traveled on their journey to heaven. One must be little, humble and empty of oneself in order to be authentic—filled with the truth and plan of God's providential love. This love in turn unites the soul powerfully to God through Christ in a spousal marriage that culminates on the Cross. One suffers with Christ to the degree she loves Him and love pushes a soul to desire to be united more and more with Him through His wounds. These wounds of Christ are a doorway that lead us into His Sacred Heart—which then consumes us with His love causing heaven to touch earth within the soul.

Christ taught the way of littleness, spousal love and the Cross not only through His words, but more profoundly by His life. Writing upon the hearts of His sheep His love story with them, He invites them to answer His call by surrendering themselves fully to the

Father in *fiat* with Him. This path leads down the road to Calvary where the soul and Christ unite as priest, victim, and altar upon the Cross and through the Sacraments. In order to be drawn into this marvelous work of the Father, a soul must be willing to respond to His grace of becoming little, lowly, empty and yet also fully possessed with His love that endures unto and through death. Ultimately, a soul must be willing to fulfill the Father's will, surrendering in *fiat* to all He wills and allows, in order to be made one with Him. In doing this, all souls can become a megaphone of the message of Jesus' love to the world simply through their lives. St. Charles de Foucauld said:

> The best way to preach the Gospel of Christ is to live it. I like those who do not preach but practice what they believe. Their lives are silent and yet they give real witness.
>
> A rose has no need to preach. It simply spreads its fragrance. Its fragrance is its sermon. That is why I say to you, let your life itself speak to us, like the rose which has no need of words but simply gives off its scent. Even the blind man who can't see the rose is attracted by its perfume. This is the secret of what I would call the "gospel of the rose." But the Gospel which Jesus preached has a perfume much more exquisite and much more penetrating than the gospel of the rose.[293]

---

[293] Kathleen of Jesus, *The Universal Brother: Charles de Foucauld Speaks to Us Today* (Hyde Park, New York: New City Press, 2019), 101.

Because of His great love for the Father, as well as for humanity, Jesus lowered Himself to take on flesh, which He used as ember in the furnace of sacrificial love in order to be our Redeemer. Our Lady, taken from His side on the Cross and transformed from being His Mother to sharing in His mission as the new Eve, helped Christ in His redemptive mission. She is the exemplar par excellence for all souls seeking to follow Christ down the road of littleness, united with Him in spousal love and ultimately partaking with Him of the Cross. By offering prayers and sacrifices incessantly in union with Him, all saints of the body of Christ follow Our Lady's discipleship in littleness, spousal love and *fiat*, which leads them as well to become co-redeemers with Jesus their Head.

Although the path of holiness that Jesus and Mary walked seems eons beyond what we poor sinners can follow, Jesus does not leave us to our own weakness. He commands us to *"be perfect as the heavenly Father is perfect"* (Mt 5:48), but at the same times calls to our weakness, saying, *"Come to me, all you who labor and are burdened, and I will give you rest. Take my yoke upon you and learn from me, for I am meek and humble of heart; and you will find rest for yourselves. For my yoke is easy, and my burden light"* (Mt 11:28–30). He offers us His Own divine love to be the bath that washes us and makes us little and innocent. His Own divine love is the thirst that draws us to Himself and is the fire that unites us one with Him. It is His Own divine love that paints His wounds upon our bodies and lives and it is His Own divine love that works through us to reach souls throughout the world allowing us through our prayer, sacrifice and union with Him to partake in the salvation of many others. Love is the means in all of this.

And so, as we look at Christ's littleness, His spousal love, His Passion and Death—we are inspired to follow His bloody footprints down Calvary as His Mother did and we beg for the grace needed to allow His love to absolutely consume us to the full. If we cling to His love, He will do the rest. If we share His love in all we do and say, it will make all things in us holy and this holiness will transform the universe. Love will transform us and love will be the measure God uses to judge us. Our work now is to surrender totally in *fiat* to the work of Christ's love poured out upon and within us, not counting the cost. For as St. John of the Cross said, *"At the end of life, we will solely be judged by love."*[294]

This work is consecrated to the Infant Weeping Heart of Jesus and the Sorrowful and Immaculate Heart of the Maria Bambina.— Mary Kloska, March 2024. Fiat. +

---

[294] "In the evening of life, they will examine you on love." See Gaucher, *John and Therese*, 33.

Works cited

Primary sources

Alphonsus de Liguori. *The Glories of Mary.* Translated and edited by Eugene Grimm. New York: Redemptorist, 1931. Translated by P. J. Kenedy. New York: Aeterna Press, 2015.

Ambrose. *On Virgins.* Edited by J. P. Migne. Patrologia Latina 16:189–91. In ICEL, *The Liturgy of the Hours,* 3:1311–12.

Angela of Foligno. *Passionate Mystic of the Double Abyss: Selected Writings.* Edited by Paul Lachance. New York: New City Press, 2006.

Aquinas, Thomas. *Commentary to St. Paul's Letter to the Philippians.* Translated by F. R. Larcher. Albany: Magi Books, 1969. Html-formatted by Joseph Kenny, https://isidore.co/aquinas/english/SSPhilippians.htm#22.

———. *Summa theologica.* Translated by the Fathers of the English Dominican Province. New York: Benziger Brothers, 1911–1925.

Augustine. *De doctrina Christiana.* Available at https://www.newadvent.org/fathers/12024.htm.

———. "Homily on the Nativity of the Lord," *Sermo Suppositus* 120:8. In Pietre, *Jesus the Bridegroom,* 93.

Benedict XV. Apostolic Letter *Inter sodalicia.* March 22, 1918. In Miravalle, *With Jesus: The Story of Mary Co-Redemptrix,* 157–58.

———. Homily for the Canonization of St. Gabriel of the Sorrowful Virgin and St. Margaret Mary Alacoque. May 13, 1920. In Calkins, "Mary Coredemptrix in the Papal Magisterium," 52.

Benedict XVI. *Behold the Pierced One.* San Francisco: Ignatius Press, 1984.

Benedict XVI. *Jesus of Nazareth—Holy Week: From the Entrance into Jerusalem to the Resurrection.* San Francisco: Ignatius Press, 2011.

Bernard of Clairvaux. Second Sermon on Advent. In Garrigou-Lagrange, "The Influence of Mary Mediatrix," 119—28.

———. Second Sermon on the Assumption. In Garrigou-Lagrange, "The Influence of Mary Mediatrix," 125.

———. *Sermo in dom. infra oct. Assumptionis.* In ICEL, *The Liturgy of the Hours,* 4:1401–2.

———. Sermon 83. In ICEL, *The Liturgy of the Hours,* 3:1333.

———. Sermon on the Nativity of the Blessed Virgin Mary. In Garrigou-Lagrange, "The Influence of Mary Mediatrix," 125.

———. *Super missus est.* in Pius XII, *Doctor mellifluus,* § 31.

Cabrini, Frances Xavier. *Parole sparse della Beata Cabrini.* Edited by Giuseppe de Luca. Rome: Istituto Grafico Tiberino, 1938. In Miravalle, *With Jesus: The Story of Mary Co-Redemptrix,* 216.

Canisius, Peter. *De Maria Incomparabili Virgine.* In Miravalle, *With Jesus: The Story of Mary Co-Redemptrix,* 109.

Catherine of Siena. *The Dialogue.* India: Tan Books, 2010.

———. *The Letters of Saint Catherine of Siena.* Translated and edited by Vida D. Scudder (1905). Re-edited by Darrell Write (2016). Scotts Valley, CA: CreateSpace Independent Publishing Platform, 2016.

Catholic Church. *Catechism of the Catholic Church.* 2nd ed. Vatican City: Vatican Press, 1997.

Peter Chrysologus, *Sermo 108*: PL 52, 499-500. In *The Liturgy of the Hours,* 2:770-772

Clare of Assisi. Letter to Blessed Agnes of Prague. *Escritos de Santa Clara*, 339–41. Madrid: 1970. In ICEL, *The Liturgy of the Hours,* 3:1311.

Claret, Anthony Mary. *Autobiography and Complementary Writings.* Bangalore, India: Claretian Publications, 2011.

Conchita. *Conchita: A Mother's Spiritual Diary.* Edited by M. M. Philipon. Translated by Aloysius J. Owen. New York: Society of St. Paul, 2007.

Cyril of Alexandria. *On the Unity of Christ.* New York: St. Vladimir's Seminary Press, 2015.

———. *Scholia on the Incarnation.* In John Anthony McGuckin, *Saint Cyril of Alexandria and the Christological Controversy,* 332-33. New York: St. Vladimir's Seminary Press, 2010.

Elizabeth of the Trinity. *Personal Notes.* November 21, 1904. In Murphy, *Always Believe in Love*, 127-128.

———. *Poems.* September 1897. In Hickey, *Drink of the Stream,* 296.

Escrivà, Jose Maria. *Amici di Dio. Omelie.* Milan: Ares, 1978.

———. *The Way.* New York: Scepter Publishers, 1982.

Eudes, John. *The Sacred Heart of Jesus.* Translated by Richard Flower. New Hampshire: Loreto Publications, 2011.

Francis de Sales. "Sermon on the Nativity of the Blessed Virgin Mary." September 10, 1620. In The Sermons of Saint Francis de Sales on Our Lady, page range. Gastonia, NC: Tan Books, 1987.

———. *Treatise on the Love of God.* Translated by Henry Benedict Mackey. Radford, VA: Wilder Publications, 2011.

Galgani, Gemma. *Estasi, Diario, Autobiografica, Scritti vari.* Rome: Passionists, 1988. In Miravale, *With Jesus: The Story of Mary Co-Redemptrix*, 214–15.

Gertrude the Great. *The Life and Revelations of St. Gertrude the Great.* Translated by the Poor Clares of Kenmare, NC. Gastonia: Tan, 2002.

Giuliani, Veronica. *The Diary of St. Veronica Giuliani.* Translated by Bret Thoman. Georgia: Icona Press, 2023.

Gregory of Nyssa. *On Virginity.* Translated by William Moore and Henry Austin Wilson. New York: Aeterna Press, 2016.

Ildephonsus of Toledo. *Crown of the Virgin: An Ancient Meditation on Mary's Beauty, Virtue, and Sanctity.* Translated by Robert Nixon. Gastonia, NC: Tan Books, 2020.

Ireneus of Lyons. *Against Heresies.* English translation in Most, *Mary In Our Life*, 25.

Isaac of Stella. *Sermo* 11. In ICEL, *The Liturgy of the Hours*, 4:246.

John Chrysostom. *De coemeterio et de cruce.* In ICEL, *The Liturgy of the Hours*, 4:1660.

———. *On the Priesthood.* Translated by W. R. W. Stephens. Monee, IL: CreateSpace Independent Publishing Platform, 2014.

John of Avila. *On the Love of God; On the Priesthood.* Edited by Idefonso Fernandez Figares. New York: IVE Press, 2012.

John of the Cross. *Selected Writings.* Edited by Kieran Kavanaugh. New York: Paulist Press, 1987.

———. *The Living Flame of Love.* Translated by Kieran Kavanaugh and O. Rodriquesz. Washington, DC: ICS Publications, 1973.

John Paul II. Address at the Marian shrine in Guayaquil. January 31, 1985. In Calkins, "Mary Coredemptrix in the Papal Magisterium," 42–43.

———. Address to the Sick in Fatebenefratelli on Rome's Tiber Island. April 5, 1981. In Calkins, "Mary Coredemptrix in the Papal Magisterium," 46.

———. Angelus for the Feast of Corpus Christi. June 5, 1983. In Calkins, "Mary Coredemptrix in the Papal Magisterium," 71.

———. Apostolic Letter *Salvifici doloris*. February 11, 1984. https://www.vatican.va/content/john-paul-ii/en/apost_letters/1984/documents/hf_jp-ii_apl_11021984_salvifici-doloris.html.

———. Catechesis. April 2, 1997. https://www.vatican.va/content/john-paul-ii/en/audiences/1997/documents/hf_jp-ii_aud_02041997.html.

———. Encyclical Letter *Redemptoris Mater*. March 25, 1987. https://www.vatican.va/content/john-paul-ii/en/encyclicals/documents/hf_jp-ii_enc_25031987_redemptoris-mater.html.

———. General Audience. January 13, 1982. in Calkins, "Mary Coredemptrix in the Papal Magisterium," 46.

———. General Audience. May 2, 1990. English translation available at https://tobinstitute.org/the-holy-spirit-and-mary-model-of-the-nuptial-union-of-god-with-humanity/.

———. General Audience. October 25, 1995. In Miravalle, *With Jesus: The Story of Mary Co-Redemptrix*, 202.

———. General Audience. October 15, 1997. https://www.vatican.va/content/john-paul-ii/en/audiences/1997/documents/hf_jp-ii_aud_15101997.html.

———. General Audience. November 19, 2003. https://www.vatican.va/content/john-paul-ii/en/audiences/2003/documents/hf_jp-ii_aud_20031119.html.

———. Homily for Canonization of St. Teresa de los Andes. March 21, 1993. https://teresadelosandes.org/1english/saint-textesjp2.php.

———. Letter to Consecrated Persons for the Marian Year. May 22, 1988. https://www.vatican.va/content/john-paul-ii/en/letters/1988/documents/hf_jp-ii_let_19880522_consecrated-persons.html.

———. *Man and Woman He Created Them: A Theology of the Body*. Translated by Michael Waldstein. Boston: Pauline Books and Media, 2006.

———. Speech in Agrigento, Sicily. May 9, 1993. In Calkins, "Mary Coredemptrix in the Papal Magisterium," 80.

John XXIII. Radio Message to Bishops of Italy in Catania on the Occasion of the 16th National Eucharistic Congress and the Consecration of Italy to the Immaculate Heart of Mary. September 13, 1959. In Calkins, "Mary Coredemptrix in the Papal Magisterium," 69.

Justin Martyr. *Dialogue with Trypho*. In Most, *Mary In Our Life*, 24.

Kateri Tekakwitha. In "Witness to Freedom: St. Kateri Tekakwitha." United States Conference of Catholic Bishops. https://usccb.org/

issues-and-action/religious-liberty/fortnight-for-freedom/upload/Kateri-Tekakwitha-Fortnight-2016.pdf.

Kolbe, Maximillian. Scritti. Translated by Cristoforo Zambelli. Rome: Militia of Mary Immaculate, 1997.

———. *The Will to Love—From the Writings of St. Maximilian Kolbe.* Translated by Regis N. Barwig. Edited by Charles Madden and Daniel Gallio. Libertyville, IL: Marytown Press, 1998.

Kowalska, Maria Faustina. *Divine Mercy in My* Soul. Stockbridge: Marians of the Immaculate Conception, 2001.

Lawrence of Brindisi. Opera omnia. Vol. 1, Mariale. Patavii: Ex Officina typograhica Seminarii, 1928.

Leo XIII. Encyclical Letter *Adiutricem populi*. September 5, 1895. https://www.vatican.va/content/leo-xiii/en/encyclicals/documents/hf_l-xiii_enc_05091895_adiutricem.html.

———. Encyclical Letter *Iucunda semper*. September 8, 1894. https://www.vatican.va/content/leo-xiii/en/encyclicals/documents/hf_l-xiii_enc_08091894_iucunda-semper-expectatione.html.

———. Encyclical Letter *Supremi apostolates*. September 1, 1883. https://www.vatican.va/content/leo-xiii/en/encyclicals/documents/hf_l-xiii_enc_01091883_supremi-apostolatus-officio.html.

Louis de Montfort. *Secret of the Rosary.* Translated by Mary Barbour. New York: Montfort Publications, 1987).

———. *True Devotion to Mary*. Coppell, TX: Christ the King Libraries, 2020.

Mandic, Leopold. *Suo umile servo in Cristo*. Vol. 2, *Scritti*, edited by P. Tieto. Padua: Portavoce di San Leopoldo Mandic, 1992.

Maximus the Confessor, "*Ambigua 41*," On Difficulties in the Church Fathers, vol. 2. Cambridge, MA: Harvard University Press, 2014. https://churchlifejournal.nd.edu/articles/st-maximus-confessors-summation-of-early-partistic-thought/.

Mechthild of Hackeborn. *Mechthild of Hackeborn and the Nuns of Helfta*. Translated by Barbara Newman. New York: Paulist Press, 2017.

Meo, Antonietta. *Lamp & Lily*. Translated by Becket Ghioto. Self-published, 2018.

Methodius of Sicily. Homily on Saint Agatha. Analecta Bollandiana 68:76–78. In *The Liturgy of the Hours*, 2:1661–62.

Newman, John Henry. *The Mystical Rose*. Strongsville, OH: Scepter Publishers, Inc. 1996.

Paul of the Cross. *Flowers of the Passion: Thoughts of St. Paul of the Cross*. Translated by Ella A. Mulligan. New York: Benziger Brothers, 1893.

Paul VI. Apostolic Exhortation Marialis cultus. February 2, 1974. https://www.vatican.va/content/paul-vi/en/apost_exhortations/documents/hf_p-vi_exh_19740202_marialis-cultus.html.

———. Apostolic Letter on the Credo of the People of God *Solemni hac liturgia*. June 30, 1968. https://www.vatican.va/content/paul-vi/en/motu_proprio/documents/hf_p-vi_motu-proprio_19680630_credo.html.

Pio of Pietrelcina. *Epistolario*. Vol. 3. Foggia: San Giovanni Rotondo, 1992.

———. *Inspiration from the Letters of Padre Pio: Words of Light.* Translated by Andrew Tulloch. Compiled by Raniero Cantalamessa. Brewster, Massachusetts: Paraclete Press, 2000.

———. *Secrets of a Soul: Padre Pio's Letters to His Spiritual Directors.* Translated by Elvira G. DiFabio. Boston: Pauline Books and Media, 2002.

Pius IX. Apostolic Constitution *Ineffabilis Deus*. December 8, 1854. https://www.papalencyclicals.net/pius09/p9ineff.htm.

Pius X. Encyclical Letter *Ad diem illum*. February 2, 1904. https://www.vatican.va/content/pius-x/en/encyclicals/documents/hf_p-x_enc_02021904_ad-diem-illum-laetissimum.html.

Pius XI. Address to Pilgrims from Vicenza. October 30, 1933. In Miravalle, *With Jesus: The Story of Mary Co-Redemptrix*, 158.

———. Encyclical Letter *Miserentissimus Redemptor*. May 8, 1928. https://www.vatican.va/content/pius-xi/en/encyclicals/documents/hf_p-xi_enc_19280508_miserentissimus-redemptor.html.

———. Letter *Auspicatus profecto*. January 28, 1933. In Calkins, "Mary Coredemptrix in the Papal Magisterium," 57.

Pius XII. Encyclical Letter *Ad Cæli Reginam*. October 11, 1954. https://www.vatican.va/content/pius-xii/en/encyclicals/documents/hf_p-xii_enc_11101954_ad-caeli-reginam.html.

———. Encyclical Letter *Doctor mellifluous*. May 24, 1953. https://www.vatican.va/content/pius-xii/en/encyclicals/documents/hf_p-xii_enc_24051953_doctor-mellifluus.html.

———. Encyclical Letter *Haurietis aquas.* May 15, 1956. https://www.vatican.va/content/pius-xii/en/encyclicals/documents/hf_p-xii_enc_15051956_haurietis-aquas.html.

———. Encyclical Letter *Mystici Corporis.* June 29, 1943. https://www.vatican.va/content/pius-xii/en/encyclicals/documents/hf_p-xii_enc_29061943_mystici-corporis-christi.html.

———. *L'Osservatore Romano.* April 22–23, 1940. In Calkins, "Mary Coredemptrix in the Papal Magisterium," 52.

———. Radio Message to Fatima. May 13, 1946. In Calkins, "Mary Coredemptrix in the Papal Magisterium," 57–58.

Raymond of Capua. *The Life of St. Catherine of Siena.* Translated by George Lamb. Charlotte, North Carolina: Tan Books, 2011.

Romanos the Melodist. "Akathist Hymn to Theotokos." In *Akathist Hymn and Small Compline,* translated by N. Michael Vaporis. Brookline, MA: Holy Cross Orthodox Press, 2015. Available at https://www.goarch.org/-/the-akathist-hymn-and-small-compline.

Rose of Lima. *Vita mirabilis.* Edited by P. Hansen. Louvain, 1668. In *Catechism,* § 618.

Stein, Edith. *The Collected Works of Edith Stein.* Vol. 2, *Essays on Woman*, translated by Freda Mary Oben. Washington, D.C.: ICS Publications, 1987.

———. *The Collected Works of Edith Stein.* Vol. 4, *The Hidden Life: Essays, Meditations and Spiritual Texts*, translated by Waltraut Stein. Washington DC: ICS Publications, 1992.

———. *The Science of the Cross.* Translated by Josephine Koeppel. Washington, DC: ICS Publications, 2002.

———. *The Science of the Cross: A Study of St. John of the Cross*. Edited by Lucy Gelber and Romaeus Leuven. Translated by Hilda C. Graef. Washington, DC: Henry Regnery Co., 1960.

Teresa of Avila. *Collected Works of St. Teresa of Avila*. Vol. 1. Translated by Kieran Kavanaugh and Otilio Rodriguez. Washington, D.C.: ICS Publications, 1987.

Teresa of Calcutta. *Come Be My Light: The Private Writings of the "Saint of Calcutta."* Edited by Brian Kolodiejchuk. New York: M.C. Doubleday, 2007.

———. "Letter to Vox Populi Mariae Mediatrici." August 14, 1993. Vox Populi Mariae Mediatrici Archives (Hopedale, Ohio). In Miravalle, *With Jesus: The Story of Mary Co-Redemptrix*, 229.

Therese of Lisieux. Letter 89, to Mother Agnes of Jesus. August 1890. Excerpt available at https://catholicismpure.wordpress.com/2017/10/03/saint-therese-of-lisieux-on-the-love-of-god/.

———. Letter 103, to Celine. October 20, 1890. Excerpt available at https://www.littleflower.org/st-therese/st-therese-quotes/.

———. Letter 203, to Fr. Roulland. May 9, 1897. Excerpt available at https://biltrix.com/2012/10/01/little-things-done-with-great-love-saint-therese-of-lisieux/.

———. *The Story of a Soul: the Autobiography of St. Therese of Lisieux*. Translated by John Clareke. Washington, DC: ICS Publications, 1996.

Secondary sources

"Akathist to the Mother of God—Softener of Evil Hearts." *Eirenikon: Towards Orthodox-Catholic Reconciliation* (blog). https://eirenikon.wordpress.com/akathist-to-the-mother-of-god-softener-of-evil-hearts/.

Alberione, G. *Maria Regina degli Apostoli*. Rome, Edizioni San Paolo, 1948.

Avcikurt, Angelica. "St. Veronica Giuliani: An Extraordinary Mystic and Victim Soul." *Mystics of the Church*. https://www.mysticsofthechurch.com/2015/07/st-veronica-giuliani-extraordinary.html.

Béchard, Henri. *The Visions of Bernard Francis de Hoyos, S. J.* New York: Vantage Press, 1959.

Calkins, Arthur Burton. "The Mystery of Mary Coredemptrix in the Papal Magisterium." In *Mary Co-redemptrix: Doctrinal Issues Today*, edited by Mark Miravalle, 25–92. Goleta, CA: Queenship Publishing, 2002.

Cavadini, John. "Spousal Vision: A Study of Text and History in the Theology of Saint Augustine." *Augustinian Studies* 43, nos.1/2 (2012): 127-48. https://doi.org/10.5840/augstudies2013431/213.

Coleridge, Henry James. *The Life and Letters of St. Francis Xavier*. Vol. 2. London: Burns Oates & Washbourne, 1921. Available at https://www.google.com/books/edition/The_Life_and_Letters_of_St_Francis_Xavie/MUoAAAAAMAAJ?hl=en&gbpv=1&bsq=%20great%20little%20things.

Conlin, Richard. "The Paradox of Divine Love: A Treatise on the Kenosis of Christ and Creation." The Prodigal Catholic Blog. November 16, 2016. https://prodigalcatholic.com/2016/11/16/the-paradox-of-divine-love-a-treatise-on-the-kenosis-of-christ-and-creation/.

Gaucher, Guy. *John and Therese: Flames of Love: The Influence of St. John of the Cross in the Life and Writings of St. Therese of Lisieux.* New York: Society of St. Paul/Alba House, 1999.

———. The Passion of St. Therese of Lisieux. New York: The Crossroad Publishing Company, 1999.

Garrigou-Lagrange, Reginald. "The Influence of Mary Mediatrix." *The Three Ages of the Interior Life.* Vol. 1, translated by M. Timothea Doyle. St. Louis: B. Herder Book Co., 1948.

Guardini, Romano. *The Lord.* Translated by Elinor Castendyk Briefs. Washington, DC: Regnery Publishing, Inc., 2013.

International Commission on English in the Liturgy (ICEL). *The Liturgy of the Hours.* 6 vols. New York: Catholic Book Publishing Co., 1975.

Kathleen of Jesus. *The Universal Brother: Charles de Foucauld Speaks to Us Today.* Hyde Park, New York: New City Press, 2019.

Lord, Bob and Penny. *Visions of Heaven, Hell and Purgatory.* Morrilton, AR: Journeys of Faith Publishing, 2009.

Mesina, Gabriel M. "Christ and Mary Revealed In Genesis 3:15." *Missio Immaculatae* 13, no. 3 (May/June 2017). https://missio-magazine.com/christ-mary-revealed-genesis-315/.

Merton, Thomas. *What are These Wounds?* Mansfield Centre, CT: Martino Publishing, 2014.

Miravalle, Mark. *With Jesus: The Story of Mary Co-Redemptrix*. Goleta: Queenship Publishing, 2003.

Morazzani, Sr. Clara Isabel. "St. Mary Magdalene de Pazzi: God Is Love, and Is Not Loved!" *Heralds of the Gospel Magazine* 43 (May 2011). https://catholicmagazine.news/st-mary-magdalene-de-pazzi-god-is-love-and-is-not-loved/.

Most, William. *Mary In Our Life*. Garden City, NY: Image Books, 1963.

"Mysterious Heart of Saint Clare of Montefalco." *Anointing Fire Catholic Ministries*. August 11, 2019. https://www.afcmmedia.org/ Mystical-07.html.

"The Mystical Marriage of St. Catherine of Alexandria." *The Madonna, the Magdalene, and the Muse: Women in Religious Art* (blog). https://madonnamagdalenemuse.wordpress.com/christian-saints/the-mystical-marriage-of-st-catherine-of-alexandria-by-pinturicchio/.

Penny, Hickey. *Drink of the Stream: Prayers of Carmelites*. San Francisco: Ignatius Press, 2002.

Philippe, Paul. *The Blessed Virgin and the Priesthood*. Translated by Dorothy Cole. Chicago: Henry Regnery Company, 1955.

Pietre, Brant. *Jesus the Bridegroom*. New York: Image, 2014.

Rowe, Margaret. *God is Love: St. Teresa Margaret Redi: Her Life* (Washington, DC: ICS Publications Institute of Carmelite Studies, 2003),

"Saint Mariam Baouardy, the Little Arab and Lily of Palestine." *Mystics of the Church*. https://www.mysticsofthechurch.com/2010/07/blessed-mariam-baouardy-little-arab-and.html.

Salvatori, Filippo Maria. *The Life of St. Veronica Giuliani, Capuchin Nun*. Potosi, WI: St. Athanasius Press, 2014.

Sheen, Fulton J. *The World's First Love, Mary the Mother of God*. San Francisco: Ignatius Press, 1952.

Sicardo, Joseph. *St. Rita of Cascia: Saint of the Impossible (Wife, Mother, Widow, Nun 1381–1457)*. Rockford, Illinois: Tan Books and Publishers, Inc., 1990.

"St. Francis of Assisi Receives Stigmata from Seraphs." Saint Mary of the Angels. https://www.sma-church.org/st-francis-of-assisi-receives-stigmata-from-seraphs/.

"St. Gemma Galgani, the Lover of Jesus." *Mystics of the Church*. https://www.mysticsofthechurch.com/2009/12/st-gemma-galgani-lover-of-jesus.html.

"St. Lutgarde of Aywières: The First Known Woman with the Stigmata." *Mystics of the Church*. https://www.mysticsofthechurch.com/2015/09/st-lutgarde-of-aywieres-first-known.html.

"St. Rose of Lima." Dominican Sisters of Saint Cecilia. https://www.nashvilledominican.org/community/our-dominican-heritage/our-saints-and-blesseds/st-rose-lima/.

"The Stigmata of Saint Francis of Assisi." Sacred Heart Catholic Church. https://sacredheartfla.org/about-us/being-franciscan/franciscan-feast-days/the-feast-of-the-stigmata-of-st-francis-of-assisi/.

Sullivan, Ray. "Saints' Quotes on Redemptive Suffering." *Catholic Stand*. April 20, 2023. https://catholicstand.com/saints-quotes-on-redemptive-suffering/.

Traflet, Dianne Marie. *St. Edith Stein: A Spiritual Portrait*. Boston: Pauline, 2008).

Von Balthasar, Hans Urs. *Priestly Spirituality*. Translated by Frank Davidson. San Francisco: Ignatius Press, 2013.

Works consulted

Primary sources

Albert the Great. *On Union with God*. Translated by a Benedictine of Princethorpe Priory. Lexington, KY: Wildside Press, 2013.

John of Avila. *Audi, filia—Listen, O Daughter*. Translated by Joan Frances Gormley. New York: Paulist Press, 2006.

John Paul II. *Mezczyzna I Niewiasta Stworzyl Ich*. Lublin: Wydawnictwo KUL, 2008.

Kolbe, Maximillian. *The Kolbe Reader: The Writings of St. Maximillian Kolbe*. Edited by Anselm W. Romb. Libertyville, IL: Marytown Press, 2007.

Louis de Montfort. *Friends of the Cross*. New York: Montfort Publications, 2008.

Pio of Pietrelcina. *Padre Pio's Spiritual Direction for Every Day*. Edited by Gianluigi Pasquale. Translated by Marsha Daigle-Williamson. Cincinnati, OH: Servant, 2011.

Teresa of Avila. *The Interior Castle*. Translated by the Benedictines of Stanbrook. Rockford, IL: Tan, 1997.

———. *The Life of St. Teresa of Avila*. Translated by J.M. Cohen. Great Britain: Penguin Books, 1957.

———. *The Way of Perfection*. Translated and prepared by Kieran Kavanaugh. Washington D.C.: ICS Publications, 2000.

Secondary sources

Ahern, Patrick. *Maurice and Therese.* New York: Image Books Doubleday, 1998.

Brunot, Amedee. *Miriam, the Little Arab: Sister Mary of Jesus Crucified.* Translated by Jeanne Dumais and Sister Miriam of Jesus, OCD. Veneta, Oregon: The Carmel of Maria Regina, 1990.

Cabrera de Armida, Concepcion, and Luis Martinez. *To Be Jesus Crucified.* New York: St. Paul's, 2013.

———. *Under the Gaze of the Father.* New York: St. Pauls, 2011.

De Foucauld, Charles. *Selected Writings.* Maryknoll, New York: Orbis Books, 1999.

De Meester, Conrad. *With Empty Hands: the Message of St. Therese of Lisieux.* London-New York: Burns & Oates, 2002.

Descouvemont, Pierre. *Therese of Lisieux and Marie of the Trinity.* Translated by Alexandra Plettenberg-Serban. New York: Alba House, 1997.

Ermatinger, Cliff. *Therese of Lisieux: Spouse and Victim.* Washington, DC: ICS Publications, 2010.

Garrigou-Lagrange, Reginald. *Our Savior and His Love for Us.* New York: Aeterna Press, 2016.

Gorres, Ida Friederike. *The Hidden Face: A Study of St. Therese of Lisieux.* San Francisco: Ignatius, 2003.

Hamans, Paul. *Edith Stein and Companions: On the Way to Auschwitz.* San Francisco: Ignatius Press, 2010.

Kauth, Matthew. *Charity as Divine and Human Friendship: A Metaphysical and Scriptural Explanation According to the Thought of St. Thomas Aquinas.* Rome: St. Benedict Press, 2021.

Kelley, Bennet. *Spiritual Direction According to St. Paul of the Cross.* Union City New Jersey: Passionist Press, 2008.

Maillard, Sr. Emmanuel. *Maryam of Bethlehem, The Little Arab.* Bosnia Herzegovina: Children of Medjugorje, Inc, 2011.

Marie-Eugene of the Child Jesus. *Under the Torrent of His Love: Therese of Lisieux, a Spiritual Genius.* Translated by Mary Thomas Noble. New York: Alba House, 1995.

Neubert, Emile. *Mary and the Priestly Ministry.* Translated by Thomas A. Stanley. New Bedford, MA: Academy of the Immaculate, 2009.

Schmidt, Joseph. *Everything is Grace: The Life and Way of Terese of Lisieux.* Frederick, MD: The Word Among Us Press, 2007.

Sheen, Fulton. *Archbishop Fulton Sheen's St. Therese: A Treasured Love Story.* Irving, TX: Basilica Press, 2007.

Germanus, C. P. *The Life of St. Gemma Galgani.* Charolette, NC: Tan, 2012.

Von Balthasar, Hans Urs. *Two Sisters in the Spirit: Therese of Lisieux and Elizabeth of the Trinity.* San Francisco: Ignatius Press, 1992.

Walz, M. F.. *Why is Thy Apparel Red? (or Glories of the Precious Blood).* Monee, IL: Christ the King Libraries, 2021.

www.ingramcontent.com/pod-product-compliance
Lightning Source LLC
Chambersburg PA
CBHW050851160426
43194CB00011B/2108